THERE PLANT EYES

Library of Congress Cataloging-in-Publication Data
Name: Godin, M. Leona, author.
Title: There plant eyes : a personal and cultural history of blindness /
M. Leona Godin.
Description: First edition. New York : Pantheon Books, 2021. Includes
bibliographical references and index.
Identifiers: LCCN 2020045789 (print). LCCN 2020045790 (ebook).
ISBN 9781524748715 (hardcover). ISBN 9781524748722 (ebook).
Subjects: LCSH: Blind—History. Blindness—Social aspects. Blind in
literature. Blind in art.
Classification: LCC HV1581 .G63 2021 (print) | LCC HV1581 (ebook) |
DDC 305.9/08109—dc23
LC record available at lccn.loc.gov/2020045789
LC ebook record available at lccn.loc.gov/2020045790

www.pantheonbooks.com

Jacket design by Janet Hansen

Printed in the United States of America

First Edition
2 4 6 8 9 7 5 3 1

For Mom, in loving gratitude
For Dad, in loving memory

Contents

Introduction

When I was ten years old, I suddenly could no longer see the writing on the blackboard from the back of the class. This at first seemed a trivial issue of my needing glasses, but it turned out that my vision could not be corrected. Several optometrist and ophthalmologist appointments came in quick succession, in which the men in white coats provided increasingly absurd explanations to cover their impotence, including one who told my mother, "Her eyes are growing too fast for her body." Or perhaps it was, "Her body is growing too fast for her eyes."

After visiting several doctors in the creaky bungalows on the outskirts of the Presidio's medical complex in San Francisco, my mother and I finally found ourselves face-to-face with a hotshot ophthalmologist in the impressive upper floors of the Letterman Army Hospital, where Lucasfilm now has its headquarters. Although I had spent my first three and a half years living in the Netherlands, after my parents' divorce, my mother and I had moved back to their hometown of San Francisco, while my father (an officer in the Air Force) continued his travels around the world. Thanks to him, I received benefits with my military dependent card, and so my mom and I often drove into the Presidio for free health care and cheap commissary groceries.

Even if doctors' appointments and shopping were not my favorite childhood activities, I never tired of the beauty of the (now decommissioned) military base. I hold in my mind's eye how our old green Ford would punch through the Arguello Gate into the cool dark fairy forest of cypress, pine, and eucalyptus, or wind along the glimmering waters of the Bay toward the bright red towers of the Golden Gate Bridge with its skirts of fog that would roll in and blanket our Outer Richmond neighborhood every afternoon.

Men of intelligence being notoriously susceptible to the kind of ignorance the ancient Greeks called blindness—an ignorance born out of fear or hubris or both, as in the famous story of Oedipus—it seems unsurprising to me now that the highly accomplished ophthalmologist at Letterman would offer the most absurd explanation, or rather accusation, yet: "Maybe she can't see because you've been taking her to so many eye doctors."

My mother, her tears and frustration welling over, responded (as if this were not the reason for our sad pilgrimage in the first place), "Then why can't she see the writing on the blackboard?"

Somehow, this simple insistence caused the doctor to look again, with fresh eyes, into his ophthalmoscope, and spot the bits of discoloration that indicated the very beginnings of blindness from retinal dystrophy—whereby the cells are not getting or processing the nutrients they need to survive. Back then, the doctors diagnosed the condition as retinitis pigmentosa (RP), a genetic degenerative disease that slowly and implacably wears away the retinas, leading eventually to blindness. Modern genetics has since made my childhood diagnosis almost meaningless, since it turns out that many gene mutations can cause retinal degeneration. RP is simply the most well known of them, and sometimes expresses itself in several members of a family. I was the only one in my family to have it, and my gene mutation turned out to be a strange one.[1]

Instead of the typical RP degeneration, which starts at the

periphery and leads to tunnel vision, I lost a bit out of the center early on, leaving me unable to read normal-size print by the time I was about sixteen. Aside from some night blindness, I would be able to walk around without assistance—no cane, no dog—for years to come. I was emphatically not blind; I was visually impaired. Now, nearly four decades since my initial visits to the eye doctors, I am blind, and yet the vision loss is incomplete. I can still sometimes glimpse light from the outside world—a very bright lamp in my far peripheral vision, the wash of daylight from an intense sun.

Although this book is not about me and my decades of vision loss (which, similar to aging, has been almost imperceptibly slow, incremental, adaptive, and frankly a bit boring), you will be hearing quite a bit from me in these pages. Blindness is not just a subject; it is a perspective.[2] Thus, it would be disingenuous of me to say that my long years of vision loss do not inform this cultural history of blindness through literary, scientific, philosophical, and autobiographical writings over roughly three millennia. They certainly do. Conversely, my study of blindness in our ocularcentric world reveals a great deal about how we—blind and sighted alike—conceptualize our abilities and disabilities.

Ocularcentrism dictates that blindness, when literal, translates into not just a different but a lesser way of perceiving the world. However, when measured in metaphorical terms, especially in religious and literary contexts, blindness signifies how eyes can get in the way of spiritual and artistic transcendence—a theme exploited by the blind poet extraordinaire John Milton in *Paradise Lost,* from which my title comes:

So much the rather thou, celestial light,
Shine inward, and the mind through all her powers

Irradiate, there plant eyes, all mist from thence
Purge and disperse, that I may see and tell
Of things invisible to mortal sight.[3]

By reading metaphorical blindness against its realities, we may begin to see how blindness has shaped our culture in myriad ways. Considering the fact that human vision is necessarily limited by our sense organs, blindness helps to give credence to the idea of perfect sightedness. By interrogating our biases, assumptions, and misconceptions about blindness, we may begin to notice cracks in our Western imagination regarding the sense that many consider to be the most important. Thus I began this book with my first loss of sight because it beautifully illustrates the relationship between literal and figurative blindness: the nearly invisible beginning of eye disease led directly to the doctors' unwillingness to admit ignorance, causing them to grow frustrated and spin yarns.

———

In the fabric of our language, sight is inevitably linked with knowledge and understanding. We inherited this connection from the ancient Greeks, whose word for "to see" (*idein*) gives us our word "idea." Our word "theory" also has a specular root; it is related to the word "theater," and comes from the Greek word for "to look at" (*theorein*). Perhaps it's no wonder, then, that the opposite of sight would also take on weighty associations. The Greeks were so obsessed with the idea that sight equals knowledge and blindness equals ignorance that they turned blind men into poets (Homer) and prophets (Tiresias), giving them transcendent vision more valuable and profound than physical sight could ever be. The blind seer in particular is so foundational that it's become a cliché: you'll be hard-pressed to read a book of science fiction or fantasy that does not include a blind character. From the *Dune* series to *A Song of Ice and Fire* (which HBO turned into *Game of Thrones*), blindness forces the sighted to see what's what.

On the other hand, the rhetorical use of the word "blind" is bandied about so frequently—blind faith, blind love, blind rage, blind drunk, etc.—that one does not often pause to consider the effect the slur may have on actual blind people. In her 1978 essay "Illness as Metaphor," Susan Sontag points out that "illness is not a metaphor, and that the most truthful way of regarding illness—and the healthiest way of being ill—is one most purified of, most resistant to, metaphoric thinking."[4]

Though I have not found metaphorical thinking to be entirely detrimental to my contending with vision loss—in fact, it's helped me to construe a bit of blind pride—I do believe that metaphors must be balanced with realities. We can "hardly take up residence" in the non-normal kingdom "unprejudiced by the lurid metaphors with which it has been landscaped," says Sontag of illness,[5] and I think it can also be said of blindness. In this case, the landscaping has been done, almost exclusively, by sighted people.

Blindness seems to have nearly irresistible appeal as a literary trope, but as such, it has lost the particularity and multiplicity of lived experience. Generally speaking, "the blind" are either idealized in theory, as being exceptionally pure or superpowered, or pitied in practice, as being inept or unaware. I think this is because blind people are rarely allowed to be the authors of their own image. Rather paradoxically, the grand exception is Homer, who stands at the starting point of Western literature.

"We may believe that Homer never existed," declares Jorge Luis Borges in his autobiographical essay "Blindness," "but that the Greeks imagined him as blind in order to insist on the fact that poetry is, above all, music; that poetry is, above all, the lyre; that the visual can or cannot exist in a poet."[6] In tracing the stunning lineage of the blind writer from Homer to Milton, Joyce, and beyond (including himself), Borges makes the flamboyant claim that "Milton's blindness was voluntary,"[7] by which I believe he means that Milton accepted his blindness as the mark of a poet. I might add that if Milton had not gone blind, it is likely that volatile seventeenth-century English politics would have continued to subsume him, so that there would have been no *Paradise Lost.*[8]

Despite the astounding genealogy of the blind bard, there simply have not been enough blind writers to greatly affect the metaphorics of blindness. I think this is because the publishing industry, perhaps prompted by the reading public, expects blind writers to produce personal narratives that follow the model of overcoming adversity, even if their ideas and opinions extend far beyond the constraints of autobiography. This kind of thing has been going on for quite some time: "Every book is in a sense autobiographical," wrote Helen Keller in her preface to *The World I Live In,* which was published more than 100 years ago, in 1908. "But while other self-recording creatures are permitted at least to seem to change the subject, apparently nobody cares what I think of the tariff, the conservation of our natural resources, or the conflicts which revolve about the name of Dreyfus."[9]

Keller wanted desperately to write about the social issues of her day, but her editors were not interested. Her preface ends with these prescient words: "Until they give me opportunity to write about matters that are not-me, the world will go on uninstructed and uninformed, and I can only do my best with the one small subject upon which I am allowed to discourse."

The World I Live In has been long out of print, though Keller's first and most famous book, *The Story of My Life,* continues to sell, but it is arguably the more interesting of the two, describing as it does the way in which Keller perceives the world, and holding in it, on almost every page, her frustration at not being taken seriously—of sometimes not even being believed—because her perceptions relied so heavily on senses that others barely experience: "The sensations of smell which cheer, inform, and broaden my life are not less pleasant merely because some critic who treads the wide, bright pathway of the eye has not cultivated his olfactive sense. Without the shy, fugitive, often unobserved sensations and the certainties which taste, smell, and touch give me, I should be obliged to take my conception of the universe wholly from others."[10]

This frustration is not found in Keller's early, more innocent autobiography, which she wrote when she was barely into her twenties and which is a perfect example of what many in the disability community call "inspiration porn"—an uplifting story that tends to leave nondisabled people feeling grateful for what they have and confident in the powers of the plucky individual to overcome obstacles. The narrative of *The Story of My Life,* and later *The Miracle Worker* (both the celebrated play and the film based on it), structures itself around Keller's sudden plunge into darkness and silence by disease and her equally sudden retrieval by education into light. This simplistic version of Keller's life ends when she is a child, causing many to forget that she grew into adulthood; in other words, inspiration porn requires an uncomplicated, optimistic ending.

I became fascinated with Helen Keller's long, dynamic adulthood (incongruously) while I was studying seventeenth- and eighteenth-century English literature as a graduate student at NYU. A few years into the program, I received a dissertation grant to continue my research on how ocular technologies such as the telescope and the microscope informed writers of the era, and found myself with too much unscheduled time on my hands. I began to wonder if academia was for me and fell in with a performance scene on the Lower East Side. Although I would eventually receive my PhD in 2009, instead of landing myself a sweet tenure-track professorship, I wrote and produced a play about Helen Keller.

"The Star of Happiness" is a one-woman, two-voiced, three-act play based on Keller's life, with her little-remembered vaudeville years (1920–24) at the heart of it. The play begins with a kind of comedic lecture on Keller's childhood, which ends with the climactic water-pump scene in *The Miracle Worker,* where Anne Sullivan ("Teacher") spells W-A-T-E-R into Helen's hand. The light dawns on the child's face, and the music swells. Bells ring, and the movie rushes to the end. Behind me on the stage, "The End" in all its Metro-Goldwyn-Mayer glory projects on the screen, and an offstage Evil Voice, who plagued me with jokes and snark in the first act, says, "That's a lovely story."

I, onstage, say with a big smile, "And that's just the beginning."

Evil Voice replies, "Nope, that's the end of the movie."

"But she's only seven at the end of the movie," I say, crestfallen. "And she lives to be eighty-seven."

The audience duly laughs. And the Evil Voice deals its final blow: "She's deaf, dumb, and blind, and she learns to *quote* talk. What more do you want?"

The spotlight constricts, and I recite the quote from *The World I Live In* that ends with "I can only do my best with the one small subject upon which I am allowed to discourse."

The point is loud and clear: wrapping Helen Keller up as a happy ending when she is seven provides a neat story that is reiterated in countless saccharine children's books and gives the impression that Keller's story is a simple matter of overcoming adversity that makes nondisabled people feel uplifted and grateful. It denies her the complexities of adulthood, which we will continue to return to in these pages.

Keller is one of my several blind spirit guides in this book, who will help unravel the inspirational narratives that sighted people so often demand from blind people. These stories have a long and ingrained lineage in our Western imagination: The triumph-over-adversity genre has its roots in the Christian symbolism of conversion, perhaps no more famously put than in the biblical text turned hymn lyric: "I once was blind, but now I see."

Blindness and sight—as well as their analogs darkness and light—constitute, in the Western imagination, a fundamental dichotomy, but that has not been my experience and is not the experience of most blind people, a very small percentage of whom were born with absolutely no sight. Furthermore, the congenitally blind generally find the equating of blindness with darkness or blackness particularly absurd, as these terms derive meaning only with the experience of their opposite. I, too, now that I am blind, find that I do not live in darkness. Rather, I am bombarded with light. The constant, hallucinogenic,[11] pulsating pixelated snow-fuzz that is the remainder of my vision actually keeps me from experiencing the blackness of night, and I'm not alone.

"One of the colors that the blind—or at least this blind man—do not see is black; another is red," explains Borges in "Blindness." "I, who was accustomed to sleeping in total darkness, was bothered for a long time at having to sleep in this world of mist, in the greenish or bluish mist, vaguely luminous, which is the world of the blind." The blind night that sighted people often assume is ours, as expressed in Shakespeare's line "Looking on darkness which the blind do see," is simply not true, or at least not universally true. As Borges says, "If we understand darkness as blackness, then Shakespeare is wrong."

The arc of my illness has taken me through nearly every notch of the sight-blindness spectrum. That spectrum, both metaphorically and literally, is what I want to reveal in these pages as a much more truthful and interesting alternative to the strict sight-blindness dichotomy. Blindness, in reality, is so often incomplete and spotty, degenerating and contingent. In what follows, with the help of examples taken from my own life and the lives of others, as well as artistic, philosophical, and scientific representations of blindness, we can begin to unravel the symbols and ideas upholding the notion that one is either sighted or blind.

I hope by the end of this book to show you, dear sighted and blind readers, how intimately connected are our histories—our stories—and how dependent we are on one another for human understanding. By tracing the complexities of metaphorical and literal blindness and sight I also hope to demonstrate how flimsy are the barriers between literally blind and sighted people. *There Plant Eyes* seeks to chip away at the pervasive ocularcentrism of our culture, to open up a space for social justice that accepts sensorial difference, to celebrate the vast, dappled regions between seeing and not-seeing, blindness and sight, darkness and light.

THERE PLANT EYES

Homer's Blind Bard

Homer, the author generally credited with the composition of *The Iliad* and *The Odyssey*—two of the oldest works of Western literature—is in large part responsible for the tradition of the blind bard, and yet so little is known about him and his life that most scholars believe him (and his blindness) to be legendary. Most accounts of Homer come to us from centuries after he purportedly lived, and even in the ancient world there existed skepticism regarding his blindness, as succinctly represented by Proclus (a philosopher of late antiquity), who in his *Life of Homer* turned the doubt into a kind of aphorism: "Those who have stated that he was blind seem to me to be mentally blind themselves, for he saw more clearly than any man ever."[1]

Although this kind of ocularcentrism (how can a blind person speak clearly about the visible world?) will be echoed about other blind writers from John Milton to Helen Keller, the idea that Homer was blind has endured.

The two great epic poems associated with the name Homer were probably composed in the eighth or seventh century BCE, about events during (*The Iliad*) and after (*The Odyssey*) the Trojan War, which itself, if historic, took place a few hundred years earlier in a distant heroic age. These epics as they've come down to us should be understood as a kind of tapestry of older legends and stories sung by many bards in many different versions, some of which were codified under the authorial name Homer.

The tradition of the blind bard in Western literature originates not in histories or biographies of Homer, but in *The Odyssey* itself. When Odysseus meets the blind bard Demodocus in the court of King Alcinous (leader of the Phaeacians) the moment feels rather meta: the fictional blind bard of the *Odyssey* as stand-in for the legendary blind author Homer: "The house boy brought the poet, whom the Muse / adored. She gave him two gifts, good and bad: / she took his sight away, but gave sweet song."[2]

This is from Emily Wilson's 2018 translation of *The Odyssey*. The famous passage sets forth the concept reiterated in Western culture again and again: the poetic gift is compensation for the physical lack of sight. Both the lack of sight and the gift of poetry come from the gods. The invocation of the Muse at the start of all great epics announces the poet's receptivity, and that receptivity is a matter of ears, not eyes. The poet demands not that the Muse show but tell: "Sing to me, O Muse!"

I first remember reading, or rather attempting to read, *The Odyssey* in the tenth grade, but by then my eyesight had deteriorated to such an extent that I did not make it very far. I confronted endless blocks of text (so perhaps it was a prose version created for high school readers) and, after just a few pages took me hours—the words breaking apart before my eyes, making comprehension nearly impossible—I attempted to write an essay about the book without having come anywhere near finishing it. I received a D for the paper, my first, and it was terrible. As an English honors student and a once-avid reader, I blamed and hated the teacher for my failure. I would not finish *The Odyssey* for several years—not until I found myself studying Greek and Latin at UC Santa Cruz (Go, Slugs!). Only then, as this anomalous creature—a classics major at a school best known for redwood groves and marijuana—did I first begin to identify with blindness in all its complexities and contradictions.

In fact, it was my Greek and Latin tutor (paid by Disabled Students Services to give me extra help outside of class) who first made me realize that blindness was not just my future calamity, but also a cultural phenomenon. "Did you know," he said, "that the ancients revered the blind as poets and prophets?"

By then I knew about Homer, of course, but I hadn't really thought about what the blind bard might have to do with me. With my CCTV—a cumbersome magnification system involving a seventeen-inch monitor that blew my Greek and Latin texts up into inch-high characters—at home, and the bulky packets of passages printed in forty-point type—which were still hard for me to read, but helped me to follow along in class—I did not feel very much like a poet or a prophet. I surely did not feel the compensatory powers set forth in *The Odyssey* and reiterated again and again in Western literature. I did not know then that my tutor's words would set me on my path to read metaphorical blindness against its realities. I did, however, have an inkling that this other blindness—the metaphorical kind—might provide some compensation after all. That I might do well to identify with metaphorical blindness in order to mitigate the intense shame I'd felt throughout my teens.

For it was shame that was—from about the age of twelve—my dominant feeling with regard to my visual impairment. Shame for the things I could not do. Shame at not being able to recognize faces, shame at not being able to see street signs, and above all, shame at not being able to read. If I had been a different kind of kid with different kinds of friends, I might have been bummed not to be able to catch a ball—and to be sure, there have been times in my life when play eluded me because of my poor sight. Mostly, however, my friends were the type of people who smoked, drank, made art, read, and frequented used record and book shops. So much of my time was spent trailing them around Green Apple, a used-book shop on Clement Street in San Francisco, inhaling that familiar scent of old paper everywhere, scrutinizing the covers in hopes of being able to find some words—a title or an author's name—large enough to recognize and perhaps purchase, maybe even show it off.

For some years to come, I would still be able to read (very) large print, and I could recognize my books by their covers, but by eleventh grade, most printed pages held only decorative lines of black ink for me. I could see the shapes of words dancing along, but without extreme magnification, no matter how much I squinted or maneuvered the page I could not read a single word.

My inability to read *The Odyssey* when I was in high school—before I was introduced to all the technology (the CCTV, the computer with speech output, later my braille display) that makes digital books accessible today, and even before I was introduced to recorded books when I was eighteen—echoes an irony at the heart of the blind Homer tradition. The books that have come to us as *The Iliad* and *The Odyssey* are written documents derived from a much older oral tradition. The dominance of the written word over that oral tradition made the reality of a blind reader, let alone a blind writer, a near impossibility, at least until the invention of first raised type and, later, braille in the eighteenth and nineteenth centuries. Even then, accessing the tools of the trade—the work of other writers, the means of writing—has hardly been easy for the blind writer.

"Believe me," Jorge Luis Borges said in an interview a year

before his death, "the benefits of blindness have been greatly exaggerated. If I could see, I would never leave the house, I'd stay indoors reading the many books that surround me. Now they're as far away from me as Iceland, although I've been to Iceland twice and I will never reach my books."3

This quote is heartbreaking, coming from a man who headed up the Argentinian National Library and wrote such intricately wrought, book-oriented stories as "The Library of Babel." The quote is also, however, surprising and a bit odd, coming as it does from someone who continued to have a wonderful career long after losing his ability to read. If reports of the benefits of blindness have indeed been exaggerated, Borges himself is not innocent: "Blindness has not been for me a total misfortune," he explains in "Blindness." "It should not be seen in a pathetic way. It should be seen as a way of life: one of the styles of living."4 This reminds me of the rallying cry of the actor and playwright Neil Marcus, who has helped to reify disability culture: "Disability is not a brave struggle or 'courage in the face of adversity.' Disability is an art."

Borges continues this train of thought by affirming that "being blind has its advantages," and credits it with many gifts, including another book "entitled, with a certain falsehood, with a certain arrogance, *In Praise of Darkness*." Then he moves on to "speak now of other cases, of illustrious cases." Beginning with the "obvious example of the friendship of poetry and blindness, with the one who has been called the greatest of poets: Homer," he goes on to mention others that we will encounter in this book: John Milton, whose "blindness was voluntary," and James Joyce, who "brought a new music to English."5

However, even with his illustrious forebearers showing him the way, Borges admits elsewhere that his blindness did adversely affect his writing. "Of course," Richard Burgin says to Borges in a 1968 interview, "it must be much more difficult for you to write now because of your blindness."

"It's not difficult, it's impossible," answers Borges. "I have to limit myself to short pieces. Yes, because I like to go over what I write; I'm very shaky about what I write . . . so I write sonnets, stories maybe one or two pages long."[6]

Although Milton famously used several amanuenses to take down and revise the epic *Paradise Lost*—Borges seemed to allow blindness to affect what and how he wrote. Why did he not use an assistant to read longer works aloud, and work with that assistant to make the necessary corrections? It remains a mystery to me. While I had a computer with speech output by the time I finished college, I often had to contend with professors' comments scribbled in the margins. When I was working on my dissertation, I liberally used human readers to slog through the chicken scratch in my revisions. Now I can read Word comments with my screenreader, and do not generally use any help in my writing process beyond the usual sorts that most writers appreciate. One exception is a final eyeball check for formatting mishaps by my sighted life partner, Alabaster Rhumb.

I can only account for Borges's path by reminding myself that we blind writers are not all alike. Moreover, as can be seen by his rather wild oscillations between bravado and insecurity, boasting and excuses, Borges illustrates how the metaphor of blindness offers solace even as dealing with its practicalities can feel overwhelming.

It is not only blind people who harbor such contradictory feelings about blindness; it is also—perhaps to an even greater extent—the sighted. What I'm wrestling with in this book is the concept of blindness that our ocularcentric culture extols on the one hand and dismisses on the other. The blind either converse with the gods or are incapable of performing the simplest tasks. The admiration sometimes mitigates the ridicule, but as we'll see when we come to the blind seer Tiresias, who prophesizes doom in the many Greek tragedies he inhabits, the sighted will shift their attention to the latter just as soon as the literally blind point out their metaphorical blindness.

For now, we are in the happy realm of the compensatory structure of the blind bard, wherein the sighted extend a helping hand in exchange for the gift of song. Here's how respectfully the blind bard Demodocus is treated in *The Odyssey,* despite his disability:

> The wine boy brought a silver-studded chair
> and propped it by a pillar, in the middle
> of all the guests, and by a peg he hung
> the poet's lyre above his head and helped him
> to reach it, and he set a table by him,
> and a bread basket and a cup of wine
> to drink whenever he desired.[7]

Once the blind bard is satisfied by food and drink, the Muse prompts him "to sing of famous actions, / an episode whose fame has touched the sky." The episode concerns Odysseus and Achilles, and it will cause our titular hero to weep because he is reminded of all his dead friends back in Troy. The tears of Odysseus prompt his host (and the employer of Demodocus), King Alcinous, to send them all outside for games, and then a different kind of song. Demodocus is not only a teller of tales but also a musician who gets people dancing:

> The house boy gave Demodocus the lyre.
> He walked into the middle, flanked by boys,

young and well trained, who tapped their feet
   performing
the holy dance, their quick legs bright with speed.[8]

Here, Demodocus presents as something that may feel more familiar to modern ears: the popular blind singer-songwriter, not so different from talented musical artists like Ray Charles and Stevie Wonder. Throughout the ages, music has offered employment for blind people who are gifted in that way, but in the time of *The Odyssey* the poet and the singer were synonymous. As Borges says, the blindness of Homer has everything to do with the idea that poetry is a musical art, and in the days of Demodocus and Odysseus it was literally so.

The character of Demodocus has been, in large part, responsible for the idea of Homer's blindness—a blindness that says much more about our preference for, and suspicion of, sight than it does about the man credited with the creation of the texts of *The Iliad* and *The Odyssey*. The author or authors who pulled together these scraps of legend and song into a codified written version were unlikely to have been blind, as it was the oral, not the written, culture in which the blind poet was most likely to thrive. Homer, as is sometimes suggested, could have been a wandering singing bard, the most famous representative of the oral tradition that lost its teeth as the written word took hold. But as the introduction to Wilson's translation suggests, the relationship between the purveyors of the oral tradition and those practicing literacy[9] remains mysterious; it has been given a name, the Homeric Question, and it has fueled much academic discourse.

There are scholars who argue that *The Odyssey* was composed by a single person. This person may have been familiar with the oral tradition and then gained literacy, making it possible for him (or her) to write the epic down. Alternatively, it could have been a group effort—several oral poets coming together with scribes to set their spoken words into indelible print. If so, this raises more questions about the relationship and the influence of these literate scribes on the final work. Were the scribes entirely passive, or did they help to shape the songs into something more in line with the new written format? It is, as Wilson's introduction cheekily asserts, "difficult to adjudicate between these various possibilities, in the absence of any solid evidence, or a time machine."[10]

I think what can be asserted without question is that if Homer was the author of the written poems with which he is credited, then he was not blind, and that if there *was* a blind Homer, who, like Demodocus, entertained the great lords and ladies of his age, then the texts that we know as *The Odyssey* and *The Iliad* were not sung by him in the form in which they come to us; they are too long to be performed.

It is, perhaps, the age-old desire of readers to inject autobiography into fiction that has allowed Homer's blindness to trickle through the centuries. Even if we learn in school that Homer is more an idea than a person, for blind people, especially blind writers, the name Homer holds a kind of talismanic power, and for most everybody, I think, Homer is the quintessential blind author. He tops Wikipedia's "List of Blind People" in the writers section,[11] for example, even though his entry clearly states in its introductory paragraph that his existence is but legendary. This suggests that what we know intellectually about the mysterious authorship of the great epics of Western literature cannot hold a candle to the powerful image of the blind poet. But why?

In other words, why is blindness tied to artistic creation in our imaginations? How is it that blindness, in a largely ocular-centric culture such as ours—such as the Greeks'—holds such (metaphorical) power? As we shall continue to witness, the blind bard will morph, or divide, into the blind prophet of Classical Greek theater who points out the metaphorical blindnesses of tragic heroes, and the philosophy of Socrates, whose paradoxical stance regarding sight suggests that it actually imperils clear thinking with its superfluous distractions. And, as we shall— dare I say—see, these two aspects of blindness together suggest the dangers of sight when it comes to seeing invisible (spiritual) truths.

Having tied blindness to transcendence—artistic, philosophical, spiritual—Western culture from the days of Homer onward has made much of the blind guide. Take, for example, Mark Danielewski's 2000 novel of obsession and filmic horror, *House of Leaves,* which invokes the blind bard on many levels. Homer, Milton, and Borges seem to be inspirations for the novel's blind guide, the character named Zampanò. I think it's not irrelevant to point out that *House of Leaves* is a perfect example of how far a sighted author will go in drawing a blind character for a presumably sighted reader. With its several fonts, multicolored print, insane repetitions of words or crossed-out phrases, pages with a single word or two, the novel is virtually unreadable—at least as the author intended—by a blind person.

I read Danielewski's haunting masterpiece several years ago and was riveted. I was also shocked to learn, after the fact, just how much I'd missed out on as a listener to the electronic book. (For obvious reasons, perhaps, there does not seem to be a commercial audio version, and for less obvious reasons, no commercial ebook[12] either.) When revisiting the novel, I make sure to have a physical copy on hand as well, so that when it comes to specific passages, I can have Alabaster check the look of them, but it's sometimes hard to know what to have him look for when it is not described. Once when I asked him generally about what he saw on the pages of the novel as he casually flipped through, he suddenly said, "There's braille on this page!" I had no idea; it was visual braille.[13]

In *House of Leaves,* Zampanò—the blind, relatively minor character whose death before the start of the novel sets its events in motion—stands in strange relationship to the two protagonists. Johnny Truant is the hapless inheritor of the blind man's trunk, and Will Navidson—a filmmaker whose work is the record of a dark, fathomless infinity ostensibly enclosed within his house—is the creation of the blind man's imagination.

The irony of the blind graphomaniac creator of a film that exists only in words (as well as much of its attendant criticism) is not lost on Johnny. As he examines the former tenant's apartment, wondering about "these strange, pale books" and "the fact that there's hardly a goddamn bulb in the whole apartment, not even one in the refrigerator" he discovers the strange truth: "Well that, of course, was Zampanò's greatest ironic gesture; love of love written by the broken hearted; love of life written by the dead: all this language of light, film and photography, and he hadn't seen a thing since the mid-fifties."

Johnny concludes, "He was blind as a bat," which, of all the clichéd phrases used to disparage blind people, seems most inept. But we'll let it go, assuming the imprecision to be that of a startled young man just beginning his journey into the dark.[14]

The (ironic) blind guide is perhaps as old an image as that of the blind poet, and he (occasionally she) appears in the guise of a prophet or seer. That image, as we shall see, has a whole other set of associations. Still, the blind poet and the blind prophet share an important characteristic: they are generally not the heroes of the tales in which they figure. Even as the myth of the great blind bard is formulated, the concept of the blind man as helper or sidekick to the sighted hero is also forged.

After Demodocus finishes entertaining the guests of King Alcinous with song that inspires dance, he and the rest of the party return to the great hall. There Odysseus, "clever mastermind of many schemes," makes a self-serving request of the blind bard, and sweetens it with compliments: "You are wonderful, Demodocus! / I praise you more than anyone."[5] He also offers Demodocus a choice piece of meat, taken from his own plate, and asks the blind bard to "sing the story / about the Wooden Horse," a story rather flattering to Odysseus himself, since it was his doing after all: "Odysseus / dragged it inside and to the citadel, / filled up with men to sack the town." He concludes, "If you / can tell that as it happened, I will say / that you truly are blessed with inspiration."[6]

Odysseus asks for a song of himself, and the blind bard, as so often happens, obliges the sighted person's need to see himself, to know himself, in the eyes—or rather out of the mouth—of the blind. In this case, the need seems quite practical. For this episode in *The Odyssey* takes place just before Odysseus reveals himself to the court. Then, for the next four books (IX–XII), Odysseus will relate his incredible tale in his own words, explaining how he came to be washed up on the shores of King Alcinous and the Phaeacians, as a destitute and naked suppliant. And those events are some of the most memorable in *The Odyssey,* including Circe turning his men into swine, Scylla and Charybdis, the Lotus Eaters, the journey into the underworld, and the blinding of the Cyclops Polyphemus. Odysseus was really asking the blind poet to set the stage for his own more extravagant and incredible tale.

Thus, I'm tempted to blame Odysseus for the predicament of the blind character, who, for nearly three millennia of Western literature, has been tasked with delineating the importance, even the existence, of the sighted hero. The blind bard, the blind prophet, and so many other archetypal blind figures are rarely the protagonists of the stories in which they find themselves. The legendary Homer aside, we can perhaps understand this predicament as being related to the fact that so few blind characters have been drawn by blind writers. It does not explain, however, why blind characters are so ubiquitous. As we continue to investigate the literary blind, we will see how it is the idea of blindness, not the experience of blind people, that is important to sighted readers and audiences.

In the following pages, we will encounter many examples of the blind character's ability to delineate or make manifest that which appears shaky in the mind of the sighted protagonist, but nowhere is the phenomenon more succinctly used (or perhaps abused) than in this brief (random) passage in Gillian Flynn's 2006 novel, *Sharp Objects,* where a blind stranger on the street reassures the protagonist, Camille, of her own existence:

> Once I was standing on a cold corner in Chicago waiting for the light to change when a blind man came clicking up. *What are the cross streets here,* he asked, and when I didn't reply he turned toward me and said, *Is anybody there?*
>
> *I'm here,* I said, and it felt shockingly comforting, those words. When I'm panicked, I say them aloud to myself. *I'm here.*[17]

The fact that the figure of the blind bard stands next to our archetypal hero explains, at least in part, why we have so much blindness to contend with in books, movies, television shows, and so on. Homer's blind bard plays a small part in *The Odyssey,* and yet his influence on the role of the blind in literature has, as Flynn's random blind man suggests, stuck.

Besides the blind bard Demodocus, there is another blind

character in *The Odyssey* who similarly represents an enduring and related type: Tiresias, the blind seer. Although he is more often associated with the tragedies of fifth-century Athens (Classical Greece), such as *Oedipus the King,* Tiresias makes a cameo appearance in *The Odyssey,* among the realms of the dead. Specifically, Tiresias will tell Odysseus about his future as well as how to talk to the other dead souls, who offer him their insights on the lives they've left behind.

Odysseus came to the underworld to learn how to get home safely. Thus, while the blind bard tells of things past, the blind seer speaks of things to come, and this makes all the difference; it's generally less jarring to hear about the past than the future. But in either case, the blind poet Demodocus and the blind prophet Tiresias make manifest things invisible, i.e., things not present. It is not easy to make out divine truths with our mortal, physical eyes, and so Odysseus also begins the tradition of calling upon the blind seer to give some clue about what the future holds, and Tiresias (like Demodocus) obliges the sighted man's need to know, saying, "I prophesy the signs of things to come."[8] Even if what Odysseus will learn is mostly about how to get through the trials facing him on his journey back to his home in Ithaca, he is comforted to know that he will eventually get there.

2

The Tenacious Grip of the Blind Seer

Oedipus the King, also known as *Oedipus Rex,* is the most famous of Sophocles' three Theban plays (which also include *Antigone* and *Oedipus at Colonus*) and was first performed around 429 BCE (some two or three hundred years after the Homeric epics were written down). In it we witness, with excruciating exactitude, the fall of the mythical king Oedipus. He begins as a man riding high on his powers, both intellectually and politically, and ends famously low, with his eyes self-gouged. If only he'd listened to the blind seer Tiresias—who told him not to look. But of course Oedipus does look—does need to know—and thus plays out his iconic destiny.

The backstory of Oedipus will sound awfully familiar, as it is an archetypal plot that fuels many myths ancient and modern. Similar to the stories of the Trojan War, the stories of Oedipus and his doomed Theban family were already very old by the time they were written and performed: Oedipus is born the son of Laius, king of Thebes, but because of a prophecy that the baby would grow up to kill his father and wed his mother, the king casts off his child, giving him (his feet pierced with metal pins) to a shepherd, with instructions to leave him on a mountain to die. The shepherd tasked with this unpleasant duty instead gives the baby to a fellow shepherd from another part of Greece. In turn, that shepherd passes him along to the childless king of Corinth, who raises him as his son and names him Oedipus—

for his swollen feet. Ignorant of the identity of his true parents, Oedipus hears of the curse, strikes out on his own, and has a run-in with a stranger, resulting in that stranger's death. That stranger, of course, is his biological father, Laius. Oedipus then wanders into Thebes, where he solves a riddle to rescue the city. The citizens are so grateful that they offer him the kingship and throw in the queen as well, who is, of course, his mother, Jocasta.

The play opens years later with Thebes suffering under another curse, which an oracle has said will last until the killer of King Laius is found and brought to justice. In order to solve the mystery, Oedipus calls for the blind seer Tiresias. But instead of helping him, Tiresias tells him to stop his search, stat. Oedipus, however, is a man who needs to know, and so he pushes the blind seer for answers, which turn out to be not exactly what Oedipus expected: "You are the curse, the corruption of the land!"[1]

Like Demodocus in *The Odyssey,* Tiresias must flesh out the personality and destiny of the sighted hero. But whereas Demodocus tells Odysseus an ego-stroking version of events past, Tiresias tells an unpleasant version of things present: "[Y]ou and your loved ones live together in infamy," he tells Oedipus, "you cannot see how far you've gone in guilt."[2]

Thus, instead of flattery and choice cuts of meat, Tiresias receives insults: "You've lost your power," Oedipus shoots back, "stone-blind, stone-deaf-senses—eyes blind as stone!"[3]

Nearly identical exchanges occur in other Greek tragedies: between Creon and Tiresias in *Antigone* (the first-written and performed of Sophocles' Theban plays), between Pentheus and Tiresias in *The Bacchae* (written by Euripides and first performed in 405 BCE), and so on. When the prophetic vision of Tiresias is called upon in these tragedies, honest responses lead to his person and blindness being ridiculed, his advice ignored. Though he is summoned by the men in power to tell them what's going on—why the gods are angry—Tiresias gives answers that are accusatory and unwelcome.

This raises the question of why the blind seer Tiresias keeps showing up when his revelations are always so distasteful to his sighted listeners. It seems the answer has something to do with the tragic structure itself: The hero falls because of his refusal to accept the truth from another. He must discover it for himself, and in doing so must suffer and (usually) die. In the case of Oedipus, the truth is that he unwittingly killed his father and married his mother. That truth, foretold by an oracle and repeated by Tiresias, must be discovered by asking practical questions, not of oracles and prophets but of ordinary men and servants. People who have firsthand information about his past.

When he finally can no longer deny the truth that he is the man he is looking for, Oedipus gouges out his eyes in a spectacularly bloody display of guilt and punishment. Although that event, like all action scenes in Greek tragedy, takes place offstage, the telling of it by the servant who witnessed it is quite enough to get one's heart rate going:

> He rips off her brooches, the long gold pins
> holding her robes—and lifting them high,
> looking straight up into the points,
> he digs them down the sockets of his eyes, crying,
>   "You,
> you'll see no more the pain I suffered, all the pain I
>   caused!
> Too long you looked on the ones you never should have
>   seen,

blind to the ones you longed to see, to know! Blind
from this hour on! Blind in the darkness—blind!"
His voice like a dirge, rising, over and over
raising the pins, raking them down his eyes.[4]

When I taught *Oedipus the King* at NYU in several semes-
ters of a general humanities course called Conversations of the
West, the students never seemed to think twice about the blindness of the prophet Tiresias or even why Oedipus gouges his eyes
at the end. Why, for example, does Oedipus not follow his wife/
mother Jocasta's lead and kill himself? Why does he poke out
his eyes with her brooches instead? He blinds himself in order to
see, of course. That impulse—to be like the blind seer Tiresias
rather than like the sighted and ignorant king that he was—
assumes he will see something with empty eye sockets that he
could not see with fully sighted eyes. And somehow this iconic
literary grotesquery has developed into one of our dominant
metaphors.

The Oedipus trope of eye-gouging—picked up by Shakespeare in *King Lear,* for example—has been ingrained in our
culture ever since. My students' blasé acceptance of the bloody
scene of sight's destruction suggests that the notion that one sees
better when one is blind is barely recognized as a myth with a
literary history.

May I speak plainly here? Although I have often joked
onstage that "I have a touch of the clairvoyance—as do all my
blind brothers and sisters," I must sadly admit that I'm just as
circumscribed to the mundane present as my sighted counterparts. Contrary to popular belief, one does not automatically
gain extrasensory abilities when one loses (or pokes out) his or
her eyes. However, I admit I don't always deny it. If a sighted

person wants to believe in my prophetic powers, why not? I mean, our practical abilities are so often doubted and distrusted in this ocularcentric world that I might as well claim the blind-seer superpower.

That said, clairvoyance has its limitations, which is perhaps why the quintessential blind seer, Tiresias, has a mythology that connects blindness with femaleness, and hence impotence. Tiresias may know the future, but he is extremely limited in what he can do about it.

Gender inflects blindness, as we shall continue to witness, but I want to point out here that classical dramatic representations of blind men have much in common with representations of women, such as a relationship with the dark (shut up in their houses as women were supposed to be) and political impotence (women were not considered citizens in Athens in the Classical Period). Impotence is a strange concept to invoke when talking about literature because to our modern minds it's almost inextricable from male sexual power. But powerlessness is not just something males can lose—it is also what women (and blind people) are culturally saddled with. If we tend to care about able-bodied male impotence, it's because we love to lament what is lost, not what appears to our imaginations as inherently missing from the outset.

Yet, a dark, nearly mad, and explicitly unknowable power belongs to both women and blind men in the plays they inhabit. The Greeks—lovers of strength and light—indulged women and blind men to parade across their stages in order to reveal truths beyond their masculine sight and outside the control of reason and law—pillars of Athenian society so admired through the ages. One does not have to look far to see how these images are still with us.

In her 1999 memoir and cultural critique, *Sight Unseen,* Georgina Kleege writes about how the Oedipus myth so easily translates from stage to film:

> Because blind men in the movies exist as passive
> objects of speculation for both the viewer and the
> viewer's on-screen surrogate, they perform the function
> that mainstream cinema usually reserves for women:
> They exist to be looked at. They are all spectacle.
> In treating blind men like women, movies reenact
> the castration that blindness has represented since
> Oedipus. The viewer contemplates the blind man
> on screen with both fascination and revulsion. The
> sighted man, the true protagonist, reassures the viewer
> by taking charge of this walking-talking castration
> symbol and diluting the horror he provokes.[5]

Happily, as living mythologies with startlingly topical archetypes, the story of Oedipus is not just for those dinosaur-like filmmakers with their (masculine) complexes. When seen through non-Freudian eyes, Oedipus (and Tiresias) can also speak to a new generation of gender-fluid mythologies that would not be a surprise to the Greeks. After all, they dressed in drag onstage and portrayed such women as Agave in *The Bacchae,* who rips apart her son, Pentheus, himself disguised as a female worshipper in order to spy on the reveling women in their nocturnal Dionysian rite.

Tiresias himself has a complicated transsexual mythology that lurks behind his appearances in Classical tragedies, which are perhaps most familiarly told in Ovid's *Metamorphoses.* In that Roman retelling, Tiresias's experience as both a man and a woman is directly linked to his blindness and prophetic vision. He starts out life as a sighted man who happens upon two huge snakes as they are mating and inexplicably strikes them. He is then transformed into a she, and for seven years remained so, until he/she encountered those mating serpents once again, and thought perhaps another strike might produce a reversal. It did, and Tiresias regained his maleness. That's the backstory.

Having enjoyed the pleasures of life as both a man and a woman, Tiresias was invited by the gods Jove and Juno to settle their dispute as to who enjoyed sex more: the man or the woman. According to Juno (and probably many women since), Tiresias gives the wrong answer, siding with Jove that in fact women enjoy sex more! The goddess, angered to excess, punishes Tiresias with blindness. Unable to undo the work of another god, Jove mitigates the penalty by giving Tiresias foresight, thereby tempering the loss of sight with the gift of prophecy.[6]

I've been fascinated by Tiresias for some time, and my first attempt at writing a novel was a retelling of his/her story. Although I never finished it, I learned quite a bit about Tiresias in the process. As a woman, Tiresias is initiated as a priestess of Hera (Juno) and gives birth to Manto, a famous prophetess in her own right. Thus I was delighted to discover Daisy Johnson's 2018 novel *Everything Under,* which is, in part, a modern reimagining of the Oedipus myth set in and around the waterways of Oxford.

In *Everything Under,* we have the dire prophecy as well as the Oedipal attempt to elude it. Physical blindness is less of a plot device in Johnson's retelling than in the original ancient stories, but it does manifest in one character, Charlie, who has premonitions of his fate: "He told you that he dreamed of going blind, of waking and being able to see nothing but night, of seeing a pin moving with speed towards his pupils."[7]

Instead of the dramatic poking out of eyeballs, Charlie will suffer from a degenerative eye disease. In Johnson's retelling, a kind of meandering mutability takes center stage alongside fate, symbolized by slow vision loss as well as the ever-flowing Oxford Canal. The mutability of human existence is also presented as gender fluidity. Two transvestite characters emerge as central figures in the novel: the Tiresias-like character arrives in female drag and delivers the terrifying prophecy, while the Oedipus-like character changes from girl to boy in the course of her adventures. Perhaps because lack of vision is not all that is at stake, blindness often takes on the cultural baggage of femininity, insofar as the blind man seems also to rely on the sighted male—even a sighted boy will do—which is a powerfully emasculating bit of collateral damage. As Demodocus is led to his seat and handed his harp in *The Odyssey,* Tiresias is led by his guide from town to town: "Lords of Thebes," Tiresias announces upon his entrance on the stage of *Antigone.* "I and the boy have come together, / hand in hand. Two see with the eyes of one . . . / so the blind must go, with a guide to lead the way."[8]

The need for a guide is almost as ubiquitous a marker for blindness as the staff or the dog, the blank or milky eyes. In Frank Herbert's *Dune* series, Paul Atreides could be said to choose the office of the blind prophet called "the Preacher" over that of emperor. Although his prophetic vision gives him perfect second sight (as it is in lockstep with the present), his lack of eyeballs makes it necessary that he have a guide—at least culturally, if not practically: "The Preacher entered the plaza at first light, finding the place already thronging with the faithful. He kept a hand lightly on the shoulder of his young guide, sensing the cynical pride in the lad's walk. Now, when the Preacher approached, people noticed every nuance of his behavior. Such attention was not entirely distasteful to the young guide."[9]

Being the guide of a blind prophet necessitates a strange kind of leading, for it is the will of the blind that dictates the actions of the sighted, suggesting a larger theme in the relationship, an unlikely codependence: The sighted guide is actually led by the needs and obligations of the blind seer, and is therefore guided by him.

The sighted guide can do no more than avoid visible obstacles, while the blind prophet navigates the obstacles of the invisible realms, or at least that is the hope. For if prophetic vision is perfect it is a kind of prison—dictating, rather than simply foretelling, the future. That is one fundamental lesson of *Oedipus the King*—that foresight can so easily turn to destiny. As the Preacher of *Dune* puts it, "If certainty is knowing absolutely an absolute future, then that's only death disguised! Such a future becomes now!"[10]

Because of the assumed impotence of blindness, extrasensory powers, including prophetic vision, are commonly understood to offer compensation for a lack. Just as divine inspiration is granted to the blind bard Demodocus, divine sight is given to the blind Tiresias. Thus the impotence of the ancient blind seer is directly connected to his power of prophecy, a power that has morphed over the centuries into a kind of superpower, much beloved in our superhero-crazed age.

Stuck in the realm of high culture and classic texts as I often am, it occurred to me that there may be an abundance of blind seers in popular culture—particularly in visual media such as comic books and television shows—that have escaped my notice. Therefore, I decided to do a quick and dirty Facebook crowdsource: "Who are your favorite blind seers (besides Tiresias)?" My question incited a lively discussion in which I learned about or was reminded of: Sensei Tomonaga, blind zombie slayer in *World War Z;* Hinoto from the Japanese comic book *X,* by the all-female artist/writer collective CLAMP; Alicia Masters, the blind sculptress (and adopted daughter of a supervillain) in *The Fantastic Four;* Eli (played by Denzel Washington) in *The Book of Eli;* Toph from *Avatar* (animated TV series), who is a twelve-year-old blind earthbender; Baba Vanga from Russia; Stick from *Daredevil,* and Daredevil himself; Aughra from *The Dark Crystal,* who isn't completely blind, but has one eye, like Odin the Norse god; Blindfold from Marvel Comics; Pamela Barnes from *Supernatural;* the Graeae, who share a single eye (and tooth), made memorable as "The Stygian Witches" in *Clash of the Titans,* and so on.

Admittedly, some of the examples blur into the realm of the physically superblind—like the superhero Daredevil, whose powers are linked to his crime-fighting abilities, or are only half blind, or are not exactly prophets—but you get the idea. I asked for blind seers, and in response I got all kinds of superblind—one friend even mentioned Milton—which suggests that the image of Tiresias has morphed through the ages into the extraordinary blind generally. We'll have more to say about the perils of the superblind later, but for now, it's important to keep in mind how the blind seer archetype retains its grip on our imaginations. At least our sighted imaginations. Interestingly, every one of the comments was from my sighted friends. Perhaps my blind friends are just a little tired of the blind seer thing.

Despite the ubiquity of the blind seer, the way Oedipus transforms into a blind seer figure akin to Tiresias is often overlooked. Again, it seems that the dual aspects of blindness—that it is a tragic horror on the one hand and a powerful gift from the gods on the other—remain stubbornly fixed in our cultural imaginations. So before we take Oedipus all the way to Colonus, to his rightful place in the blind seer pantheon, we must dwell for a while longer with him in his darkness, where we leave him after the eye-gouging. At the end of *Oedipus the King,* he is led back onstage by a boy and laments his fate:

> Dark, horror of darkness
> my darkness, drowning, swirling around me
> crashing wave on wave—unspeakable, irresistible
> headwind, fatal harbor! Oh again,
> the misery, all at once, over and over
> the stabbing daggers, stab of memory
> raking me insane.[11]

This blind misery at the end of *Oedipus the King* is what most of us remember, and it seems to amplify the response of many sighted people to the horror of blindness that is akin to death—a theme that remains just as fixedly in our cultural imagination as the extrasensory powers of the superblind, and in some ways the opposing forces feed each other.

Take, for example, Stephen King's *The Langoliers,* in which the little blind seer, Dinah, saves the time-suspended stragglers of American Pride's Flight 29 with her mysterious powers. Then (spoiler alert) she dies, happy, because she, at last, sees: "Don't worry about me," she tells her companion. "I got . . . what I wanted." To drive the point home, she smiles and says, "Everything was beautiful . . . even the things that were dead. It was so wonderful to . . . you know . . . just to see."[12]

Of course, Dinah's dying words say very little about the sentiments of actual blind people and much more about the fears and hyperbolic claims of sighted people that they'd rather be dead than blind.

It's not only popular fiction that expresses the theme with

such vehemence. For example, in *Blindness,* an allegorical novel by the Nobel Prize–winning author José Saramago, nearly all the inhabitants of an unnamed city suddenly go blind from a mysterious "white mist" descending upon their vision. The "first blind man" succinctly expresses the all-too-common sentiment "If I have to stay like this, I'd rather be dead."

That blindness is worse than death is the overwhelming conclusion at the end of *Oedipus the King.* In fact, it's the reason Oedipus gives for choosing to gouge his eyes as punishment for his crimes—"crimes too huge for hanging."[3]

However, Oedipus's end as a despised and blind fallen king at the close of this tragedy is not the end of him. He will be redeemed in the final play of Sophocles' Theban trilogy, *Oedipus at Colonus,* arguably the least read, least performed of the three plays.

Oedipus at Colonus was Sophocles' last play, written in his ninetieth year and produced posthumously. It is a kind of inverse of its more famous prequel. In *Colonus,* Oedipus himself becomes a Tiresias-like figure, who accepts his destiny with the fore-knowledge that's reserved for blind seers. He begins to see, to have prophetic vision, and even, at its conclusion, to walk alone to his true destiny as an instrument of power. Though he dies as the conventions of tragedy dictate, it is not exactly a tragic end, but rather an apotheosis:

> No blazing bolt of the god took him off,
> no whirlwind sweeping inland off the seas,
> not in his last hour. No, it was some escort
> sent by the gods or the dark world of the dead,
> the lightless depths of Earth bursting open in kindness
> to receive him. That man went on his way,
> I tell you, not with trains of mourners,

not with suffering or with sickness, no,
if the death of any mortal ever was one,
his departure was a marvel![14]

How different this play's ending is from that of its predeces-
sor. It is surely not coincidence that amongst the three Theban
plays, this is the only one in which Tiresias does not appear. Why
should he? Oedipus now plays his part. It is also interesting to
note how many readers forget that the hapless unseeing victim
of fate becomes, in the end, the blind seer, beloved by the gods.

I was eighteen or nineteen when my mom took us to see
the American Conservatory Theater production of *The Gospel
at Colonus* (created by Lee Breuer). The modern musical sets
the story of *Oedipus at Colonus* in an African American church,
complete with preacher, choir, organ, and a dynamic cast including The Blind Boys of Alabama collectively playing Oedipus.
The gospel interpretation of the final days of Oedipus helped
me to understand what perhaps keeps us moderns from appreciating *Oedipus at Colonus:* its strong religious symbolism. In the
gospel reimagining, the final joyful number—complete with
warbling organ and hand-clapping—"Now Let the Weeping
Cease," beautifully enacts the happy religious ending: "When I
was blind and could not see, he touched my eyes and now I can
see . . ."[15]

As we'll continue to witness, the ancient Greek tradition of
the blind seer neatly translates into a Christian context. When
you are literally sighted you are likely blind to eternal truths, and
so self-blinding is the quickest way to see those truths that exist
beyond mortal sight.

After all, Oedipus is not the only ancient to gouge out his
eyes. Democritus, a.k.a. "the Laughing Philosopher," was born
about thirty years after Sophocles. He came up with the idea of

atoms. Democritus, Robert Burton tells us in his 1621 *Anatomy of Melancholy,* was a great scholar with encyclopedic interests. And, Burton explains, it is related by some that in order to "better contemplate," Democritus "put out his eyes, and was in his old age voluntarily blind, yet saw more than all Greece besides."[6]

Perhaps the lesson of the self-blinded has much to do with the disconcerting knowledge of how much lies beyond human sight, and our often hubristic refusal to accept this truth. Nonetheless, we must investigate, or grope around, all the same. When it comes to issues relating to invisible truths, the blind seer may be called upon to guide us through the superficial, oddly extraneous external world. Blinding oneself therefore is a symbol of acknowledging our inherent blindnesses, and the ancient Greeks made a habit and an art of it, which we have inherited.

3.

I Once Was Blind, but Now I See

It's no secret that Christianity has helped to shape our (presumably) secular culture. Thus it should come as no surprise that its assumptions and biases about the blind being more spiritual and less prone to sin (as so much temptation comes through the eyes) continue to influence our culture high and low. But before we get to the iconic New Testament instances of blindness such as Jesus's healing of the blind man and Paul's blindness on the road to Damascus, I should remind you that Christianity grew up in a Greek-speaking world. The Gospels were written in Koine (common Greek) in the early centuries of the first millennium CE. Thus, we must spend a little more time with the ancient Greeks, specifically the philosophy of Plato, whose life spanned the fifth and fourth centuries BCE, and whose dialogues involving Socrates are at least in part responsible for the Christian Bible's near obsession with the dualities of darkness and light, blindness and sight, which gained momentum through the Christian Middle Ages, with its numerous blind saints.

In the Conversations of the West course I taught several times as a PhD candidate at NYU, we almost always read Sophocles' plays back to back with Plato's dialogues featuring Socrates. Inevitably some students would get those two names mixed up. It was understandable, as they were contemporaries in Athens—Sophocles ca. 496–406 BCE and Socrates ca. 470–399 BCE. And in their different ways—as dramatist and as philosopher—each extolled the virtues of the seeing blind, or rather, the unseeing sighted that so dominate Western religious thought.

Phaedo, the Platonic dialogue that ends with the death of Socrates, makes explicit the importance of acknowledging the separation between body and soul. The body, Socrates says, participates in the visible world, "oppressive and heavy and earthy and visible." The soul's element is invisible and airy, but can be "made heavy and dragged back into the visible region through terror of the Unseen and of Hades." These souls clinging to the visible turn out to be a nice explanation for ghosts, which are "the sort of souls that weren't released in purity but participate in the Visible—which is why they too are visible."[1]

In this way Western ideas have conceived body and soul as separate and antithetical entities, often symbolized and enhanced by sight and blindness—the soul reaching for light, the body mucking around in the dark. Furthermore, while being overly concerned with the body can corrupt the soul, the soul, with its invisible and immortal relationship to the gods, is the superior element. That the soul is unchangeable and deathless is precisely what is at stake in *Phaedo.* The friends of Socrates yearn to believe that after his death, which is looming over them—the hemlock with which he will be executed putting a precise and irrevocable endpoint to this particular dialogue—something of the great philosopher will remain.

During the course of his arguments, Socrates tells how he came to be a philosopher—or rather, how he came to adopt philosophy as the means to grasping truths. When he was young, he had investigated the nature of things and the things of nature. He looked at them directly and tried to understand them. But at some point he became afraid of this direct looking, that it would tend to blindness. "Since I had had it with this looking into beings," he tells his friends, "it seemed to me I had to be on my guard so as not to suffer the very thing those people do who behold and look at the sun during an eclipse. For surely some of them have their eyes destroyed if they don't look at the sun's likeness in water or in some other such thing." Socrates seems to be saying that one must look at the reflection of the eclipse, of the sun, in order not to be blinded. And yet even reflections are not to be trusted. "I thought this sort of thing over and feared I might be totally soul-blinded if I looked at things with my eyes and attempted to grasp them by each of the senses."[2]

One may be reminded of Plato's famous "Allegory of the Cave" from *The Republic*. In the cave we find prisoners chained and unable to move their heads, staring at shadows cast on the wall by the people walking in front of a fire behind and above them. Yet, if one of these prisoners were to be freed, to stand and turn around and look up at the light, he would be dazzled by the light and doubtful that these new images were real. And if he were compelled to take the steep path out of the cave and into the sunlight, he would, for some time, be blinded by the light. Thus the metaphorics of light and dark are, from the outset, complicated, as one may be blinded by darkness just as easily as by light.

The infinite reversals of seeing and not-seeing are revealed in a continual looping exchange. One thing remains constant in these reversals: it is better to see (understand) metaphorically than to see physically (with one's eyes), just as it is better to tend to the soul rather than the body.

Here enters the paradox that drives so many assumptions swirling around blind people: Soul blindness, diametrically opposed to physical blindness, can be brought about by paying too much attention to the perceptions of the eyes and other senses. As the paradox is transmuted into a Christian context, blindness is understood to be a concern when it is spiritual, and a situation ripe for miracles when it is physical. In either case, what is at stake is truth—the kind of truth that philosophy and religion concern themselves with.

In her consideration of the age-old antagonism between facts and truth in *The Art of Cruelty* (2011), Maggie Nelson writes, "The idea that the visible, palpable, or present world is but a shadow of a different, 'truer' world that exists elsewhere lies at the heart of the Platonic universe."[3]

"It also undergirds the biblical notion that in the here and now, we must 'see through a glass, darkly,'" she writes, "but that on Judgment Day, our vision will clear."[4] Truth, then, is not only separate from but also often diametrically opposed to perceptible facts (of the senses and intellect). And because humans tend to put so much stock in physical sight, it is sight that is often accused of leading us away from truth.

Nelson invokes the eighteenth-century illustrator and poet William Blake and quotes his *Marriage of Heaven and Hell* (1793): "If the doors of perception were cleansed every thing would appear to man as it is, infinite. For man has closed himself up, till he sees all things thro' narrow chinks of his cavern."[5]

These narrow chinks resonate with me literally, as I sometimes still catch a bit of physical light in my far left peripheral vision, but it is also the plain fact that all physical seeing is dictated by the anatomy of our eyes. We see no more and no less than what is physically possible without technological aids such as reading glasses, telescopes, microscopes, and X-rays. Nelson calls attention to this limitation: "Blake says man has 'closed himself up'; a less pointed diagnosis might treat these 'narrow chinks' as our inevitably limited senses, the apertures through which we must apprehend and construct the world, a world we presume to exist independently of us, 'out there.'"[6]

As I said, Christian thought grew up in a Greek-speaking world, and so Jesus's teachings (at least as they've come down to us) were influenced by Greek as well as Jewish traditions. Like Socrates before him, Jesus emphasized a fundamental paradox: physical death brings spiritual life. In the related teachings of both Socrates and Jesus, the emphasis on realms beyond the physical threatens the authority of state and empire and leads to death—by hemlock and crucifixion, respectively. In both cases, blindness can symbolize either spiritual ignorance—i.e., a blinding by the physical world to spiritual truths—or its opposite, a physical blindness that can aid in seeing spiritual truths.

In John 9, Jesus and his disciples come upon a man who has been blind from birth, and the disciples ask their teacher if it was by the man's own sin or his parents' sin that he was made blind. But Jesus answers, "Neither this man nor his parents sinned; he was born blind so that God's works might be revealed in him." Then he spits on the ground and makes mud with his saliva and puts it on the blind man's eyes. After washing off the mud, the blind man is able to see. The skeptical Pharisees interrogate the previously blind man, who'd been known to beg on the streets, and the man answers, "One thing I do know, that though I was blind, now I see."[7]

Thus, the curing of the blind man makes manifest the power of God through Jesus. "Since the world began was it not heard that any man opened the eyes of one that was born blind," the formerly blind man testifies. "If this man were not of God, he could do nothing."[8] The Pharisees are angered by his attempts to teach them, and they cast him out.

The chapter ends with an open-ended threat to the Pharisees and other unbelievers: "And Jesus said, for judgment I am come into this world, that they which see not might see; and that they which see might be made blind."[9]

Like Socrates before him, Jesus invokes the paradox of blindness, wherein physical sight may lead to spiritual blindness. But in this biblical story he heals a physically blind man in order to show both the power of God and the folly of thinking too much of one's physical sight. The Pharisees and other unbelievers may see with their eyes, but they are soul-blind. Perhaps here lies the origin of the idea of physical blindness as holding curative powers for spiritual blindness. And through the centuries this has been extrapolated to mean that blind people are less prone to sin, particularly of the sort that comes from worldliness.

"I once was lost, but now I'm found," sang the busker at the West Fourth Street subway every morning as I made my way from Brooklyn to NYU during my first year of grad school, "Was blind but now I see." Having some limited vision at the time, I could just make out the big black man with the joyful voice, standing in his corner of the station between the street entrance and the ramp down to the C train, but I never saw his white cane. A friend finally told me he was blind. No wonder he sang that song. Every day the same song, and I'd always hum along. How can you not? Written in 1779, "Amazing Grace" is arguably the most popular Christian hymn, and it perfectly illustrates how, at the heart of Christianity, lies blindness. Who better, then, to sing rapturously of the curing of soul-blindness than a blind man?

To say that I, a blind atheist, am an anomaly, or that blind people tend to be religious, is perhaps going too far. Yet it cannot be denied that blindness is embedded in Christian theology in such a fundamental way that it influences how sighted people (Christian and not) think of blind people. Similar to the blind bard and the blind prophet, the blind Christian seems to offer a locus for divine compensation. In this case, the compensation is a kind of blessed innocence: eyes and ears open to spiritual truths and closed to corruption and sin. This presumed innocence and blessedness can be a burden even for blind Christians.

Rebecca Redmile-Blaevoet, a blind woman in Canada who describes herself as a devout Christian, reached out to me after I did an interview with *Tapestry* (a Canadian radio show)[10] about how adopting a punk aesthetic can help mitigate the pity that sighted people so often throw our way. It might seem strange that my attempts to unravel stereotypes of the blind by way of in-your-face, irreverent performance art would resonate with her, a former Orthodox church choir director, but indeed they did. Rebecca wrote that she feels there is something "insidious" in remarks she's heard from other Christians such as, "Because you can't see, you don't sin, right?"

Such presumed innocence in the blind is not only misplaced but demeaning. Equating blindness with sinlessness negates the struggles a blind Christian also faces to balance the spiritual and physical parts of herself. As Rebecca says, "The minute society equates blindness with sinlessness, there's a whole suitcase of other assumptions that go with it."

I think these assumptions can generally be thought of as being about innocence and purity, even incorruptibility. As I've noted, this has a lot to do with the paradoxical position that many sighted people have with regard to vision: it is believed to be on the one hand our most useful and important sense and on the other hand the most distracting, superficial, and temptation-laden sense. It was precisely the assumptions of sighted people that prompted me to write the Blind Punks article (that led to the CBC interview) in the first place. A woman saw me with my white cane preparing to go onstage with my accordion and said, "You must sing like an angel." I assured her that I do not, and proceeded to assault my audience's ears with my "avant accordion brain smash" act.

I find it troubling that, in our now largely secular world, blindness remains a prime locus for transcendence. It is not just the Christians on the street who cry, "Bless you!" as I pass, but all kinds of people—from avuncular types to young professionals—who have these expectations for what it means to be blind, when really what it means is no more and no less than a lack of sight.

Lack of sight does not give rise to specific types of personalities, behaviors, drives, ambitions, ingenuities, insights, or conversions. As the religious scholar John Hull wrote in his 1990 memoir, *Touching the Rock:* "Blind people differ from each other as much as sighted people do."[1] Being blind in a sighted world inflects personality just as much (or as little) as such things as gender, ethnicity, or socioeconomic status, and there is no way of knowing how all these intersecting factors will play out. Unraveling stereotypes of blindness depends on the realization that blindness is just one aspect of our humanity, albeit one laden with hundreds of years of intense religious iconography wrought into seemingly indelible truths by literature and art.

The tradition of the blind saints in particular seems to have helped to codify the relationship between purity and blindness. The most famous of these is Saint Lucy (a.k.a. Lucia) of Syracuse, whose vow of virginity led to her martyrdom in 304 CE. Born a wealthy Sicilian, she refused marriage and instead gave her goods to the poor. A disappointed suitor accused her of being a Christian, not a light matter as this was during the Great Persecution of Diocletian—the last ferocious attempt by the Roman Empire to stomp out the upstart religion. The judge ordered her to be violated in a brothel, but she was made miraculously immovable. He then condemned her to death by fire (which did not take), and finally she was killed by sword. In some versions of her story she blinded herself to avoid marriage, and in others her eyes were gouged out by the authorities (and miraculously restored after death).

Although not all of the versions of Saint Lucy's story feature blindness (and in fact the blindness bits seem to have emerged centuries after her death), she nonetheless became the patron saint of the blind and is often depicted holding out a plate of eyeballs, as if to say, "I don't need these, you take them." Saint Lucy's name comes from the Latin word for light, "lux," which makes her a perfect example of that neoplatonic tendency to exchange physical light for spiritual light, and those weighty metaphorics play out in the celebration of Saint Lucy's Day on December 13, in the darkest time of the year.

During a recent visit to my hometown of San Francisco, Alabaster and I stepped into Saints Peter and Paul Church in North Beach. We bought a candle and put it in front of a sculpture of Lucy with her plate of eyeballs, and Alabaster took a picture of me with her. I like Saint Lucy, and, although I'm not a believer, I can understand the relationship people have with saints who, unlike God and Jesus, are human and relatable role models.

Saint Lucy is not the only female saint associated with blindness. There's also Saint Odile (660–720 CE), who was supposedly born blind but regained her sight after baptism. Odile, like Lucy, is often depicted holding forth eyeballs, but hers are placed on a book rather than a platter.

Perhaps the blind saint tradition originated with Paul the Apostle. Paul started life as a Jew named Saul, who persecuted Christians, and ended it as one of the church fathers martyred for his faith. According to the ninth chapter of *Acts,* Saul was on that famous road to Damascus when "suddenly there shined round about him a light from heaven. He fell to the ground and heard a voice: 'Saul, Saul, why persecutest thou me?' "[12]

Saul asks who it is and the voice answers, "I am Jesus whom thou persecutes." When Saul arises and opens his eyes, he is blind, "but they led him by the hand, and brought him into Damascus," where he spends three days without sight, until a Christian named Ananias helps him.[13]

Having been instructed by the Lord to restore Saul's sight in order to transform the former persecutor into an effective preacher, Ananias puts his hands on him and says, "Brother Saul, the Lord, even Jesus, that appeared unto thee in the way as thou camest, hath sent me, that thou mightest receive thy sight, and be filled with the Holy Ghost."[14]

Then the scales fell from Saul's eyes and he was baptized. As Paul, he teaches the word of Jesus. Tradition ascribes the writing of 1 Corinthians to him, in which we find a famous quote that describes our limited human vision: "For now we see through a glass, darkly." Paul's story lays out the corrective power of blindness, but perhaps its most important lesson is recognizing our fundamentally dark and imperfect sight even (or especially) when we believe it to be most perfect, connecting sight with hubris, pride, and self-righteousness forevermore.

———

You, dear reader, may be a heathen like me, and do not read the Bible much, but that does not mean you have not been indoctrinated into the belief that being blinded is a useful corrective. Take the blinding of Rochester in the novel *Jane Eyre,* in which Charlotte Brontë (the daughter of a curate) explicitly uses the Christian symbolism of blindness to reveal relationships between superficiality and sin, true and false loves.

Jane Eyre (1847) is the story of an undersized, plain-looking orphan who struggles through unkind treatment by relatives and brutal schoolmasters to gain a cushy job as the governess of the ward of the rich, aristocratic Mr. Rochester in his impressive Thornfield Hall. She also manages to win his love, but unfortunately he is already married to the poor mad Bertha Antoinetta Mason (who will finally get to tell her own story in Jean Rhys's *Wide Sargasso Sea*). That does not stop Rochester from trying to marry Jane anyway, but before he can do so, the truth is revealed, causing Jane to flee. After she does, Bertha sets fire to Thornfield, killing herself and maiming and blinding Rochester.

When Jane hears that her beloved Mr. Rochester is now blind (and a widower), she rushes to visit him but, anxious not to startle him, she is content at first to play the part of the voyeur, and there is something empowering in her bold—one might even say male—gaze, watching the blind man, who cannot know that he is being watched:

> He descended the one step, and advanced slowly
> and gropingly towards the grass-plat. Where was his
> daring stride now? Then he paused, as if he knew not
> which way to turn. He lifted his hand and opened his
> eyelids; gazed blank, and with a straining effort, on
> the sky, and towards the amphitheatre of trees: one
> saw that all to him was void darkness. He stretched
> his right hand (the left arm, the mutilated one, he kept
> hidden in his bosom); he seemed to wish by touch
> to gain an idea of what lay around him: he met but
> vacancy still; for the trees were some yards off where
> he stood. He relinquished the endeavour, folded his
> arms, and stood quiet and mute in the rain, now
> falling fast on his uncovered head.[15]

I was nine years old and sat in a comfortable window seat in a little public library around the corner from where my mom sold expensive imported women's fashion when I first read these last sad chapters. The tears were falling freely. I felt very adult, and I remember the tears best of all. As a sighted child I could not relate to Rochester as I did to the pitying Jane, but now I feel kinship with the newly blinded man. How many times have I attempted to venture outside, only to be thwarted by an immediate confusion and reluctance to grope around. How often have I, in recent years, resigned myself to crossing my arms on my chest to signal to any potential onlookers, "This is precisely where I meant to be, rain falling on my head be damned."

My mom and I often had picnics on her bed and watched old movies together. Once, after I'd read the novel, the beautiful black-and-white 1943 film version of *Jane Eyre* (starring Joan Fontaine and Orson Welles and featuring a stunning child Elizabeth Taylor) came on the television. Since then, I've occasionally shared this film with (deprived) friends over the years. Now when I watch it, it is with my ears, but I remember most of the scenes in my mind's eye. The film makes me a little weepy also.

Though the film adaptation essentially ends with Jane's emotional return to Thornfield, in the novel she elaborates on their life together, and suggests that it was his blindness "that drew us so very near—that knit us so very close!" She explains then how she helped him to see the world, reading books and describing nature to him. "Literally," she says, "I was (what he often called me) the apple of his eye." And she assures her readers: "Never did I weary of reading to him; never did I weary of conducting him where he wished to go: of doing for him what he wished to be done. And there was a pleasure in my services, most full, most exquisite, even though sad—because he claimed these services without painful shame or damping humiliation."[16]

What an extraordinarily idealized version of helpmate! I adore Alabaster, but such perfect helpfulness on one side and perfect gratitude without humiliation on the other seem quite beyond the reach of mortals. However, it is possible that I am wrong, and that other blind/sighted pairs experience Jane and Rochester's kind of marital bliss. I should not speak for all.

Interestingly, Rochester, Jane tells us, will not remain blind, but rather he will end as a visually impaired person: "He had the advice of an eminent oculist; and he eventually recovered the sight of that one eye. He cannot now see very distinctly: he cannot read or write much; but he can find his way without being led by the hand: the sky is no longer a blank to him—the earth no longer a void. When his first-born was put into his arms, he could see that the boy had inherited his own eyes, as they once were—large, brilliant, and black."[17]

Temporary, incomplete blindness is the perfect solution in a plot that depends on us feeling that "God had tempered judgment with mercy," as Rochester acknowledges at the sight of his son. The lesson of blindness, once learned, is apparently enough to keep the erring soul on the right path thenceforward, as the Saul/Paul conversion testifies.

Whenever the calamity of blindness—temporary or permanent—drops suddenly upon the head of a main character, you can pretty much bet your bottom dollar that that character will learn something very important—a life lesson that could not have been seen with working eyes. From Gloucester's violent eye-gouging in *King Lear* to Fonzie's accidental blindness in *Happy Days* to Arya's swift and sudden punishment by blindness in *A Song of Ice and Fire* (that HBO turned into *Game of Thrones*), a lesson—sometimes profound, sometimes schmaltzy—will certainly result. Thus, the Christian symbolism of conversion under duress offers charming, seemingly universal potential for compensation: blindness in exchange for true sight.

I have thought about this lesson—a favorite of books, movies and television shows—quite a bit in recent years and have cried out to the blank heavens that I feel as though I've learned what there is to be learned from blindness, and it would suit me fine to now reenter the sighted world, exuding my understanding like a happy blue aura of humility and wisdom. Because if blindness is actually a fix for wrongheadedness and sinfulness, then all of us blind should be quite infallible and angelic, right?

To me, however, these lessons of blindness have everything to do with our forgetfulness that all our senses are limited by physicality—hearing and touch are not necessarily more profound than sight, no more prone to lead toward or away from spirituality. That is to say that if blind people are interested in transcending the physical, we ought to find our own ways rather than be pigeonholed by the sighted.

John Hull taught religious studies at the University of Birmingham and, after decades of eye problems and operations due to cataracts and resultant detached retinas, he lost his vision completely. His memoir, *Touching the Rock,* is organized around the journal he dictated into a tape recorder during the years 1983–86. Although in his introduction Hull gives an abbreviated sketch of his life up until he becomes totally blind, *Touching the Rock* takes place over the course of the three years following: "In 1983 the last light sensations faded and the dark discs had finally overwhelmed me. I had fought them bravely, as it seemed to me, for thirty-six years, but all to no avail. It was then I began to sink into the deep ocean, and finally learned how to touch the rock on the far side of despair."[18]

At the end of his memoir, Hull describes his stay at Iona Abbey, a medieval nunnery in Scotland, as a visiting scholar. While there, he made solitary visits to the abbey proper, in which he found and inspected, by feel and incrementally night after night, its enormous marble altar, and this "whole-body seeing" seems to offer him a unique compensation:

> The top was as smooth as silk, but how far back did it go? I stretched my arms out over it but could not reach the back. This was incredible. It must have a back somewhere. Pushing myself up on to it, my feet hanging out over the front, I could reach the back. I did this again and again, measuring it with my body, till at last I began to have some idea of its proportions. It was bigger than me and much older. There were several places on the polished surface which were marked with long, rather irregular indentations, not cracks, but imperfections of some kind. . . . The contrast between the rough depressions and the huge polished areas was extraordinary. Here was the work of people, grinding this thing, smoothing it to an almost greasy, slightly dusty finish which went slippery when I licked it. Here were these abrasions, something more primitive, the naked heart of the rock.[19]

I very much appreciate Hull's unusual experience of touch-based transcendence. Although, as we've seen, Christianity (largely thanks to Greek philosophy) encourages its followers to get over the body and look with the inner eye, the stunning and imposing churches of the world indicate a deep hypocrisy; why make a church beautiful when the eye is so easily led astray by beauty? I do not mean to be cynical. My point is simply to acknowledge how complicated is the idea that the senses lead us away from God or truth or soul. And, although religious transcendence may seem encouraging to blind people—suggesting a kind of fast track to the divine—it is extremely limiting. I think it is also based on a fundamental misconception that itself is rooted in the entrenched soul-body dualism.

Our senses may be inaccurate and limited, but without them how can we learn enough to begin to imagine or construct that which lies beyond or beneath, let alone trouble the assumptions that prompt desires for transcendence in the first place? It seems to me that it is only our bodies and their groping and fallible senses that can give us the world—from reading scripture to hearing hymns to stretching oneself out on an altar. Yet until our cultural productions widen their scope and enjoy these larger, more-complex metaphors of the senses and transcendence, blind people will continue to enjoy the dubious distinction of remaining aloof from the body and its temptations, a mind-set that gives them many difficulties in the practical, literal realm, and a leg up when it comes to the spiritual.

4.

Out, Vile Jelly!

The Tragedy of King Lear, written by William Shakespeare and first performed in the Court of King James in 1606, is the story of a king who wishes to retire and divide his kingdom among his three daughters—but only after they proclaim in a public, ostentatious way how much they love him. Lear will accept the superficial declarations of his two conniving daughters (Regan and Goneril) as true affection, and despise the honest words of his one loving daughter (Cordelia) until it is too late. It is also about the Earl of Gloucester, who is duped by his ambitious bastard son (Edmund) into believing that his honest legitimate son (Edgar) is plotting against him, also until it is too late.

Thus the play actually contains two tragedies—and many deaths—that revolve around two foolish old men; one will go mad and the other blind on their journey to see the situation and their children correctly. So much is doubled and multiplied in this play: two fathers, two evil daughters, two worthy (but mistrusted) children, two brothers, two husbands, two plots, at least two fools, several madnesses, and many, many blindnesses.

The excess has not always been appreciated by critics. George Orwell, in his 1947 essay "Lear, Tolstoy, and the Fool," does not agree with Leo Tolstoy's disdain for *King Lear* (nor for Shakespeare generally, whom Tolstoy finds overrated at best), but admits there are some fundamental flaws: "*Lear* is not a very good play, as a play. It is too drawn-out and has too many characters and sub-plots. One wicked daughter would have been quite enough, and Edgar is a superfluous character: indeed it would probably be a better play if Gloucester and both his sons were eliminated.'"[1]

With all due respect to Orwell, I take issue with his flip dismissal of Gloucester—in fact, I take it personally. The representation of Gloucester's blindness was another one of those early moments in my reading history that revealed to me the metaphorical weightiness of sightlessness. Gloucester's eye-gouging by the Duke of Cornwall (husband of Lear's evil daughter Regan) bombastically represents the play's heavy-handed allegory: if you look upon loved ones with superficial eyes, you are figuratively blind, and one good corrective for that problem is losing the eyeballs. As with Oedipus and Paul the Apostle, blindness brings true sight. However, something that I didn't notice when I first read *King Lear* back in my first college English class was how the blindness to which Gloucester is subjected brings a kind of bumbling buffoonery along with insight, so that his ability to see his sons clearly is tempered by his inability to do almost anything else.

That first encounter with *King Lear* took place at City College of San Francisco (a two-year community college). I have often felt that I'm the only person to drop out of high school and then go on to obtain a PhD eventually. Everything took longer, as I was always needing to adjust how I did things as my vision faded. I had dropped out of high school mostly out of frustration with underperforming—not because it was too difficult, but because I could no longer see well enough to do the work. Yet I had never once considered not going to college, so I immediately enrolled at CCSF. There, finally, I got some help from Disabled Students Services and got hooked up with books on tape from nonprofit and public libraries for the blind. Coincidentally, I also made use of a computer for the first time. (Before that I'd been blindly writing papers—for I could touch-type but not proof my work—on my mother's 1950s manual typewriter.)

My wonderfully geeky boyfriend of the time had moved in with me and brought his computer with him. He downloaded free text-enlargement software, and he even convinced me to take an MS-DOS class to learn about the far-from-intuitive command-line interface. This was probably 1991. Which was how it came to pass that the first time I ever used a computer to write an essay was in that general English literature class at CCSF. The essay was about Gloucester and the strange paradox of needing to be blinded in order to see the light. While the giant luminous letters, green on black, scrolled across the screen in that distinctive DOS-system minimalism, I realized that I might make a career out of writing about literature. I don't think it had ever before occurred to me that people did such things. In other words, Gloucester's blindness and my first accessible computer were my gateway drugs to academia.

"*The Tragedy of Hamlet Prince of Denmark* and *The Tragedy of King Lear* rival each other as the two ultimate dramas yet conceived by humankind,"[2] announces the late, great literary critic Harold Bloom in his usual superlative tone at the start of his 2008 analysis, simply called *Lear*. If Bloom does not put as much pressure on the importance of Gloucester as I might like, he does raise the father by raising the son. "It is infrequently realized that, after Lear himself, the crucial personality in the drama is Edgar, legitimate son of Gloucester, and godson of Lear. Lear speaks 749 lines, Edgar 392, which is more than anyone else."[3] Although Gloucester speaks only 338 lines, I would argue that this is because after the plucking of his eyes and the revelation that he'd banished the wrong son, he falls directly into a suicidal depression, generally not the most verbose state of mind, while his son Edgar disguises himself and pretends a kind of madness marked by the playful and provoking loquaciousness of the wise fool—an oxymoronic type not unlike the blind seer.

In the opening lines of *King Lear* we meet Gloucester as the first of our misguided fathers, and—let's not mince words—he's kind of an ass. It's no wonder his bastard son, Edmund, does not love him. To the Earl of Kent's perfectly polite question "Is not this your son, my lord?" Gloucester answers, "His breeding, sir, hath been at my charge. I have so often blushed to acknowledge him that now I am brazed to't." In other words, he's hardened himself to the idea of his bastard son. And it doesn't stop there. When Kent asks for clarification with the innocent statement "I cannot conceive you," Gloucester makes a crass pun: "Sir, this young fellow's mother could," and continues by informing Kent that Edmund's mother had "a son for her cradle ere she had a husband for her bed."[4]

Meanwhile, the bastard in question is standing by, no doubt taking solace in his own conception: a scheme to trick Gloucester into believing that his legitimate and sweet son, Edgar, is plotting against him. Gloucester has no trouble swallowing the story, and it must be said that Edgar is also easily duped into acting in accordance with his brother's plot. Edmund gleefully rejoices in their respective blindnesses: "A credulous father," he calls Gloucester, and Edgar is "a brother noble," who has a nature that's "so far from doing harms / That he suspects none; on whose foolish honesty / My practices ride easy."[5]

That is to say, Edgar is blinded by goodness—unable to see his brother's evil intentions because he harbors none in himself. The idea that innocence has not the ability to see duplicity will be echoed in Milton's *Paradise Lost,* where even "the sharpest sighted spirit of all in Heav'n" cannot recognize Satan in disguise.[6]

This play is all about appearances versus realities: when we meet Lear, he is ready to let go of the ruling of his kingdom and to divide it between his three daughters in accordance with their professions of love. "Sir, I love you more than word can wield the matter, / Dearer than eyesight, space, and liberty," pronounces the evil Goneril.[7]

Her hyperbolic declaration of affection is precisely what Lear wants from all three of his daughters, but will receive from only two. With his pompous and pathetic need to have the love painted on thick, he is unable to see Goneril's hypocrisy nor that of his other evil daughter, Regan, nor (most important to the tragedy) the unvarnished love of his favorite daughter, Cordelia, who in an aside speaks her truth: "I am sure my love's / More ponderous than my tongue."[8]

Shortly, Lear will learn that Goneril's and Regan's pretty words do not go deeper than their lips, for they do not treat him well. He quarrels with one and then the other of them and ends up wandering the heath, where he'll lose his wits. For both Lear and Gloucester, evil must be made plain before they begin to see correctly. Gloucester is literally punished for helping Lear (and perhaps metaphorically punished for trifling with infidelity), and it is not until after the punishment is dealt that he will learn the truth about his two sons.

After Cornwall and Lear's daughters apprehend Gloucester, we hear, as Bloom puts it, "a litany of evil unsurpassed in Shakespeare."[9] In fact it is the very same sister—Goneril, who had earlier declared Lear to be "Dearer than eyesight"—who now diabolically demands Gloucester's punishment: "Pluck out his eyes."[10]

Though she does not wait around for her idea to be executed, her sister Regan does. After Gloucester admits that he sent Lear to Dover, Regan asks why, to which he answers with unconscious irony, "Because I would not see thy cruel nails / Pluck out his poor old eyes, nor thy fierce sister / In his anointed flesh stick boarish fangs."[11]

Gloucester continues for several more lines in this vein, setting up Cornwall's cruel retort: "See't shalt thou never.— Fellows, hold the chair.—/ Upon these eyes of thine I'll set my foot."[12]

And with that, the first of Gloucester's eyes is plucked. A servant without a name (but with a conscience) tries to intervene and a scuffle ensues. Regan puts an end to it by stabbing the servant in the back.

> 1st Servant: O, I am slain! My lord, you have one eye
>   left
> To see some mischief on him. O!
> [He dies.]
> Cornwall: Lest it see more, prevent it. Out, vile jelly!
> Where is thy luster now?
> Gloucester: All dark and comfortless! Where's my son
>   Edmund?[13]

Which is precisely when Gloucester begins to learn the truth: his son Edmund, the bastard, is the villain, and his true son, Edgar, is the falsely accused one.

"I have seen several stage performances of *King Lear*," says Bloom. "The gouging of Gloucester's eyes is not to be borne. Why did Shakespeare inflict this scene upon us, and indeed, upon himself?"[14]

I, on the other hand, appreciate the idea of the horror, even if I have never (strictly speaking) seen it. This brutal scene, with its darkly humorous "vile jelly"—a reference to what many of us consider to be our most precious and poetic sense organ—

violently underscores the uselessness of functioning sight when it is trapped on the surface of things. Bloom was not, like me, weaned on David Lynch and Quentin Tarantino (whose disturbing images and slick brutality remain indelible in my mind's eye), and so perhaps he prefers his gore to happen offstage, as in *Oedipus*. But, as we saw earlier, even in its retelling, Oedipus's self-blinding is pretty gruesome: "raising the pins, raking them down his eyes," recounts the messenger who witnessed it. "And at each stroke blood spurts from the roots, / splashing his beard, a swirl of it, nerves and clots— / black hail of blood pulsing, gushing down."[5]

Often dismissed as mere pulp, horror has been part of our literary tradition since the beginning. The eye-gouging in particular is an old motif: consider, in *The Odyssey,* Odysseus's treatment of the cyclops Polyphemus. In revenge for Polyphemus's cannibalizing of Odysseus's men, Odysseus makes the one-eyed giant drunk, very drunk, on delicious Greek wine. Then he and his men heat a sharp log in the fire and plunge it into the eye of the sleeping cyclops "so that His blood / poured out around the stake, and blazing fire / sizzled his lids and brows, and fried the roots," finally making "his eyeball crackle on the spear."[6]

Perhaps we need to be occasionally reminded just how physically vulnerable the precious eye is. Perhaps that is why Homer and Sophocles and Shakespeare inflict eye-sizzling and -gouging and -plucking upon us. So many of us rely on our eyes so much that we believe them to be more than sense organs— they have come to be "windows on the soul," a popular phrase that seems to have taken inspiration from Matthew 6:22–23: "The light of the body is the eye: if therefore thine eye be single, thy whole body shall be full of light. But if thine eye be evil, thy whole body shall be full of darkness. If therefore the light that is in thee be darkness, how great is that darkness!"

It has also been attributed to Shakespeare, but I cannot find this exact phrase. He certainly makes much of the idea in his sonnets, though, for example in Sonnet 1: "But thou, contracted to thine own bright eyes, / Feed'st thy light's flame with self-substantial fuel."[7]

The American sculptor Hiram Powers (1805–73) is on record for putting the phrase into the form that we all recognize (and overuse): "The eye is the window of the soul, the mouth the door. The intellect, the will, are seen in the eye; the emotions, sensibilities, and affections, in the mouth. The animals look for man's intentions right into his eyes. Even a rat, when you hunt him and bring him to bay, looks you in the eye."[8]

Sometimes I feel oppressed by the preciousness, the endless harping on the beauty and soulfulness of the eye. How much time in literature is spent extolling the beauty of the eye, particularly the color of the iris, which is, I am always happy to remind my sighted friends, mostly just a muscle, delightfully called the iris sphincter muscle.

Though our culture may put a great deal of emphasis (poetic or clichéd) on what the eyes can reveal about a person's (or animal's) inner depths, it is sometimes useful to remember that the eyes are made of the same stuff as the rest of the body: tissues and cells, muscles and vessels and goo. And though some might like to shy away from such things as the violent destruction of "vile jelly," I believe the horrific moments in canonized texts illustrate how our modern notions of high and low culture are more of a trend than an inherent quality of art.

Similarly, the analogous distinctions between tragic and comic are not so distinct as we sometimes pretend. Shakespeare, of course, is a masterful scrambler of these extremes of high and low, tragic and comic, so that one is hard-pressed to know where one ends and the other begins, something to keep in mind as we follow the brisk tonal shifts from Gloucester's first appearance as a tragic blind figure to a comically helpless and gullible one.

Gloucester, after his eye-plucking, meets an old man, who wishes to help him on his way, to which Gloucester touchingly replies: "I have no way and therefore want no eyes. / I stumbled when I saw."[19]

Then he elaborates on how he mistook his good son Edgar for bad, wishing that he could make amends: "Might I but live to see thee in my touch, / I'd say I had eyes again."[20]

Cue Edgar, who has been standing by, to reveal himself—or rather himself in the guise of "Poor Tom." Why exactly Edgar goes to such lengths to keep his father from recognizing him is rather mysterious, but we must assume that he disguises his voice as well as putting on his madman's costume of nakedness, because Gloucester does not know him. Even so, he insists that this "Poor Tom" be clothed and then lead him to the Cliffs of Dover, where Gloucester plans to end his own suffering. When the old man protests this decision, Gloucester says, "'Tis the time's plague when madmen lead the blind."[21]

The son pretends to lead the father to his death with a ruse that cannot help but strike one as comical. Dressed as Poor Tom, Edgar leads his blind father to the "Cliffs of Dover" and the father accepts his sighted companion's word on the matter, as if the Cliffs of Dover are a thing to be seen only, not felt and heard (and smelled), giving the scene a slapstick feel.

Gloucester: When shall I come to th' top of that same hill?
Edgar: You do climb up it now. Look how we labor.
Gloucester: Methinks the ground is even.
Edgar: Horrible steep.
Hark, do you hear the sea?

Gloucester: No, truly.
Edgar: Why then, your other senses grow imperfect
By your eyes' anguish.
Gloucester: So may it be indeed.[22]

It is interesting how Shakespeare plays with the idea of compensation here: instead of his other senses growing more acute, Edgar insists (and Gloucester capitulates) that he has lost them entirely, along with his eyeballs. Of course we must doubt the veracity of this, as Gloucester attempts to argue the point using those very senses—the flatness of the path, the lack of wind—but Edgar slaps him down. It's rather painful for me to read this as a blind person because it seems to perfectly illustrate how we, the blind, are so often denied any knowledge of the world, as if the world were merely visible. Worse, it shows how we are ready to deny the accuracy of our other senses in the face of the certainty of the sighted.

Soon we will turn to the science of the seventeenth century—the origin of the science of our modern era—and consider how the empirical impulse to investigate the vast cosmos on the one hand, and the smallest biological organisms on the other, requires a certain amount of humility. Human vision is necessarily circumscribed by our sense organs, which is why the telescope and the microscope—invented in the century of Shakespeare's death—were so startling and powerful. I pause here to say that the humility that makes for the best kind of science—arguably making science possible—is often forgotten by the sighted when dealing with the blind. It's as if the information coming through the other senses is so pale compared to the information coming through the eyes that it compels the sighted person to spin himself a false sense of security. And that security, the insistence that what is seen is necessarily true and correct, withers the blind person's attempts to contradict it.

Shakespeare seems to be playing with this notion in this scene with Gloucester and Edgar, but I think Gloucester's ultimate credulity is what is most memorable, rather than his initial, albeit weak, attempt to contradict his sighted companion. Even if it is all metaphorical, the absurdity of a blind man being so uncertain of his other senses as to be unable to distinguish a cliff from a flat footpath undoubtedly affects how actual blind people have been seen and treated in the real world from Shakespeare's Renaissance to today.

Jacob Twersky, a blind historian and novelist, whose ninety-two-year life spanned the greater part of the twentieth century and spilled over into the twenty-first (1922–2014), also takes Shakespeare's depiction of Gloucester personally. In his 1955 book *Blindness in Literature,* he writes: "The blinded Earl of Gloucester in *King Lear* offers nothing to marvel at, save to those who know anything about the sightless."[23]

Though it's hard to swallow, Gloucester's credulity leads him to leap off the supposed cliff of Dover, where Edgar assumes another vocal disguise and marvels at his survival. This finally causes Gloucester to accept his situation: "Henceforth I'll bear / Affliction till it do cry out itself / 'Enough, enough!' and die."[24]

This seems to me to be an important aspect of Christian-inflected narratives of disability, even a kind of prototype of inspiration porn: our ability to "buck up" in the face of affliction and adversity with dignified acceptance. These stories have come to be clichéd in their efforts to make (nondisabled) people feel better—to teach them to accept their own relatively minimal suffering. The inspiration derives meaning from the supposed extremity of suffering of disabled people. All humans suffer, but somehow being reminded that others suffer more helps people to bear their own lot more easily. This is an old story, of course, and Shakespeare merely uses Gloucester's blindness (and Lear's madness) to illustrate an outrageous and mundane fact of life: we suffer and die, and we can do it well or ill.

Twersky goes a bit further in blaming Shakespeare for contributing to the image of the helpless, inept blind person as viewed through the eyes of the sighted: "Yet since the seeing generally assume that an individual upon losing his sight takes on immediately somehow the characteristics of the blind as a class, Gloucester's confusion is automatically ascribed to that class." And "from a source so greatly looked upon as gospel," the depiction of Gloucester has, as Twersky suggests, "probably done a good deal of harm to the sightless and still can do more."[25]

Assuming that we will continue to read *King Lear* in classrooms and perform the play on brave stages, may I offer a possible corrective? We need more blind and visually impaired teachers, critics, and actors to guide the sighted reader or viewer away from simple ableist assumptions about the implicit and explicit meanings of Gloucester's blindness.

That said, Shakespeare did not invent the tricking-of-the-blind-man trope any more than he ended it. It is an old story, at least as old as compensation (poetic/prophetic gifts in exchange for the loss of sight). It may be that Shakespeare had in mind the tricking of old Isaac in the Hebrew Bible when he drew the scene of Gloucester on the supposed Cliffs of Dover.

Having made the excellent trade of a bowl of lentils for the birthright of his elder brother, Esau, Jacob worries that his future will still be uncertain unless he also receives the blessing that their father, Isaac, would bestow upon Esau by virtue of his being the firstborn. With the help of his mother, Rebecca, Jacob carries out a plan to do just that, a plan that can work only because his father, Isaac, is blind. To deceive the old blind man, Jacob puts the skin of a goat on his arms and neck, thus posing as Esau, whose hairiness was a distinguishing feature. His arms must have been very hairy indeed.

Twersky (who happens to have been the son of a rabbi) critiques Isaac's gullibility in this biblical scenario in a way that sounds suspiciously similar to what he has to say about Gloucester's credulity later in his book and here calls attention to the dubious nature of such a deception: "Isaac's other senses are not impaired. Nor is he witless. Quite the contrary; he is still the head of the family and makes decisions for it. Some theologians struck by the incredibility of the story explain the success of the deception on the grounds that Isaac wanted or pretended to be deceived or that it was God's will."[26]

Twersky concludes, "Taken literally, however, it implies that the blind are very easily deceived indeed, that impairment of the other senses, or confusion as to the information they gather, necessarily follows the loss of sight."[27]

Gloucester's gullibility regarding both his physical whereabouts and his insight into the true character of each of his sons comes immediately after losing his eyes. And the two states of being—both more and less aware—perfectly represent those wild oscillations of blindness that so dominate our culture. These two seemingly oppositional characteristics of blindness—the bumbling and the knowing—coexist in our imaginations and loosely follow the extremes of theatrical emotion, mixing and mingling them, as Twersky points out: "Of course Shakespeare's tone and intent do not make Gloucester comical in a way that can be called humorous. His tragedy is too highlighted for that. He is tragically comical, as is Lear when mad."[28]

The Gloucester/Isaac syndrome comes down to us through the ages, making it possible for a person as widely respected as Helen Keller to have a mind-boggling number of jokes told about her blindness (and a few about her deafness). I can explain these seeming contradictions only by saying that if blindness speaks to an inherent fear on the part of the sighted—on the part of all of us—that we are circumscribed by our limited human senses, then the release of laughter that arises from making fun of those who are lacking a sense (or two) perhaps helps to cover over that fear.

5

Telescopes, Microscopes, Spectacles, and Speculations

Four years after *King Lear* was first performed and six years before Shakespeare died, an Italian astronomer named Galileo published a little treatise called *Sidereus Nuncius* (1610), which has the ambiguous meaning of either *The Starry Message* or *The Starry Messenger*. In either case, his observations, which include the discovery of four moons circling Jupiter that had never before been observed by humans, made plain the weakness inherent in human vision—a weakness revealed only by looking through powerful lenses. The telescope, as a visual prosthesis,[1] starkly demonstrated how the limited focal range of humans limited our understanding of the cosmos: "It remains for us to reveal and make known what appears to be most important in the present matter: four planets never seen since the beginning of the world right up to our day, the occasion of their discovery and observation, their positions, and the observations made over the past 2 months concerning their behavior and changes."[2]

Galileo's observations are presented as a journal of the newly sighted scientific eye. There can be no doubt that the truly startling aspect of *Sidereus Nuncius* was the revelation that discoveries could be made by augmenting mortal sight with powerful lenses. Galileo makes manifest an inherent blindness in human vision and the means to correct it—a correction that will forever lack finality. Things exist in the universe beyond the scope of unaided human vision, but by merely extending that vision, one could now see what had been previously invisible, suggesting a new kind of (secular) revelation.

Interestingly, it was not only the discovery of the moons of Jupiter that astounded his readers, but also his description of our own moon, which, since the dawn of poetic contemplation, has inspired thoughts of austere beauty and divine perfection. Through his telescope Galileo saw that the moon is "most evidently not at all of an even, smooth, and regular surface, as a great many people believe of it and of the other heavenly bodies, but on the contrary it is rough and unequal." In a letter dated January 7, 1610, Galileo concludes that the moon "is full of prominences and cavities similar, but much larger, to the mountains and valleys spread over the Earth's surface."[3]

The moon turned out to be, through the eye of the telescope, a "spotty globe," as Milton would later put it in *Paradise Lost*. Galileo's drawings and descriptions of the lunar surface dispelled a powerful illusion regarding the substance of heavenly bodies, which had traditionally been connected more closely to the divine rather than the earthly. It was not pleasant for Galileo's contemporaries to admit their limited (naked) vision. They preferred to think that the telescope lied rather than their eyes. And I think this unwillingness to admit such limitations is still very much a part of our modern culture. We like to think that when we open our eyes, we see the world (and the universe) as it is, when in fact, we see the world precisely as well as our eyes and brain working together allow us to see it—usually just what is needed to get along in a world created by like-sighted individuals, and not much more.[4]

As we have now widened our study of blindness in Western culture to include science as well as literature and religion, we do well to remember that science as we understand it today grew out of the impulse to study the world empirically—that is to say, through the senses, namely through the eyes. But this "new science," or new way of learning, developed out of philosophy—was in fact called "natural philosophy." There were those who realized from the start that a certain amount of humility regarding the limitations of our God-given senses ought not to be forgotten.

"But much the greatest obstacle and distortion of human understanding comes from the dullness, limitations and deceptions of the senses," wrote Francis Bacon, the great seventeenth-century cheerleader for empiricism and the new science, in his 1620 *New Organon.* This treatise was a kind of update on Aristotle (384–322 BCE), whose original *Organon* (Greek for "instrument") was a collection of his works on logic. Bacon kick-started ideas of modern science in *New Organon* by emphasizing inductive reasoning while at the same time casting doubt on the abilities of our sense organs, particularly our eyes: "Things that strike the senses have greater influence than even powerful things which do not directly strike the senses. And therefore thought virtually stops at sight; so that there is little or no notice taken of things that cannot be seen."[5]

Bacon insists that the weakness of our sense organs—together with our confidence in our intellect and reliance on ancient treatises (such as those by Aristotle)—fundamentally throttled the advancement of learning. Bacon wanted to convince his contemporaries that they should learn to rely on instruments and the inductive methods that arise from experimentation. Although empiricists like Galileo were already using instruments to discover new phenomena, it was Bacon who began to theorize the movement that was to become modern science. In particular, he notes the importance of the augmentation of sight because "it is evident that sight holds first place among the senses, as far as information is concerned." And he identifies the three main functions of scientific visual instruments: "to see what has not been seen; or to see further; or to see more accurately and distinctly."[6]

As an example of the first kind of instrument—that which reveals what is ordinarily invisible to the human eye—he presents the microscope, "which (by remarkably increasing the size of the specimens) reveal[s] the hidden, invisible small parts of bodies, and their latent structures and motions."[7]

When I think about microscopic vision, I am taken back to a fourth-grade animal report for school. While my fellow students chose to write about such glamorous animals as wolves and bears and horses, I chose the rotifer, a microscopic creature of about a thousand cells. I made a shoebox diorama featuring my rotifer, which was modeled after the photo in our textbook. I believe this photo of the little alien among us was what prompted me to choose him in the first place. I talked about my darling rotifer every chance I got. My mom encouraged me in this as well, appreciating the oddity of a ten-year-old getting excited about a pseudocoelomate animal invisible to the naked human eye.

The rotifer isn't just a species or genera, but an entire phylum of mostly freshwater animals that boast microscopic body parts like eyes, jaws, stomachs, and even penises! It was first described at the end of the seventeenth century, a few short decades after the microscope was invented, and was named for its wheel-like head with its distinguishing cilia—tiny bristles or tufts—that pull the rotifer forward or help sweep food into its mouth.

Perhaps, then, I have always been intrigued by the idea of that which escapes the naked human eye. Or, since my rotifer report took place in the same school year as my first ophthalmology appointments, perhaps it was that the two ideas—of the limitless realms of life teeming beyond our normal sight, and of my own barely perceptible vision loss—were from then on fused in some fundamental part of my unconscious. Growing up, I felt I could never be a scientist—discomforting biology classes throughout middle and high school during which I pretended to see or got the information I needed mostly secondhand reinforced that perception glaringly—but I would later find myself face-to-face with the wonders of the microscopic world, improbably, through my studies of seventeenth-century literature.

In a graduate school class I read some of the major scientific texts of the seventeenth century, such as Galileo and Bacon as well as Robert Boyle (known as the Father of Modern Chemistry), William Harvey (who first demonstrated the circulation of blood), and Robert Hooke (first curator of experiments at the Royal Society—a learned society founded in 1660 in London to promote and disseminate the new science). It was Hooke and his early use of the microscope, along with Galileo and his telescope, who had a starring role in the dissertation that I would (after much doubt and distraction) finish.

The microscope, even more dramatically than the telescope, demonstrated the startling worlds discoverable by the augmentation of human vision. Hooke used the brand-new technology to dazzling effect in his 1665 book, *Micrographia.*

When I first discovered *Micrographia,* I could see Hooke's drawings—their extravagant effect, if not their detail—and hold those images in my mind's eye. In particular I remember his famous louse—a centerfold illustration of all its never-before-seen parts that accordioned out of the already large folio volume. Alongside his startling visionscapes, Hooke set forth a kind of ideology of seeing that made it clear that our notions of surface were but an illusion. He put the most common and insignificant things under his microscope in order to reveal just how unseeing humans really are. His microscopic drawings must have been as alarming to his contemporaries as a magician pulling a rabbit-sized fly out of his hat. But Hooke starts his readers off easy, with a simple household object.

"We shall begin with a physical point," he announces in his first observation, on the point of a needle, and proceeds to explain how although the needle appears to be "made so sharp, that the naked eye cannot distinguish any parts of it," if viewed under a "very good microscope," the top "appears broad, blunt and very irregular." It does not, Hooke assures us, look anything like a cone, as we might imagine, "but only a piece of a tapering body with a great part of the top remov'd or deficient."[8]

The reader cannot help but notice that she is being ushered into a new world, not only of the senses but of thought; the metaphorical and rhetorical power of this first observation is shamelessly obvious. We will start with a point—a literal point—that reveals just how much we cannot see with the naked eye, our limited human vision. By removing our certainty that the sharpness and smoothness that we see are its true attributes or final reality, the microscope relegates our perception of a smooth surface as relative to our own size, distance, and acuity of sense. This realization will forever trouble the once-fixed polarities of the visible and the invisible.

"There are but few Artificial things that are worth observing with a Microscope and therefore I shall speak but briefly concerning them," Hooke announces. "For the productions of art are such rude mis-shapen things, that when view'd with a Microscope, there is little else observable, but their deformity."[9] Thus, the man-made productions of art appear to us perfect only because we do not have a microscopic eye, and so Hooke will juxtapose the rude and misshapen things of human industry with the marvelous symmetry of the creatures that humans had always thought very ugly and deformed, from the louse to the fly. In *Micrographia,* we accompany Hooke on a journey that uncovers inconceivable imperfections on the one hand and limitless divisibility on the other. It is, in fact, in Hooke's book that the word "cell" as a term for biological structure—a structure that, with its roomy implications, indicates further divisibility—is coined.

Even though Hooke's *Micrographia* was a dark-horse best seller in the decades following its publication, not everyone would find the ideas and images of the microscope profound. "Why has not Man a microscopic eye?" asks Alexander Pope in his 1734 poem *Essay on Man,* answering with a snappy rhyme that completes the snarky couplet, "For this plain reason, Man is not a Fly." To drive the point home, he continues: "Say what the use, were finer optics giv'n, / T' inspect a mite, not comprehend the heav'n?"[10]

The men of English letters who wrote in the decades after Hooke—such as Pope, who through his translations of Homer and his own poetry was actually the first Englishman to benefit enough from early copyright laws to make a small fortune from his pen, and Jonathan Swift, the satirist extraordinaire, whose oft anthologized "A Modest Proposal" (a satirical proposal to just go ahead and eat the Irish babies and be done with it) found microscopic vision to be a useless endeavor, though a useful new metaphor. Microscopic vision suggests blindness by way of too much proximity, similar to being dazzled by too much light (like one exiting Plato's Cave). Thus microscopic vision—in the hands of a great satirist like Swift—becomes an elaborate metaphor for the ridiculousness of looking with the eye of a fly, or rather, in the case of Gulliver in the land of giants, the eye of a creature approximately the size of a rat. And the whole endeavor is made more ridiculous by such a creature displaying the hubris of one who is scientifically inclined.

Swift's 1726 *Gulliver's Travels* is the story of a man keen on adventure, both for its potential to make his fortune and for its potential to quench his thirst for knowledge. Perhaps Gulliver's first voyage to the land of the tiny Lilliputians is most memorable, but it should be remembered that in his very next voyage the roles will be reversed, and he will be the tiny creature in Brobdingnag, a land of giants. In both cases, Swift calls attention not just to the ludicrousness of being a body terribly out of whack with the society around it, but also to the ways in which the shift in perspective necessarily transforms how much one sees.

In Brobdingnag Gulliver instantly loses touch with his manhood, his adulthood, and nearly his personhood too. His only defense is to wax scientific and philosophical in order to retain some sense of power and control in a world where he is the size of a rat or a doll, where he is dangled and coddled like a baby—privy even to breast-feeding from a baby's-eye view:

> I must confess no object ever disgusted me so much as the sight of her monstrous breast, which I cannot tell what to compare with, so as to give the curious reader an idea of its bulk, shape and colour. It stood prominent six feet, and could not be less than sixteen in circumference. The nipple was about half the Bigness of my head, and the hue both of that and the dug,[11] so varied with spots, pimples and freckles, that nothing could appear more nauseous.[12]

Since Gulliver is a man of reflection, this distressing impression causes him to consider "the fair skins of our *English* ladies, who appear so beautiful to us, only because they are of our own size, and their defects not to be seen but through a magnifying glass; where we find by experiment that the smoothest and whitest skins look rough and coarse, and ill coloured."[3]

This is a rather blatant allusion to Hooke's discoveries sixty years earlier, as well as a jab at Swift's contemporaries who looked with a microscopic eye to find faults and defects, particularly the micro-eyed critic who picked apart bits of the great literary works, rendering them unrecognizable. Though Hooke, a scientist, did his best to convey the fascinating world of the microscopic, Swift, the satirist, cleric, and man of letters, presents Gulliver's observations as obvious, unedifying, and ridiculous. Of course one's skin looks disgusting when viewed through magnification—who cares? Swift, like Pope, seems to suggest that looking with the eye of a fly is not only disquieting but absurd. Much better to accept the blindness of un-augmented human vision. Yet perhaps there is one lesson to be learned, and that is one of relativism.

Gulliver's experience as a tiny creature in the land of giants causes him to reflect back on his own time as a giant in Lilliput, where he thought "the complexion of those diminutive people" to be "the fairest in the world." He had made this observation to one of the Lilliputians—"a Person of Learning there, who was an intimate friend of mine"—who informed him that in fact the ladies of whom Gulliver spoke were riddled with defects. More pointedly, he informed Gulliver of the impression he made when "I took him up in my hand, and brought him close, which he confessed was at first a very shocking sight. He said he could discover great holes in my Skin, that the stumps of my beard were ten times stronger than the Bristles of a boar, and my complexion made up of several colours altogether disagreeable." Gulliver, with a fair degree of ego, does not want to leave his readers with this distasteful impression, so he "must beg leave to say for myself, that I am as fair as most of my Sex and Country, and very little Sunburnt by all my Travels."[14]

Despite his attempts to be an objective and disinterested observer, Gulliver's relative size while in Brobdingnag makes him hardly more consequential than a fly. This inconsequence leads to his being treated as a specimen, a spectacle, whom the natives view with vision-enhancing prosthetics: "I was immediately produced, and placed upon a table, where I walked as I was commanded, drew my Hanger,[15] put it up again, made my Reverence to my Master's Guest, asked him in his own Language how he did, and told him he was welcome. . . . This Man, who was old and dim-sighted, put on his Spectacles to behold me better; at which I could not forbear laughing very heartily, for his Eyes appeared like the Full Moon shining into a Chamber at two Windows."[16]

Though in this instance Gulliver manages to laugh at the situation he finds himself in, the laughter feels strange and forced. His tabletop performance is just one more seemingly unavoidable humiliation of the sort that arise when you are plopped into the role of specimen. I am reminded of T. S. Eliot's modernist construction of this position in "The Love Song of J. Alfred Prufrock":

And I have known the eyes already, known them all—
The eyes that fix you in a formulated phrase,
And when I am formulated, sprawling on a pin,
When I am pinned and wriggling on the wall,
Then how should I begin
To spit out all the butt-ends of my days and ways?
And how should I presume?[17]

The discomfort of a specimen stuck but not yet dead, still presuming subjecthood, and yet ostensibly in no position to claim it, is one that I, as a blind person, can easily relate to, especially when I venture out alone. A blind person is necessarily urged into the position of the specimen under the gaze of the sighted observer. And yet blindness tends to present as a monolith, causing the sighted observer to neglect our complex interiorities as thinking, feeling creatures (just like them).

Swift ended quite blind (and mad) himself. In his 1779 "Life of Swift," the eminent eighteenth-century biographer (famous also for his dictionary) Samuel Johnson (often referred to simply as Dr. Johnson), ridicules Swift for refusing to wear spectacles in his old age. For "having by some ridiculous resolution, or mad vow," writes Johnson, "determined never to wear spectacles, he could make little use of books in his latter years." Thus, concludes Johnson, his ideas "being neither renovated by discourse, nor increased by reading, wore gradually away, and left his mind vacant to the vexations of the hour, till at last his anger was heightened into madness."[18]

Although others have speculated that Swift's madness was a result of his lifelong battle with Ménière's disease (a problem of the inner ear that often causes vertigo and deafness, among other symptoms), in the mind of Dr. Johnson, Swift's acceptance of blindness led directly to his madness. Johnson, the quintessential sociable and curious man of letters, understood books (along with conversation, which Swift also refused in his later mad years) to be a kind of balm that soothes or even covers over inner torments. Thus, Swift's refusal to wear spectacles was tantamount to cutting himself off from the human race.

In considering sight's prosthetics, we must not forget the commonplace. The telescope and the microscope had developed from the simple eyeglasses that helped countless middle-aged scholars keep up with their reading.

In his introduction to Galileo's *Starry Messenger,* Albert Van Helden tells how "before the end of the thirteenth century craftsmen in Italy had begun making thin, plano-convex glasses and putting them into frames so that they could be worn in front of the eyes." The spectacles were thicker in the middle than at the edges—lentil-shaped—and hence were named for the Latin word for lentil: "lens." And by the middle of the fifteenth century Italian spectacle makers could also correct myopia with concave lenses, although "it appears that these early versions could only correct mild degrees of myopia because it was difficult to grind and polish highly curved concave glasses."[19]

Now nearsighted and farsighted vision could be corrected, at least to some extent. The technology spread from Italy to other parts of Europe, and according to Van Helden, it was not only city-folk who benefited: "Itinerant peddlers hawked their optical wares throughout the countryside's small settlements, markets, and fairs."[20]

As most of my heretofore perfectly sighted friends now find themselves hitting the drugstore for reading glasses, I can understand how the phenomenon must have spread like medieval wildfire amongst the over-forty set.

As the telescope was mostly just a matter of putting the two types of lenses—convex and concave—together, delay in its invention had mainly been due to lack of quality in the lenses, which was corrected by Galileo and others. In other words, the necessity of "correcting" vision in individual humans led directly to enhancing the vision of humankind. In considering the blindnesses inherent in the anatomy of our eyes, we would do well to remember how embracing this realization can help break down the strict polarities of blindness and sight.

Although we'll remain in England for a while yet before we venture to France—the birthplace of the first school for the blind and Louis Braille—there is one early seventeenth-century French philosopher we should be familiar with. René Descartes not only famously wrote "I think, therefore I am" in his 1637 *Discourse on Method,* but he was also keenly interested in the science of his day. In fact, the *Discourse* was meant to serve as an introduction to his treatises on meteorology, geometry, and optics. This last, called *La Dioptrique,* was inspired by the telescope and, among other things, encouraged the construction of more such devices by giving detailed (and illustrated) instructions. Although his theories on light would soon be supplanted by those of Sir Isaac Newton, Descartes's thoughts on sight that called upon a hypothetical blind man for answers would have a lasting effect on philosophy into the eighteenth century—the Age of Enlightenment.

Descartes is considered by many to be "the founding father of the modern visualist paradigm," writes the intellectual historian Martin Jay in *Downcast Eyes* (1993).[21] As Jay puts it, he is a "quintessentially visual philosopher, who tacitly adopted the position of a perspectivalist painter using a camera obscura to reproduce the observed world." The term "camera obscura" (meaning "dark room") was coined by the astronomer Johannes Kepler in 1604 to designate the projection of an image onto a wall through a small aperture, not unlike the pinhole cameras people use to view eclipses without going blind. Camera obscuras could be used by artists to virtually trace an image creating strikingly lifelike paintings. In other words, Jay likens Descartes to the painters of his day who copied from nature by way of a visual device, and notes that in doing so his methods "may nicely serve as a shorthand way to characterize the dominant scopic regime of the modern era."[22]

I should probably admit that Jay has been haunting the pages of this book since the beginning, as it was within *Downcast Eyes* that I (and I think many others) first encountered the words "ocularcentric" and "ocularcentrism," which (rare among) neologisms seem so obvious as to need no explanation. I recently visited Rice University via Zoom (due to the COVID-19 quarantine) and was astounded to find the students in a History of the Senses course throwing around the term "ocularcentrism" with seeming glee. It had been years since I'd heard or used the word—not since grad school—but its revivification by these young people (thanks to their professor, Lan Li) reminded me how useful it is to have a single word to designate something so deep and entrenched as to almost go unnoticed in our society.

While the vast majority of blind people from the days of Homer to our own never heard the word "ocularcentrism," they certainly suffered its effects, for Descartes is surely not alone in believing sight to be "the noblest sense," as he calls it: "All the management of our lives depends on the senses, and since that of sight is the most comprehensive and the noblest of these, there is no doubt that the inventions which serve to augment its power are among the most useful that there can be."[23]

Thus, Descartes may be considered a major purveyor of ocularcentrism. Strange, then, to find the blind man and his sticks in Descartes's book about optics, but indeed he is there in *Dioptrique,* complete with illustrations. I hold a strong (if not precise) memory of the illustrations of the blind man in *Dioptrique* from when my reader first read, described, and showed me the passage. The sticks of the blind man are meant to make an analogy between the sense of touch and the sense of sight—to show how the feeling sticks of the blind are akin to the rays of light hitting our eyes. What will turn out to be more interesting and influential (and in some measure correct, as borne out by modern brain imaging) is that sight as we understand it happens largely in the mind.

Descartes got hold of an actual eyeball—in this case, a cow's eye—and sliced through it, to witness the strange phenomenon of the upside-down and right-left reversed retinal image, which perplexed early scientists: why do we not experience objects in the world as upside-down or reversed? We'll return to this question again when we consider our blind spots, but for now, I simply point out that Descartes speculated that the eye does not properly "see" the world as it is, but rather it is the mind—the thinking part of humans—that actually sees.

Although Descartes emphasizes seeing in the mind, which would seem to negate the importance of the *physical* eye, the *mind's* eye retains its ocular primacy. This remains true even today: It is commonplace to talk about the mind's eye, a bit of a stretch to speak of the mind's ear, and the mind's ability to hold and consider subjects as if by way of the other senses is basically unheard of—the mind's nose sounds silly, and the mind's finger absurd. The blind man and his sticks may be analogous to sight, but they are by no means equivalent.

Early modern science initiated an attempt to learn about the world through the senses—through experiential and experimental knowledge rather than received wisdom. And this empirical impulse spurred a kind of schism in representations of the blind: the blind poet or prophet on the one hand, and the blind man as specimen, as observable object of speculation on the other. These two starkly different images continue to dominate our ideas of blindness and the blind to this very day.

6

Darkness Visible

Sing to me, O Muse, of the great blind poet of the seventeenth century, the bard of whose existence, unlike Homer's, we are assured. John Milton was born in London in 1608 and died in 1674. He went blind, like me, in his forties, after which he composed *Paradise Lost* (1667), one of the great epics of world literature. He composed in the solitude of his bed, and stored the lines in his head until they could be written down. One of his amanuenses, Cyriack Skinner, wrote that Milton would wake early "as is the use of temperate men" and have a "good stock of verses" ready to dictate, "which if it happened to be later than ordinary, he would complain, Saying he wanted to be milked."[1]

Although we will be able to consider only some of the 10,565 lines of *Paradise Lost,* and will not venture beyond that poem, Milton did: he went on to compose another combined 3,828 lines of *Paradise Regained* (the admittedly less exciting sequel) and the closet drama (a play written for the page rather than the stage) *Samson Agonistes.* There is much to say about Milton and his blindness, particularly with regard to *Samson,* whose situation of blindness often feels highly personal, but I must be circumspect, for the danger of falling into the fiery quagmire that is Milton and the 350-year-long scholarship surrounding his oeuvre is very real.

If you've so far managed to avoid reading *Paradise Lost,* or have tried and failed—because let's face it, Dr. Johnson was not completely off his rocker when he wrote, "*Paradise Lost* is one of the books which the reader admires and lays down, and forgets to take up again"[2]—allow me to introduce you to its opening lines, which, in the style of the blind bard Homer, begins with the invocation to the Muse, or, I should say, it sort of begins with the Homeric invocation, because actually that's on line six. The first five lines introduce the subject of the poem, namely, Adam, Eve, their fall, and their eventual redemption by Christ:

Of man's first disobedience, and the fruit
Of that forbidden tree, whose mortal taste
Brought death into the world, and all our woe,
With loss of Eden, till one greater man
Restore us, and regain the blissful seat,
Sing heav'nly Muse.[3]

As you can see, Milton, as Johnson suggests, is not an easy read. I used to ask my students to find the verb in these opening lines (answer: it's "sing"). Besides perhaps being baffled by Milton's ability to compose such complex (tortured) syntax in his head, I feel it's important to pause right here and say that although Milton is (rightly) thought of as a blind poet, he spent his first four decades as a sighted person, and a scholar of the most intense variety. It is nearly impossible to imagine him receiving the knowledge he had stored up by the time he composed *Paradise Lost* without having studied with his eyes in those days before braille, before the systematic education of the blind—the conception of which would have to wait more than a hundred years to appear, and even then not in England but in France. I point this out because I think sometimes it's forgotten that Milton was not born blind, and that he had the benefit of vast reading—in several ancient and modern languages—behind him. If we like the idea of the blind bard, we must remember that he, like his sighted counterpart, also needs education to succeed. Milton may invoke the Muse, but his poetry is not the result of divine inspiration alone.

Paradise Lost is the story of Adam and Eve and their temptation to eat the forbidden fruit, but it is also about the backstory: the war in heaven that resulted in the fall of the rebel angels led by Lucifer (Satan), who subsequently plans to corrupt man as revenge for his expulsion. Not many lines pass before we move from the taste of the forbidden fruit to the flames of hell, where we meet up with Satan and his companions blinking in their new surroundings, their new fiery home that's not much to look at or, more precisely, not look-at-able:

> A dungeon horrible, on all sides round
> As one great furnace flamed, yet from those flames
> No light, but rather darkness visible
> Served only to discover sights of woe.[4]

The expression "darkness visible" has a nice ring to it precisely because it feels almost meaningless, perhaps paradoxical. Some commentators have even called it sublime and thought of it as an expression of the very limits of our visual imagination, where perception stretches into the infinite horizon of the unknowable and unseeable.

"When I was fourteen, I discovered the sound of iniquity on a long-playing record for the blind from the Library of Congress," writes the poet and memoirist Stephen Kuusisto in his memoir *Eavesdropping*. Kuusisto, having been born premature in 1955, lost most of his vision due to an overly oxygenated incubator (a not-uncommon occurrence at the time). "I listened to *Paradise Lost,* and sometimes after hours of playing the story of Satan I'd walk to the driveway's edge and feel the elaborate work of sunlight and wind and imagine, the way only a teenager can, the falling of Satan in a blackness so pure you could feel it in the bones of your face."[5]

With Kuusisto, we sense that there is something palpable about the darkness of hell. It is a darkness of the heart and the mind that one feels rather than sees. This is a metaphorical darkness that can be experienced alike by the sighted and the blind.

"Blindness is often perceived by the sighted as an either/or condition," writes Kuusisto in his first memoir, *Planet of the Blind*. "One sees or does not see. But often a blind person experiences a series of veils: I stare at the world through smeared and broken windowpanes. Ahead of me the shapes and colors suggest the sails of Tristan's ship or an elephant's ear floating in air, though in reality it is a middle-aged man in a London Fog raincoat that billows behind him in the April wind. He is like the great dead Greeks in Homer's descriptions of the underworld. In the heliographic distortions of sunlight or dusk, everyone I meet is crossing Charon's river."[6]

Similar to Kuusisto's, similar to mine, Milton's blindness was at least for some time incomplete and nearly hallucinatory. "As sight daily diminished, colors proportionately darker would burst forth with violence and a sort of crash from within," Milton explained in a letter to his friend Philaras (a Greek physician who promised to pass the description on to an acclaimed oculist in Paris), "but now, pure black, marked as if with extinguished or ashy light, and as if interwoven with it, pours forth. Yet the mist which always hovers before my eyes both night and day seems always to be approaching white rather than black; and upon the eyes turning, it admits a minute quantity of light as if through a crack."[7]

It's hard to imagine a pure black that approaches white as anything other than a paradox, akin to the darkness visible of *Paradise Lost*'s hell, unless you interpret that pure black as a metaphorical loss of the visible world. The loss manifests not as blackness, not as darkness, but rather as a kind of too-muchness of light, a dazzlement like that experienced by the man who climbs out of Plato's Cave only to be confronted by the blinding sun.

I pause here to say that although the age-old tendency is to equate blindness with darkness or blackness, that is generally not the experience of the blind—not for Milton, Kuusisto, nor myself. Yet you may be wondering about those born completely blind, or who went blind so early in life that no memories remain of having been sighted: Surely they live in a dark world? I will let the philosopher Martin Milligan, who lost his eyes to cancer when he was eighteen months old, answer: "Perhaps it's just worth dwelling for a moment on the word 'darkness,' to emphasize that for blind-from-birth people and people like me this word doesn't have any direct experiential significance. We don't live, as is sometimes supposed, in a 'world of darkness,' because, not knowing directly from our own experience anything about light, we don't have any direct experience of darkness."[8]

Yet the language of darkness is so pervasive in our culture that it is almost impossible not to use the word just as sighted people do. Milligan argues that even if blind people cannot have an experiential knowledge of darkness and light, the secondary, metaphorical meanings of the terms are completely accessible "because of the ways in which such words are so frequently used by sighted people in common talk, stories, and abstract argument." Thus, he maintains, darkness has all the same associations for blind people as it does for the sighted: "associations with difficulty in perception, with the unknown and the incomprehensible, with threat and danger, and also sometimes with warmth, privacy and safety against intrusive perceptions by others."[9]

These quotes come from a collection of letters between Milligan and the sighted broadcaster and writer Bryan Magee, originally published as *On Blindness,* but later renamed *Sight Unseen* (a darkness-visible type of pun that seems to resonate with blind and sighted authors alike, as the title is shared with a mind-boggling number of works of both nonfiction and fiction that almost always have something to do with blindness). In this exchange, Magee is very skeptical—to the point of being offensive—about Milligan's assertion: "I have to say that I do not believe that blind people can understand visual terms to a major extent, though you demonstrate impressively that they can do so to some extent."[10]

The bold stance that enforces the notion that sighted people can speak with confidence about the world of the blind, while blind people cannot talk sensibly about the world of the sighted, is rather common and creates an infuriating asymmetry: blind characters are everywhere drawn by sighted writers, and blind people's real experiences seem then to fall short of sighted expectations. A fundamental sight-centric bias makes it very difficult for blind writers to tell their truths. I think this in part explains the dearth of blind writers, and the scrutiny that follows those brave enough to write.

There is a long tradition in Milton scholarship that falls victim to this kind of ocularcentrism. From Johnson, who wrote that Milton's "images and descriptions of the scenes or operations of Nature do not seem to be always copied from original form, nor to have the freshness, raciness, and energy of immediate observation,"[11] to T. S. Eliot's "At no period is the visual imagination conspicuous in Milton's poetry,"[12] critics have been citing Milton's loss of sight as the reason for his lack (as they see it) of visual imagery. I do not agree with Johnson and Eliot, but rather find myself allied with Stephen Dobranski, who in *Milton's Visual Imagination* argues that Milton was actually very good at rendering the "invisible visible," and, as "evidence of Milton's ability to create rich visual details," offers "the more than 150 artists who have illustrated *Paradise Lost,* from the first illustrated edition in 1688 to works by such diverse artists as Gustave Doré, William Blake, J. M. W. Turner, and Salvador Dalí."[3]

You don't have to go to the illustrators and artists that Milton inspired to prove this point. Just consider the following image from Book I of *Paradise Lost,* which is utterly cinematic in its effect, a kind of long shot of Satan pulling himself out of the burning lake of hell:

> [T]he superior fiend
> Was moving toward the shore; his ponderous shield
> Ethereal temper, massy, large and round,
> Behind him cast; the broad circumference
> Hung on his shoulders like the moon, whose orb
> Through optic glass the Tuscan artist views
> At evening from the top of Fesole,
> Or in Valdarno, to descry new lands,
> Rivers or mountains in her spotty globe.[14]

The imagery may seem a little obscure until you realize that the "Tuscan artist" alludes to Galileo. Satan is seen as if through a telescope: he and his moon-like shield are magnified and yet seen at a distance, a quite extraordinary visual that suggests how hard Milton worked to accommodate the descriptions of his non-physical worlds (hell as well as heaven) to the minds of his readers. Far from ignoring the visuals of his contemporary world, Milton adopted Galileo's telescope—a prosthetic for the human eye—and used it in his poetic imagery.

Milton had long been attracted to the Tuscan artist, and, in 1638, when he was young and still sighted, he journeyed to Italy. "There it was that I found and visited the famous Galileo grown old," as he tells it in *Areopagitica* (an anti-censorship tract), "a prisoner to the Inquisition, for thinking in astronomy otherwise than the Franciscan and Dominican licensers thought."[5]

As we've seen, Galileo's discovery through the telescope that the perfect-seeming moon was in fact craggy and uneven— "spotty," as Milton puts it—was very discomforting to his contemporaries, as was the revelation of Jupiter's moons, never before seen by the naked eye, made suddenly manifest by the telescope. What was the purpose of God's creating worlds that the human could not see without an "optic glass"? If, since the beginning of time, human vision had been capable of perceiving only a fraction of God's creation, then what was the use of so much superfluity—of so much stuff beyond the scope of the natural eye? These questions provide the backdrop for Adam's curiosity in the opening lines of Book VIII of Milton's epic. Adam asks the angel Gabriel why there appears to be such excess in the universe as to have countless heavenly bodies circling Earth, herself merely "a spot, a grain, / An Atom."[6]

The seventeenth century's prosthetics of the eye—the microscope as well as the telescope—rocked the minds of Milton's peers, and had much to do with ushering in the modern era. The fact that Milton in his blindness appreciated the enormous significance of augmented vision allied him, to a certain extent, with the empiricists of his age, even if the puritanical poet would not have appreciated how empiricism would help to dismantle Christianity. I think Milton's use of the "optic glass" is a clue to understanding how complex were his views of seeing and not-seeing. Although he participated in and perpetuated the power of the notion of the blind seer's inner illumination, he also appreciated the observations of the New Science of the seventeenth century, whose proponents, through investigation and dissemination, paved the way for the eighteenth-century "enlightenment" impulse and to modern science as we understand it today.

It may be that Johnson, Eliot, and others who criticized Milton for a perceived lack of visual imagination did so because they took the blind bard at his word regarding the compensation of a more profound, inner vision. "Hail, holy light, offspring of Heav'n first-born,"[17] cries the speaker of *Paradise Lost* as he turns his attention from the goings-on in hell to those in heaven, at the start of Book III. Although for him, "wisdom at one entrance [is] quite shut out," it is preferable that the inner eye be able to see: "There plant eyes."[18]

These lines feel autobiographical, and most readers have taken them as such. Within the long invocation of the muse that opens Book III, the compensation structure is elaborated, and we learn what exactly is lost and what gained. Although the blind speaker leaves the darkness of hell, it is not exactly for the light of day:

> I sung of Chaos and eternal Night,
> Taught by the Heav'nly Muse to venture down
> The dark descent, and up to reascend,
> Though hard and rare: thee I revisit safe,
> And feel thy sov'reign vital lamp; but thou
> Revisit'st not these eyes, that roll in vain
> To find thy piercing ray, and find no dawn;
> So thick a drop serene hath quenched their orbs, . . .[19]

Although Milton is obviously engaging with the light versus dark/sight versus blindness metaphorics we've been talking about all along, he does not forget the physicality of his eyes—the "drop serene" in the above lines alludes to his own blindness. In *Milton's Blindness* (1934), a remarkable book that one might consider an early example in the field that today is called disability studies, Eleanor Brown (herself blind from an untreated infection when she was just a few days old) points out that "drop serene" is the translation of the medical term "gutta serena"; in seventeenth-century medicine, this referred to a blindness in which the eye retained a normal appearance.[20] In other words, Milton's blindness was invisible to others, and that "deception" niggled: When he was wrapped up in his earlier political pamphleteering and new to blindness, he wrote in "Second Defense," a pro-Cromwell, pro-Parliament, anti-royalist political tract, that his eyes "are as clear and bright, without a cloud, as the eyes of men who see most keenly." This fact reveals a rare insecurity: "In this respect alone, against my will, do I deceive."[21]

Brown, incidentally, was the first blind person to graduate from Ohio University, the first blind woman in the United States to receive her PhD, the first person in Dayton with a guide dog, from the Seeing Eye (the first guide dog school in the United States, where I also was partnered and trained with my two guide dogs). She taught German, Latin, and history to sighted high school students and was arguably one of Milton's most influential blind readers. I want to highlight her relationship to Milton because her premise—that she could add to the mountain of Milton scholarship on account of her knowing a thing or two about being blind—could be taken for my own. In her preface to *Milton's Blindness,* she wrote: "To the interpretation of Milton's life and writings after the loss of sight, I add my knowledge of blindness."[22] This gives her thoughts a personal touch that's missing from what sighted scholars have written on the same issue: "No one would deny that blindness has its deprivations. That it has compensations is recognized by every sightless person. To Milton these compensations meant a great deal, and it is, I believe, the thought of these benefits that he would leave with the reader."[23]

Milton was not only the subject of Brown's book; he also gave her courage throughout her life. When she was quite young, a chorus of well-meaning voices—trying to spare her from disappointment—attempted to persuade her to leave the school for the blind that she was attending and take up residence in a safe home for women where she'd spent her summers. She refused and not only finished school, but also went on to college, and later graduate school. Through all of this, she took comfort from the fact that "Milton had written," and that she "had always wanted to write."[24]

These words were my first encounter with the explicit invocation of Milton by a female voice—blind men writers such as Borges look to Milton's greatness for inspiration, but Brown is the only woman writer to do so that I yet know of. That he was a man, or that she, as a woman, might be hindered from achieving greatness, does not seem to enter the equation. However, Brown wrote in her autobiography, *Corridors of Light,* about how she had once been tempted by marriage, but gave it up. She remained single and a faithful Christian, even if independently minded, throughout her long life. I sometimes worry that if a woman were to enter the annals of the blind bard, it would have to be as a kind of androgynous robed figure, because blind women, even more than blind men, have historically been encouraged to be circumspect in their desires—for either literary greatness or marital normalcy—and to have both was almost unthinkable.

Critics have sometimes felt that Milton's invocation of the

Muse of light that opens Book III would be heartbreakingly poignant—if it weren't so packed with conventional pastoral tropes that are literary rather than experiential, ending with:

> Seasons return, but not to me returns
> Day, or the sweet approach of ev'n or morn,
> Or sight of vernal bloom, or summer's rose,
> Or flocks, or herds, or human face divine;
> But cloud instead, and ever-during dark
> Surrounds me, from the cheerful ways of men
> Cut off, and for the book of knowledge fair
> Presented with a universal blank
> Of Nature's works to me expunged and razed,
> And wisdom at one entrance quite shut out.[25]

Critics have pounced on this passage, and in particular its "book of knowledge," to testify to the fact that Milton is not talking about the things he's seen but the things he's read about. T. S. Eliot roundly dismissed Milton as someone who, even before blindness, "may be said never to have seen anything."[26] And though it seems fairly clear that Milton is not talking about what he once saw in the streets of seventeenth-century London, there is something poignant about the loss of nature as it appears in books. Both aspects of learning about the world come through that single entrance (sight) and are now, for the blind Milton, vicarious acts. His eyes can no longer read the book of nature, nor words on a page, and I empathize with that double loss.

———

The road to the study of literature, including *Paradise Lost,* and an eventual PhD was a long and winding one for me. Having dropped out of high school, I spent some time at City College of San Francisco, where I first learned of books on tape from Recording for the Blind and Dyslexic (now called Learning Ally) and the National Library Service for the Blind (NLS). These long-playing cassette tapes were immensely valuable to me. Valuable, and yet terribly shameful. I hid those tacky blue and green boxes in drawers along with the plastic tape player with colored buttons that looked like a pitifully uninspired government-issued toy. Thus, I marvel at the bravery and self-confidence of Stephen Kuusisto, who, when his progressive high school music teacher asked the class to bring in their favorite albums, and the other students were bringing in rock records that inspired such degenerative discussions as "Who's got the better guitar solos, Clapton or Hendrix?," lugged in his special record player from the Library of Congress (this was before the innovation of cassette tapes), and played a recording of, yes, *Paradise Lost*.

Kuusisto let the side play out, and the needle rasp against the paper label. Then he picked up the record triumphantly, announcing to the class that there was braille on the label because it was for blind people. "Can you imagine how solitary John Milton must have been in the days when there was no Braille and no blind person could read a book without help? He had to listen to voices. He had to figure out who was telling the truth without seeing their faces." Not surprisingly, his presentation was greeted with silence. "I was in the midst of people whose ways were not my own," Kuusisto concludes. He was alone with the spirit of Milton.[27]

I'm not sure what prompted me to take a class on Milton in my first year at UC Santa Cruz (where I'd transferred as a junior), but given that I also took Dante's *Divine Comedy* and The Hebrew Bible as Literature, I must have caught up with my reading enough to have a sense of the importance of the good old Western canon. I think my choices in courses were also partly determined by my realization that getting the "classics," as I naively called them (until I became a classics major), on tape would always be more doable than getting the new stuff, even if the "new" stuff had been written two decades earlier—I distinctly remember being disappointed that I could not, in the 1990s, get *Zen and the Art of Motorcycle Maintenance* as an audiobook, even though it had been available in print since 1974!

I don't believe I knew about Milton's blindness until I took that first college seminar. And aside from glimpses of the complexities of blindness that I'd encountered in the character of Gloucester in *King Lear,* it was in reading Milton that I discovered the first inkling of comfort a blind person could take from the idea of compensation. This was definitely just a tiny spark at the time because I certainly did not identify as a blind person then. I was visually impaired and could see most things. As yet I did not use a cane or a dog (that would not begin until my third year of grad school). I was merely facing a future blindness. Yet it was enough to start me thinking about the cultural significance of blindness, and to prime me for Homer and the classics.

College Milton was the first time I had to sit in a circle, the only one without the ability to refer to a book, and talk about reading—basically do a close reading without being able to point to the text, as I did not bring my clunky tape player to class, of course. So the text I'd refer to would be read out loud by the professor, or other students, or be plucked out of my head. My fellow students got used to it, and so did I, but it is amazing to me that I was able to say anything relevant at all. Somehow, I felt strangely at home in these conversations about this remote book, and I would continue this method all the way through graduate school, until I started teaching and finally had a laptop on which I could access the texts and my notes, and listen, one earbud in, to the electronic voice read them out to me.

When I started teaching undergraduate survey classes and had only a few hours to discuss the epic that has inspired hundreds of books and the study of which can easily take up an entire career, I would never neglect to bring my students to the famous SATAN acrostic in Book IX (and quoted below—that appears just before that character, disguised as a "pleasing and lovely serpent," gallantly introduces himself to Eve. This passage, in its allusion-packed simile, likens Satan's serpent costume to other divine disguises and metamorphoses, and ends with the acrostic:

> He with Olympias, this with her who bore
> Scipio the highth of Rome. With tract oblique
> At first, as one who sought access, but feared
> To interrupt, sidelong he works his way.
> As when a ship by skillful steersmen wrought
> Nigh river's mouth or foreland, where the wind
> Veers oft, as oft so steers, and shifts her sail;
> So varied he, and of his tortuous train
> Curled many a wanton wreath in sight of Eve,
> To lure her eye.[28]

I asked my students to use their eyes and see what Eve must see, but does not: that behind the glamour of the serpent's appearance and the twisting allusions, SATAN is here! Yet the SATAN acrostic (from the Scipio line to "Nigh river's mouth") actually tests not Eve but rather Milton's readers—specifically his sighted readers.

Eve will, of course, be beguiled by the beauty of the serpent, convinced by his flattery that his words come from a place of benevolence—but we, as readers, should not be duped. I like to think of it as a blind man's joke, a joke that is as much on himself as on his sighted reader. It reminds one of the ineffectiveness of the prophets who show and tell the sighted where to look and what to look for, and are yet unheeded, as so often happened with Tiresias. "Here is SATAN," Milton the blind poet seems to say, "right in front of your eyes, and yet you fall."

I sometimes wonder about the reaction of the amanuensis who, on the day Milton composed the above lines, had come to "milk" the poet for his verse. Did Milton tell him to pay attention, or laugh at his not noticing? Did the poet have to point it out, say, "Make sure those lines start S-A-T-A-N"? What the SATAN acrostic suggests to me is that Milton was not only still a very visual person when he wrote *Paradise Lost,* but was in fact obsessed with seeing.

Milton's blindness, and its expression through the speaker of *Paradise Lost,* is important not only for the relationship it establishes with Homer, but for its thematic fit into the epic's interest in the limitation of sight, of not being able to see the important things that lie beneath or beyond the surface. For example, in Book III, Satan disguises himself as a humble angel who is simply curious to get to "see and know" God's new creations, Adam and Eve. Apparently the disguise is persuasive because the angel Uriel, who was "held the sharpest-sighted Spirit of all in Heaven," does not recognize him and therefore lets him pass into Paradise. If even an archangel cannot see Satan in disguise, we ought to sympathize with Eve.

Once admitted into their happy domain, Satan spies on Adam and Eve, and is tormented by their innocent intimacy. He cries, "Sight hateful, sight tormenting!"[29] Adam and Eve seem to represent all that Satan, a fallen angel, has lost. They might also represent all that we humans, also fallen, have lost. Perhaps this is why Milton goes to such lengths to describe the mother and father of all mankind as pretty darn hot:

> His fair large front and eye sublime declared
> Absolute rule; and hyacinthine locks
> Round from his parted forelock manly hung
> Clust'ring, but not beneath his shoulders broad:
> She as a veil down to the slender waist
> Her unadornèd golden tresses wore
> Disheveled, but in wanton ringlets waved.[30]

Though both Adam and Eve are attractive, it is Eve who is explicitly more so, and it is she, therefore, who must learn to love someone who is her inferior—at least on the surface. In my first Milton class, I struggled with an essay about Eve's Narcissus moment, her story of meeting her own lovely reflection. As she tells Adam, she would have "pined with vain desire" if she were not led away by the voice of God to meet him. But Adam, being "less fair, / Less winning soft, less amiably mild," prompts her to want to run back to her own reflection. When Adam calls to her with words of love and seizes her hand, Eve yields and from that moment forward sees "How beauty is excelled by manly grace, / And wisdom, which alone is truly fair."[31]

Perhaps it was something in me just starting to try to reconcile the blind bard trope with the blind woman trope, but I saw an irony in Eve's position as the one who is loved for her beauty, but who in turn must love Adam for the divine within him: "He for God only, she for God in him."[32] The irony strikes me as not dissimilar from how Jesus indulges in spectacular healings while emphasizing the humility of belief. If women are supposed to be the more superficial sex, then why is it that Eve must love Adam for what he is on the inside, while he is given a partner who is the more outwardly beautiful? Even if Milton did not intend for us to see Eve's predicament as ironic, it's absolutely true that sight plays a strange role in *Paradise Lost* precisely because it is everywhere indulged. I dare you to read the description of Eden, as seen through the eyes of Satan in Book IV, without getting some really fantastic images stuck in your mind's eye.

Ordinary sight is denigrated in *Paradise Lost* because the poem is primarily a Christian epic, and as we've seen, Christianity is fairly skeptical of sight. However, through the eyes of Satan we glimpse beauties that suggest Milton's complex (and quite modern) relationship to that lost sense. As William Blake so famously put it in *The Marriage of Heaven and Hell,* "Milton was of the Devil's party without knowing it." And the devil, as we have seen, is fully sighted, to his sorrow: "O Hell! what do mine eyes with grief behold!"[33]

Milton's visual imagination shares an appreciation for the materiality of his world with the empiricism of his age. Yet he remains a Christian, and therefore skeptical of the physical eye. His position toward sight—that which he laments and that which he loses in order to achieve greatness—is as complicated as his position with regard to Eve's temptation.

It is knowledge that Eve seeks and that Milton sought for the first forty years of his life. Thus Milton the scholar does not dismiss Satan's temptation lightly. The taste of the tree of knowledge is a kind of first sight—like the blind man restored to sight or the naive traveler in foreign lands. In both cases there is a presumption of true, uncorrupted sight, an idealization that will, as we'll soon witness, enliven philosophical discussions from the late seventeenth century onward.

In *Paradise Lost,* first sight will be given to the first knowing humans. Or at least that is Satan's promise to Eve. The tree of knowledge was forbidden because God "knows that in the day /

Ye eat thereof, your eyes that seem so clear, / Yet are but dim, shall perfectly be then / Opened."[34] The promise should resonate with Christian readers; yes, as Corinthians says, we see through a glass darkly, but don't we all want to see clearly, perfectly? Who among us would be able to resist? Eve may be forgiven, then, perhaps, for tasting the fruit and persuading Adam, too, for, as she tells him, the tree has a "divine effect" and will "open eyes, and make them Gods who taste."[35]

7

The Molyneux Man

About twenty years after Milton published *Paradise Lost,* the philosopher John Locke published *An Essay Concerning Human Understanding* (1689), which expanded the fundamentals of empiricism. Locke himself was involved in the science that was happening around him at the Royal Society and elsewhere, and he thought to formulate a philosophical basis for these observational and experimental impulses. Crucial to these impulses—which made modern science possible—was his argument that there is no such thing as innate knowledge; rather, it is the senses that furnish our minds with ideas.

Locke elaborates on the writing tablet, a.k.a. the blank slate or tabula rasa,[1] which he calls "white paper," to explain how ideas come from experience. "Let us then suppose the mind to be, as we say, white paper, void of all characters, without any ideas," he writes in Book II of *Essay.* "How comes it to be furnished? Whence comes it by that vast store which the busy and boundless fancy of man has painted on it with an almost endless variety? Whence has it all the materials of reason and knowledge? To this I answer, in one word: Experience."[2]

The issue of experience versus innate ideas spurred a fellow philosopher in Scotland, William Molyneux (sometimes spelled "Molineux"), to write to Locke with what would become a famous philosophical question involving "a man born blind, and now adult, and taught by his touch to distinguish between a cube and a sphere": If that blind man were suddenly made to see, would he, by sight alone, be able to "distinguish and tell which is the globe, which the cube?"[3]

Molyneux's question was likely prompted by his wife having gone blind shortly after their marriage. So, ironically, a blind woman is behind the famous "Molyneux Man," as the hypothetical blind man came to be called in philosophy and beyond. In any case, Molyneux answers his own question with a firm no. He explains, "For though he has obtain'd the experience of, how a Globe, how a Cube affects his touch; yet he has not yet attained the Experience, that what affects his touch so or so, must affect his sight so or so."[4]

Locke included Molyneux's thought experiment in his second edition of *Essay* (1694) and all subsequent editions. "I agree with this thinking Gent, whom I am proud to call my Friend," he writes in response, "and am of opinion, that the Blind Man, at first sight, would not be able with certainty to say, which was the Globe, which the Cube, whilst he only saw them: though he could unerringly name them by his touch, and certainly distinguish them by the difference of their Figures felt. This I have set down, and leave with my Reader, as an occasion for him to consider, how much he may be beholding [sic] to experience, improvement, and acquired notions, where he thinks, he has not the least use of, or help from them."[5]

In other words Locke asserts that although the perspicacious philosopher may guess at the truth of the matter—that a blind man made to see may not actually be able to see much of anything at first—most people who have not thought on it will assume that if the eyes are working one can see. As medical "miracles" would shortly demonstrate, things are not so simple. The brain must also learn to see or, as Locke would have it, judgment and experience play a part in what we commonly think of as sight. Locke concludes the section by telling how when Molyneux has asked the question of others, they invariably answer that the blind man would be able to tell the cube from the sphere at first sight until "by hearing his reasons they were convinced."[6]

And it does take convincing! Most sighted people—from Molyneux's seventeenth century to our own—still believe that the answer would be "Yes, of course." The idea that we do not simply open our eyes and see is counterintuitive. I had this very conversation with a friend a few years ago. "Think about how this table, with its checkered red and white plastic covering and all the glasses and plates would present to the eye that had never seen before—as just so many colors of squares and circles," I said in a SoHo café. "And then, behind me the light and shapes of all that Manhattan offers, and you'll realize that all those shapes and colors and plays of light will be totally indistinguishable— unreadable—to a newly sighted blind person as actual objects. We spend much of our early childhood relating the sense of sight to the sense of touch in order to read those plays of light and color as recognizable, nameable objects."

I think my friend tentatively capitulated, but perhaps you, dear sighted reader, remain skeptical? Perhaps you must be reminded how imperfect and biased is your "normal" vision, which is so vulnerable to the expediencies of usefulness over the complexities of truthfulness.

I turn to the works of the prolific writer and neurologist Oliver Sacks for help. He meditates on the complexities of see- ing—on just how difficult it is to recognize objects out of the chaos of perceptions—in an essay called "A Man of Letters": "We are all faced with a world of sights and sounds and other stimuli," Sacks writes, "and our survival depends on making a rapid and accurate appraisal of these."[7] The judgments that make ordinary seeing possible are a kind of shorthand based on experience, as Locke intuited and as we'll continue to observe through modern medical "miracles" of "restored" sight.

As Sacks says, "Although seeing objects, defining them visually, seems to be instantaneous and innate, it represents a great perceptual achievement, one that requires a whole hierarchy of functions." When we look at an object, we are not exactly seeing that object, but rather infer objecthood from a chaotic cluster of visual sensations: "We see shapes, surfaces, contours, and boundaries, presenting themselves in different illumination or contexts, changing perspective with their movement or ours."[8]

Sacks likens these shortcuts of the mind to perceive the world quickly to language. We learn to see as we learn to read, so that the building blocks of sight are analogous to the building blocks of language: "The power of combination must be called on; one needs a finite set or vocabulary of shapes that can be combined in an infinite number of ways, much as the twenty-six letters of the alphabet can be assembled (within certain rules and constraints) into as many words or sentences as a language ever needs."[9]

Once we learn to read fluently, we are no longer aware of the effort it took to learn the individual letters and words when we were young. The effort is in fact covered over by the fluency. But that also makes it very easy to assume what a word is—to misread, as I was made painfully aware of when I used to depend on readers a lot for my textbooks; not all of them were good readers. The bad ones would translate my obscure literary jargon into familiar words as they read. I'd have to question them and ask them to reread passages. Once you begin to recognize the shapes of words, the flow of written text, anomalies tend to disappear.

Just as with language, there is much in our vision that is

provisional, arbitrary, and a matter of custom and convention. That is to say, while what we see is useful, it is not exactly true. As Molyneux and Locke had intuited, judgment plays a crucial role in what we see. After a lifetime of building up associations, our vision, though useful, often and easily deceives us.

Michael Pollan, in his 2018 book about the power of psychedelics, *How to Change Your Mind,* conducts an experiment during one of his guided psilocybin journeys in order to see if he can dismantle learned visual tricks the mind uses to make sense of the world on a daily basis: "Loaded on my laptop was a brief video of a rotating face mask, used in a psychological test called the binocular depth inversion illusion. As the mask rotates in space, its convex side turning to reveal its concave back, something remarkable happens: the hollow mask appears to pop out to become convex again. This is a trick performed by the mind, which assumes all faces to be convex, and so automatically corrects for the seeming error—unless, as a neuroscientist had told me, one was under the influence of a psychedelic."[10]

Pollan stops his internal trip (under eyeshade) to test whether or not he can circumnavigate the brain's stubborn refusal to accept visuals that do not make sense. The adult (non-tripping, sane) mind adjusts to or compensates for those things that do not jibe with preconceived (learned) notions about how the world works. Pollan attempts through psychedelics to see things as they really are, but his adult brain is already too entrenched: "As the convex face rotated to reveal its concave back, the mask popped back out, only a bit more slowly than it did before I ate the mushroom."[11]

These shortcuts that the brain learns to make are necessary to everyday seeing, thus rendering it very difficult for the blind person "restored to sight" to learn to see in a practical sense. The person born blind will have functioning eyes but not the neural pathways to see with either ease or efficiency, while the sighted mind will see easily and efficiently, and with the sense that it is seeing the world as it is. However, as Pollan's concave/convex mask and many other visual illusions demonstrate, the functioning eye is easily tricked into believing what it's been trained to see with useful expediency rather than situational truthfulness.

It is in these seemingly extraordinary cases—the "normally" seeing mind under the influence of psychedelics, the blind man "restored" to sight—that we learn how counterintuitive and contingent sight really is. Though we often do not remember doing so as babies and very young children, we learn to see just as we learn to read. Sometimes extraordinary circumstances are what are needed to jolt us out of the complacency that everyday, ordinary seeing incites.

Visual impairment may also illustrate the strange relationship between the eye and the brain. When I was young and still had lots of useable vision, I quickly realized how the visual cortex attempts to guess at objecthood when the information coming to it from the retina is limited and sketchy. As I've mentioned, although I was originally diagnosed with RP (and told people through much of my life that that was my eye disease), it turns out that I actually have a cone-rod dystrophy, which means that I lost functioning of both kinds of photoreceptors early on. Though it was minimal, it was still markedly different from typical RP.

RP usually begins with night blindness and a constricted peripheral vision (tunnel vision) due to loss of functioning rods. The rods are the photoreceptors most common in the periphery of our retinas. They are sensitive to movement and largely responsible for our ability to see in low-light situations. While I did experience some night blindness, the more significant symptom was a loss of central vision, indicating the loss of cones.

Cones cluster in the center of the retina (called the fovea), and are photoreceptors specialized in perceiving fine detail and color. In other words, a person born with no cones is unable to read standard-size print and is completely colorblind. This is called achromatopsia.[12] Although my fovea were basically blown by the time I was sixteen or seventeen, I could still detect some color with the (more sparse) cones outside of the fovea, albeit with less accuracy for many years to come (basically until I could see almost nothing at all). I would often confuse blue and green or pink and orange.

The destruction of my central photoreceptors left me with a hole in the center of my vision that might be called donut vision (as opposed to tunnel vision). That is not to say that I perceived the missing bits of retinas as blackness or darkness, any more than you, sighted reader, perceive your blind spots as black holes. Just as you must be reminded of your inability to see in that area in your periphery where the optic nerve leaves the retina when you are learning to drive, it was only by deliberately placing objects into the missing part of my visual field that I was aware of the blind spots. In fancy cars these days, there are electronics to tell you when there is an object in your blind spot—often called blind-spot monitoring—but I had to find mine on my own.

I was in tenth-grade drama class when I made my discovery. We were spread out across the auditorium, doing some kind of movement exercise, and I noticed that although the scene appeared complete, if I put the teacher standing at some distance from me at the front of the class into the center of my vision, I could make her disappear into a scintillating pixelated tear in my visionscape (that did not present itself until I did so). Likewise, when I moved my eyes around to "focus" on one student or another, I could make that student disappear and the rest would then appear—not perfectly, as they were relegated to the periphery where detail is lost, but they were very definitely there. I was able to recognize all of them, not by seeing their facial features, but by their clothes, height and weight, stance, hair length and color, and the shapes of their faces. I experimented with this little game of perception. I do not remember being scared, just curious—even a little excited to tell others about my oddity.

It was then that I realized why people had been asking why I wasn't looking at them, and would often glance over their shoulders to find where I was looking. Until I made my discovery, I had unconsciously been putting people's faces outside my central blind spot. After that, I learned to fake eye contact in conversational situations by looking around the room to see the person's face better while I talked, and then looked directly at them (without seeing them) while they talked in order to make them feel the attention of my gaze, for which sighted people seem so needy. This worked for decades.

The blind spots of the "normal" eye offer us insights into how what we see is a construct rather than a faithful rendering of the world. "Each retina has a surprisingly large blind region where the nerves and blood vessels leave the eyes, called the blind spots," explains Richard Gregory in his seminal 1966 book about the psychology of seeing, *Eye and Brain*. "They are so large one can make a person's head disappear, when they are sitting across the room!"[3] The brain fills in the information, and it is only while learning to drive or by conducting little experiments that we notice these missing pieces.

In a section titled "The Intelligent Eye," Gregory explains how the act of seeing takes practice to master. Seeing is not simply a matter of translating impulses into pictures, but rather a learned ability to make intelligent decisions based on information from our other senses and prior knowledge about what we see: "The essential point is that sensory signals are not adequate for direct or certain perceptions; so intelligent guessing is needed for seeing objects. The view taken here is that perceptions are predictive, never entirely certain, hypotheses of what may be out there."[4]

If we assume images to be discrete photographic representations of the world, then our usual inability to see our blind spots makes no sense; but if we understand that seeing requires a brain and that in fact, the brain fills in, as best it can, the information that's not there, our unseen blind spots—as well as other peculiarities—do not trouble us. "Some puzzles of vision disappear with a little thought," explains Gregory. "It is no special problem that the eyes' images are upside down and optically right-left reversed—for they are not seen, as pictures, by an inner eye." The fact that the image is not an "object of perception" means that "it does not matter that it is inverted." It is not the brain's task to see retinal images, but "to relate signals from the eyes to objects of the external world, as essentially known by touch. Exploratory touch is very important for vision."[5]

I only read *Eye and Brain* in the last few years, and yet I have long understood the important relationship between touch and sight. For example, when I was visually impaired, knowing the objects in a room or on a kitchen table magically made them seeable. Once when I was having dinner with roommates, I said, "So you're drinking a beer?" implying that it would have been nice to share. I saw a beer can–shaped object that had some red lettering and assumed it was a Bud, but my roommate responded, "I'm not drinking a beer!" I reached out and touched the plastic—not aluminum—cylindrical object and it instantly appeared to my eyes as what it was: a container of Parmesan cheese!

A lesson from the visually impaired: humans cannot see what they cannot see. Because seeing is a function of the brain as much as it is a function of working eyes, magical (and sometimes funny) conversations happen between the electrical impulses of the retina and the brain's gestaltian endeavors of creating order and coherence. Gestalt psychology, which arose in the late nineteenth century and sought to explain how we perceive order out of chaos, helps us understand our tendency to group things together, its famous and oft-misquoted tenet being "the whole is something else than the sum of its parts." From connecting dots on a page to seeing a tree as a tree and not a mad jumble of individual leaves, our brains translate a vast amount of visual information into coherent pictures.

My visual impairment made Lockean judgment and the inferences that gathered around the Molyneux Man pop out at me as being correct, and nearly obvious. But because it still feels counterintuitive to many that we learn to see and that vision is largely a matter of the brain's ability to infer objecthood from the chaos of visual stimuli, the Molyneux Man is often trotted out when new blind men (occasionally women) have been made to "see." Each generation, it seems, needs to remind itself of the philosophical context to decipher what feels like a riddle: how can the blind man restored to sight not see?

I believe that it was my NYU reader (an excellent reader) who first introduced me to Oliver Sacks. After doing so many searches with me in the library databases for blindness and literature, he thought to bring in an article he'd read a few years earlier—a 1993 *New Yorker* piece called "To See and Not See."[16] We were in one of the more spacious study rooms when he first read to me Sacks's account of a middle-aged man named Virgil who somehow managed to live his whole life having never had his cataracts removed—an operation that had been around since the early eighteenth century.

"To See and Not See" begins as so many of Sacks's essays do: with a letter, this one from Virgil's soon-to-be father-in-law.

Virgil had been living as a blind man for more than forty years due to thick cataracts, and was also thought to have retinitis pigmentosa.

Virgil had a comfortable, circumspect life as a massage therapist at the local Y and was not particularly interested in regaining his sight. However, his fiancée, Amy, took him to see her own ophthalmologist, who suggested an operation for the cataracts, but had no way of knowing if the RP was there or not: "It was difficult to be certain at this stage, because the retinas could no longer be seen beneath the thick cataracts, but Virgil could still see light and dark, the direction from which light came, and the shadow of a hand moving in front of his eyes, so obviously there was not a total destruction of the retina. And cataract extraction was a relatively simple procedure, done under local anesthesia, with very little surgical risk. There was nothing to lose—and there might be much to gain."[7]

Of course, letters to Dr. Oliver Sacks were rarely written during moments of pure and obvious joy, but rather from places of mystery and confusion. Although the operation seemed to be a success—the cataract was removed from Virgil's right eye and there were the expected tears and excitement of a man blind from birth suddenly being able to see—the joy hardly lasted.

Sacks turns to Amy's journal to tell the tale: "Virgil can SEE! . . . Entire office in tears, first time Virgil has sight for forty years. . . . Virgil's family so excited, crying, can't believe it! . . . Miracle of sight restored incredible!"[8]

As early as the next day, the seemingly straightforward act of giving sight to the blind becomes troubled: "Trying to adjust to being sighted, tough to go from blindness to sighted. Has to think faster, not able to trust vision yet. . . . Like baby just learning to see, everything new, exciting, scary, unsure of what seeing means."[9]

In the minds of most, the restoration of sight might be assumed to be an unmitigated improvement over blindness. For, as Sacks puts it, "This is the commonsensical notion—that the eyes will be opened, the scales will fall from them, and (in the words of the New Testament) the blind man will 'receive' sight."[20]

However, as with so many things, the truth of the matter is much more complex. "Was not experience necessary to see?" asks Sacks. "Did one not have to learn to see?"[21]

The simple answer, correctly guessed at by Locke and Molyneux, is yes. We must learn to see.

Sacks refers to the Molyneux Man explicitly in "To See and Not See" because Virgil's experiences seem to prove that a man born blind (or one blind since early childhood) and "restored" to sight not only cannot distinguish a cube from a sphere by sight alone, but cannot, in fact, make out much of anything at all. But Virgil was neither the first nor the last person to undergo such an operation followed by philosophical inquiry.

In telling Virgil's story, Sacks turns to one of the earliest cataract operations, performed by an English surgeon named William Cheselden on a thirteen-year-old boy, in 1728. The boy, despite his "high intelligence and youth, . . . encountered profound difficulties with the simplest visual perceptions." He struggled with distance, space, and size. "And he was bizarrely confused by drawings and paintings, by the idea of a two-dimensional representation of reality." Like Virgil, the boy was able to make sense of the visual world only slowly, by building up connections between it and the world he understood by touch. "It had been similar with many other patients in the two hundred and fifty years since Cheselden's operation," writes Sacks: "nearly all had experienced the most profound, Lockean confusion and bewilderment."[22]

Thus neuroscience suggests that the blind man suddenly

made to see is not capable of seeing in the proper sense because his brain has not learned how to interpret the electrical impulses from the retina. Healthy as the eye may be, the brain plays a crucial role in what we think of as sight. Also, the brain learns to make more of the sense of touch in a blind person than it does in a sighted person. For Virgil, learning to see was complicated by his habitual use of touch as a primary mode of investigating the world.

"A major conflict in Virgil," Sacks explains, "as in all newly sighted people, was the uneasy relation of touch and sight—not knowing whether to feel or look."[23] Five weeks after Virgil's operation, Sacks and his ophthalmologist friend visited him and his wife, Amy, in their home. Now, "he often felt more disabled than he had felt when he was blind, and he had lost the confidence, the ease of moving, that he had possessed then. But he hoped all this would sort itself out with time."[24] Sacks, however, was "not so sure." From the early eighteenth century onward, "every patient described in the literature had faced great difficulties after surgery in the apprehension of space and distance—for months, even years."[25]

Even in the quotidian recognition of one's pets, there is learning to be done. "Virgil's cat and dog bounded in to greet and check us," Sacks relates, "and Virgil, we noted, had some difficulty telling which was which. This comic and embarrassing problem had persisted since he returned home from surgery: both animals, as it happened, were black and white, and he kept confusing them—to their annoyance—until he could touch them, too. Sometimes, Amy said, she would see him examining the cat carefully, looking at its head, its ears, its paws, its tail, and touching each part gently as he did so."[26]

Interestingly, Dr. Cheselden's young patient experienced almost the exact same thing as Virgil. Sacks quotes this early observation: "Having often forgot which was the cat, and which the dog, he was ashamed to ask; but catching the cat, which he knew by feeling, he was observed to look at her steadfastly, and then, setting her down, said, 'So, puss, I shall know you another time.'"[27]

The man born blind and made to see must—like a baby—build up the associations between touch and sight in order to train the brain to recognize objects in this new way, and to trust the new perception. After all, as Sacks points out, Virgil had been, before his operation, "a touch person through and through."[28]

Poor Virgil would not go very far in learning to see or functioning with sight. He had been a comfortable blind man with forty years' experience. He had cultivated an uncomplicated and satisfying life for himself as a massage therapist and baseball enthusiast—he loved to listen to games on the radio. Perhaps because he had not been particularly keen to regain his sight in the first place, or because he simply was not mentally equipped to undergo such a profound change, the stress of learning to see proved too much for him. It also did not help that he had underlying visual impairment from RP. Sacks's story of Virgil's "restored" sight did not end well. He became gravely ill and much less able to function as a sighted (or rather partially sighted) person than he had been as a blind person.

Even with high motivation and intelligence, however, it is not always possible for a blind man to learn to see. The extraordinary 2007 book *Crashing Through,* by Robert Kurson, is a journalistic account of Mike May, a forty-six-year-old entrepreneur who, in 2000, became another Molyneux Man. He received stem cells that allowed him to see for the first time since he was three, when he had been accidentally blinded by chemicals. I happened to have met May years ago when I still lived in San

Francisco. His company had put together my first computer—built by and for blind people—and he later came to give an inspirational talk at a summer camp for the blind, where I was volunteering. (Yes, it's a small blind world after all.)

May was a successful entrepreneur and avid skier, and was married with two boys when an ophthalmologist (his wife's, actually, because, like so many people who are totally blind, what's the point of having an eye doctor?) asked to look into his eyes and delivered the startling information that there was a new and rare stem cell transplant procedure that might be able to restore his vision. It was successful in treating very few types of blindness, but a chemical burn such as what May had experienced was one of them.

Similar to Virgil, May was not immediately taken with the idea of an operation. Though it may seem like a no-brainer to many sighted people, he spent many months considering the possibility before he took the plunge. Also similar to Virgil, for him the operation at first seemed to be an instant and unmitigated miracle.

The bandages were removed, and immediately "a cataclysm of white light exploded into May's eye." He experienced an initial shock and joy of brightness, and within seconds, objects began to emerge: "There was a bright shape in front of his face [that] he knew must be the office door[;] he remembered where it had shut, and there were walls around him, he knew it because the light to his sides was different from the light above and he didn't have to think about why it was different, he just knew it was a different color—color!—his old friend color, color was right there and it was turned on . . . whoa!—the black blob on the left was sharpening, it was getting lines and edges, it was becoming something more than color and something more than light, it was an object."[29]

The stunning description of May's first sight spectacularly demonstrates how the brain makes familiar objects out of the chaos of light, color, and shape. However, it must be kept in mind that even though May had no memory of sight, his brain had perhaps retained some connection to the visible world—learned in the first three years of his life before blindness—that made some instant restored sight possible. But sight is not just one thing, it is many.

It turned out that after two months of perfectly functioning eyes, there were still many things Mike May could not see. In a conversation with his wife, he said, "I don't know, Jen. It took me about five seconds to see colors. It took me a day before I could catch a ball on the run." But although he could recognize individual letters, he still couldn't read or recognize faces—even those of his own sons. He could not make sense of it.

Strangely, even after six months, what May could and could not see gave a complex answer to the old Molyneux question. When shown a picture of a cube, he said, "It's a square with lines."[30]

Without a clear question in mind, the research scientist (Dr. Ione Fine) who was testing him started the image rotating. May recognized it immediately. "That's a cube!"[31]

Mike May's ability to detect motion and color were as good as that of people who had been sighted all their lives, but after six months, recognizing faces, reading, and other higher-level modes of seeing continued to elude him, even after he had worked so hard to improve. After the tests, Fine delivered some hard news about how much of what we call vision actually happens in the brain, and how much of the knowledge that we unconsciously use to see in an everyday sense was built up in early childhood. Perhaps May had once had some of this knowledge but had forgotten it after decades of blindness. The upshot was that without that knowledge, a person could not see normally no matter how perfectly his eyes worked.

Mike's response was at first a eureka moment. His new, unpredictable vision had been a mystery to him and now it began to make sense: "If a person couldn't bring this massive bank of knowledge to a visual scene, it stood to reason that he would bring whatever knowledge he could. That's why he yearned to touch everything. That's why he strained for context, leaned so heavily on color, motion, and his other senses. It was all to bring whatever knowledge he could to the raw data streaming into his eye."[32]

But how would he learn or (re-learn) how to see?

Fine was noncommittal. If the neurons May needed to perceive faces, depth, and objects had died or wandered off to perform other jobs, then he might never be able to see normally. A couple of weeks later, brain imaging using fMRI would confirm her suspicion.

Mike was a younger, healthier, and more resilient recipient of sight than Virgil, and yet they both struggled to learn to see. In my opinion, what is important about their journeys from total blindness to partial sight is how starkly they reveal that "restoring" sight is necessarily a complicated and messy business, that should avoid, at all costs, the metaphorical complacencies of moving from the melancholy darkness into joyful light. "Restoring sight" is not a reenactment of a biblical parable, and thus fixing the physical apparatus of the eyes ought not to cue the angels to sing hallelujah.

I think those ancient constructions of sight and blindness too often color our ambitions as "modern" empiricists. If brain imaging shows that a blind man made to see might not actually see, it also shows what new developments can occur in the brains of those born blind, as well as those, like me, who go blind later in life. As we'll continue to witness when we consider braille and echolocation and music, blind people's brains can tell us about different ways of perceiving the world that ought not to be interpreted as attributing value but rather difference. The things blind people perceive as blind people (not newly sighted people) are generally dismissed as lesser realities on the one hand or fetishized as superpowers on the other. Neither of these attitudes does anything to teach us about our brains, our perceptions, or our human understanding.

––––––

Before we move from England to France to see how the seeds planted by Locke and Molyneux sprouted divergent projects of enlightenment (not just "restoring" sight but educating the blind), I feel it is important to point out that these three-hundred-year-old questions circling the man born blind and made to see have been, for the most part, asked, hypothesized, experimentalized, and answered by sighted people. Happily, this is beginning to change. In *The Senses and the History of Philosophy* (2019), I was astounded and delighted to find that philosophers have begun to consider what blind people might have to say about the man born blind and "made to see."

"Considerations of people with blindness have a history of oppression," the editors explain in their introduction, "and a reclamation of their voices not only broadens what might be considered as answers to Molyneux's question but also avoids a common fallacy that numerous answers fall into: a content/vehicle conflation where the representation provided by a sense is confused with the sense itself."[33]

In order to dismantle this conflation, Brian Glenney (also one of the volume's editors) considers in his essay the words of two blind authors: Thérèse-Adèle Husson (1803–31), who wrote novels as well as a philosophical, sociological autobiography, and Pierre Villey (1879–1933), who was a professor of literature at the Sorbonne. Both of these authors present blindness as "neither abnormal to human perception, nor suboptimal." The point of Glenney's piece is that "people with blindness, in fact, do not view their disability as the 'ocularist' culture at large does, as neither a deficit nor difference, but rather as merely different," which allows for a neutrality "such that some individual people with blindness can view their disability as advantage and others as disadvantage."[34]

The editors point out that the real disadvantage faced by people with blindness derives from "the ocularism prevalent in society that fails to see difference as anything but deficient." They conclude that Glenney's essay about what blind people might have to say about the Molyneux question not only gives novel and important answers to that old inquiry, but also "provides a space of justice for people with disabilities in philosophical thought."[35] In other words, we need blind philosophers (and scientists) to theorize and hypothesize—not just be—the Molyneux Man.

Until we recognize that being "made to see" is not the same as being a sight-oriented person, or that being a sighted person in the dark is not the same as blindness, we will never, as a culture, be able to say anything intelligent about blindness as a perceptual experience that is as full of variety as sightedness. We must learn to translate the blind experience into language with as much effort, as much intellectual rigor, as we invest when we attempt to translate what we see into language. Blindness lies outside the experience of most sighted people precisely because it is not the same thing to open one's eyes as it is to be made suddenly and irrevocably sighted.

8.

Performing Enlightenment

In 1771, a young Valentin Haüy, who would later open the first school for the blind and thus be remembered by history as "the father and apostle of the blind," was strolling down a Paris street when he found himself at Saint Ovid's Fair. There, a raucous crowd was jeering and cheering ten blind men. A group from Quinze-Vingts (the hospice for blind people since medieval times) were wearing dunce caps and asses' ears and mock-playing broken cellos and violas. Stands of music faced the audience, who were banging tankards and drunkenly dancing. There were even cheap playbills with some lines of tasteless verse to promote the event, which lasted a month. Haüy was horrified by the spectacle, which was dubbed the "Café of the Blind." In response he vowed to "substitute the truth for this mockery" and "make the blind read."[1]

Though Haüy would slightly revise the details of the story through the years, his encounter with the Café of the Blind stuck as the flamboyant first inspiration for his eventual school. Seeing the spectacle prompted him to make a promise to himself: "I will put in their hands volumes printed by themselves. They will trace the true characters and will read their own writing, and they will be enabled to give harmonious concerts." Then with a theatrical flourish he addresses the impresario—the presumably sighted man who had gathered and costumed his blind performers and advertised their show: "Yes, atrocious maligner, whoever thou art, the ears of the ass with which thou would'st degrade the head of misfortune, shall be attached to thine own."[2]

Despite the ire and disgust Haüy felt that day in 1771, it would be more than a decade before his plan to turn the exhibition on its head—by presenting literate and musically trained blind students instead of blind dunces—would become a reality. But the spark came at the Café of the Blind when he saw in the spectacle something that others in the presumably uneducated or poorly educated crowd could not. Though Haüy came from a modest country home, thanks in large part to his brilliant brother he received an excellent education. He followed that brother to Paris, where both became immersed in the arts and sciences of the day. An orthographer by trade, Haüy specialized in deciphering ancient handwriting. His brother, René Just, a mineralogist (who was called by his detractors "the Crystaloclast" because, after smashing a lot of crystals, he began to understand their unique structure), eventually helped Valentin gain the attention of the intellectuals of Paris whom he would need to open his school—the first of its kind in the world.

I was in the basement of NYU's Bobst Library, in its little padded (soundproofed) cell—wherein I and other visually impaired and blind students had access to a computer with text-to-speech and text-enlargement software, a CCTV magnification system, and a giant Kurzweil reading machine (a scanner loaded with speech and OCR software)—when I first read about the Café of the Blind. The vivid spectacle seemed to me at least as delightful as it was dreadful. I think I am not alone in feeling conflicted. There is a guilty glee in the recounting of this origin story; though it may seem to some to be exploitative, it is nevertheless seldom left out of histories of the education of the blind.

For Ishbel Ross and other mid-twentieth-century chroniclers of blind education, progress marches in a straight line to betterment, as the title of her book, *Journey into Light,* suggests. Given such a point of view, there is but one enlightened response to the "mummery"—that of Haüy: to correct it. As Ross puts it, "Because of the ire aroused in Haüy, this carnival scene in a Paris street became the true starting point of the systematic education of the blind, although the way had already been prepared by the French and English philosophers, and brilliant blind individuals from time immemorial had found their own way to fame and scholarship. But Haüy's cry of protest at St. Ovide's Fair was prophetic."[3]

I am not arguing. Haüy's response was a good one and fortuitous for the blind students who would enter his school and others that would follow. However, I think it's important to remember that another perspective is possible; to forget this is to forget the experience of the blind performers themselves. What if we flip the scene to their point of view on the stage? There is nothing in the literature to suggest that the men were unwilling performers—they were not prisoners, after all. It must have provided an exciting change from dull hospice life to be the center of such attention: "Now and again a drunken couple rose and danced in the street to the fantastic music. The rowdies who gathered at night stormed the blind men's platform and would have demolished it in their exuberance but for a cordon of guards called in to keep order."[4]

Sounds pretty good to me! I have never experienced such enthusiasm from an audience, and I can't help but feel that this kind of response is one that I and most of my performer friends would consider a success (which is why it has inspired so many writings and performances of my own). I like how the Café of the Blind juxtaposes the hilarity of the burlesque blind "musicians" with the sobriety of Haüy's impulse to educate them, the outrageous spectacle with Enlightenment humanitarianism and reason.

It cannot be overstated how the prevailing Enlightenment thinking of the day informed Haüy's impression of the Café of the Blind spectacle. In particular, Denis Diderot, more than any other of his fellow eighteenth-century philosophers, helped to shape the world in which the first school for the blind was founded, and thus he always has a starring role in histories of the education of the blind.

As we've witnessed, the endeavor to "restore" sight is a prevailing—even foundational—myth of the modern era. Here's how Michel Foucault puts it in *Birth of the Clinic:* "What allows man to resume contact with childhood and to rediscover the permanent birth of truth is this bright, distant, open naivety of the gaze. Hence the two great mythical experiences on which the philosophy of the eighteenth century had wished to base its beginning: the foreign spectator in an unknown country, and the man born blind restored to light."[5]

However, Diderot did not subscribe to this "myth" of modernity. "People try to give those born blind the gift of sight, but, rightly considered, science would be equally advanced by questioning a sensible blind man," he asserts in his 1749 "Letter on the Blind for the Use of Those Who See." Diderot argues that we should compare our (sighted) psychology with that of the blind in order to "come to a solution of the difficulties that make the theory of vision and of the senses so intricate and so confused." Thinking perhaps of Locke and the Molyneux Man, Diderot concludes: "But I own I cannot conceive what information we could expect from a blind man who had just undergone a painful operation upon a very delicate organ which is deranged by the smallest accident and which when sound is a very untrustworthy guide to those who have for a long time enjoyed its use."[6]

Diderot, quintessential philosophe, was a rare creature: a man of reason and light who loved the dark and believed in the power of that which cannot be seen. Perhaps it is for this reason that he is so often credited with putting the spotlight on the potential of blind people. "Where those who came before him had seen but a theoretical problem," writes Zina Weygand in *The Blind in French Society from the Middle Ages to the Century of Louis Braille* (2009), "Diderot saw a human one."[7] Thus Diderot planted the seeds for the education—rather than the curing—of the blind.

Because *The Letter on the Blind* is, as its title proclaims, "for the use of those who see," I think it's safe to say that Diderot assumed that experiences from the world of the blind would be educational for his sighted readers. He begins by introducing us to the Blind Man of Puiseaux, who "is possessed of good solid sense, is known to great numbers of persons, understands a little chemistry, and has attended the botanical lectures at the Jardin du Roi with some profit to himself." Although he had a father who was a professor of philosophy and left him means "sufficient to have satisfied his remaining senses," a "taste for pleasure led him into some excesses in his youth," and so "he withdrew to a little town in the provinces." He now visits Paris once a year to sell his liqueurs, which "give great satisfaction."[8]

Although Diderot concedes that these details are "not philosophical," he informs his reader that "for that very reason" they are "likely to convince you that the person I am speaking of is not imaginary."[9] In other words, Diderot's blind man is not a hypothetical Molyneux Man.

Diderot and his companion gently interrogate the blind man and are astonished by his definitions and explanations of such things as mirrors and eyes. Diderot even goes so far as to compare his answers favorably with the thoughts of René Descartes—the seventeenth-century philosopher whose treaty on optics was so influential. When they ask if the blind man would not like to have eyes, he answers that if it were not for curiosity, "I would just as soon have long arms: it seems to me my hands would tell me more of what goes on in the moon than your eyes or your telescopes; and besides, eyes cease to see sooner than hands to touch. I would be as well off if I perfected the organ I possess, as if I obtained the organ which I am deprived of."[10]

Later in the *Letter,* Diderot introduces us to the celebrated English blind mathematician Nicholas Saunderson, who had died ten years earlier. Saunderson, like Newton before him (and Stephen Hawking long after), held the prestigious Lucasian Chair at Cambridge, and had had to invent a new notation system to do his calculations. Diderot astutely exclaims, "It is much easier to use symbols already invented than to invent them, as one is obliged to do when there are none current. What an advantage it would have been for Saunderson to find an arithmetic arranged with signs for the touch all ready to hand at the age of five, instead of having to invent it at twenty-five!"[11] No wonder so many scholars of blind education hold Diderot up as the man who kick-started the endeavor. Like Louis Braille in the following century, a substantial effort had to be made to invent the tools of learning before Saunderson could get down to the business of learning, of catching up to (and surpassing) his sighted colleagues.

Saunderson lectured on light, lenses, optics, the phenomenon of the rainbow, and other subjects connected with sight. He also helped to make Newton's theories of the *Principia Mathematica* and other works accessible to students of Cambridge. Unlike Newton, however, Saunderson was famously (or infamously) irreligious, which adds another layer to Diderot's interest in this blind man. Diderot ends his *Letter* with a fiction—an imagined scene of Saunderson on his deathbed, with a clergyman named Mr. Holmes trying to convert him.

The sighted clergyman begins by pontificating on the wonders of nature—visible everywhere as evidence of God's existence, which the blind mathematician dismisses: "Ah, sir," replies the blind philosopher, "don't talk to me of this magnificent spectacle, which it has never been my lot to enjoy. I have been condemned to spend my life in darkness, and you cite wonders quite out of my understanding, and which are only evidence for you and for those who see as you do. If you want to make me believe in God you must make me touch Him."[12]

Thus, Diderot, skeptical of religion and the existence of God, presents Saunderson as an oppositional force to the blind men of the Christian Bible, creating instead a bold atheist. When Holmes responds by urging Saunderson to "touch yourself" in order to know something of God's miracle of creation, Saunderson will have none of it: "What relation is there between such mechanism and a supremely intelligent Being? If it fills you with astonishment, that is perhaps because you are accustomed to treat as miraculous everything which strikes you as beyond your own powers. I have been myself so often an object of admiration to you, that I have not a very high idea of your idea of the miraculous."[13]

I am astounded by Diderot's intuition here. Every blind person I know has been gawked at and congratulated for the silliest things—hearing a smile in a voice, recognizing by feel the turn in a road, getting one's fork into the mouth—that, although he created Saunderson's response out of his imagination, it feels very authentic. The sighted tend to admire the blind for things that are not at all marvelous to us, and yet they still want to tell us that what we can't see represents the true state of things.

The clergyman goes on to speak of the faith of Newton and

Leibnitz and other great scientists, but still Saunderson remains unconvinced. Rather, the blind mathematician puts forward a proto-Darwinian evolutionary theory in order to explain how great a part chance (not God) plays in the present "perfect" order of the universe: "Think, if you choose, that the design which strikes you so powerfully has always subsisted, but allow me my own contrary opinion, and allow me to believe that if we went back to the origin of things and scenes and perceived matter in motion and the evolution from chaos, we should meet with a number of shapeless creatures, instead of a few creatures highly organized."[4]

Sixty years before Charles Darwin was born, Diderot uses the blind scientist—part historic, part fictionalized—to hypothesize a theory of evolution that suggests humans are the result of chance generation, not evidence of intelligent design. And in doing so, Diderot links one of the most controversial discoveries of our modern era to the wisdom of the blind—a wisdom that stands in direct opposition to Christian fundamentalism—then and now.

Saunderson then moves to his final blow—his own blindness is evidence that the universe is, as yet, unfinished, a work in progress: "If shapeless creatures had never existed, you would not fail to assert that none will ever appear, and that I am throwing myself headlong into chimerical fancies, but the order is not even now so perfect as to exclude the occasional appearance of monstrosities." Diderot cannot resist a touch of melodrama to clinch the blind man's atheistic convictions. Saunderson turns to the clergyman and earnestly says, "Look at me, Mr. Holmes. I have no eyes. What have we done, you and I, to God, that one of us has this organ while the other has not?"[5]

In response, Holmes and the rest of the company weep. Saunderson dies. And thus ends the fictionalized life of this blind atheist who defiantly proclaims that blindness is not a punishment or a playing field for divine justice, but simply a situation of physical happenstance, unraveling centuries of belief that blindness leads to spiritual truth. In this case, if blindness leads anywhere, it leads to science, not religion.

Not unsurprisingly, *The Letter on the Blind,* together with *The Indiscreet Jewels* (a dirty philosophical novel—*Les Bijoux Indiscrets* in French—involving a ring that magically compels ladies' nether regions to speak), landed Diderot in Vincennes prison for a few months.[16] "Shortly before he was released," writes Andrew Curran in his lively 2019 biography, *Diderot and the Art of Thinking Freely,* "the lieutenant-général de police made a special trip to the prison to warn the writer that any further immoral or irreligious publications would bring about a jail sentence measured in decades, not months."[7]

Diderot was a sociable man of salons and the theater, a lover of women, wine, and food; he died reaching for another helping of stewed cherries, i.e., for more dessert! It is not surprising, then, that he did not do well in prison, and did not want to return. He resolved to keep his fanciful, controversial writings to himself, which is why the novels he is now known for—such as *Rameau's Nephew* and *Jacques the Fatalist*—were not published in his lifetime but merely circulated among his friends.

After *Letter on the Blind,* Diderot turned his public attention to slightly less offensive—if no less spectacular—endeavors, namely the *Encyclopédie,* the first attempt to bring all the spheres of learning into a multivolume set. Diderot edited and wrote many articles for the *Encyclopédie* from 1747 to 1772. Within its pages, high and low learning came together. For the first time, entries for priests and philosophers shared space with those for weavers and blacksmiths. It is the inclusion of all humankind's endeavors and ideas together in one book that made it so special and so well remembered as a weapon in the simmering war between the classes. It was in this milieu—the mid decades of the eighteenth century, when democratic thinking was fomenting in France and becoming a reality in America—that the blind (and those with other disabilities) came to be seen as a population ripe for education rather than pity or derision.

————

Although Valentin Haüy conceived his idea to educate the blind at the Café of the Blind in 1771, it was another kind of spectacle—a more gentrified kind—thirteen years later that gave him the final push to realize his dream. That push came in the form of a girl, a Viennese musical prodigy named Maria Theresia von Paradis whom he would meet in 1784, when she was on a European tour performing and demonstrating her tactile methods of education. Their meeting would finally convince him of the viability of his plan. But before we move to discuss his founding of the world's first school for the blind, let's take a little detour to learn about Maria Theresia von Paradis, a wonderfully colorful character in the story of blind education.

Paradis was born in 1759 to an aristocratic family in Vienna and mysteriously went blind at the age of three. According to most accounts, she experienced some kind of violence or fright and suffered a convulsive fit. Others said her blindness was caused by badly cared-for eyes. Still others simply diagnosed her with "gutta serena," a vaguely scientific term that merely indicates blindness without external (visible) sign in the eyes (Milton was also "diagnosed" with gutta serena). Although she had access to the finest oculists of Vienna, there appeared to be no cure.

Paradis's musical gifts revealed themselves quite early, and she was introduced to singing and to keyboard instruments such as the organ and harpsichord. At age sixteen she performed for Empress Maria Theresa, who was so impressed that she endowed the young woman with an annual pension—a pension that allowed her parents to supply her with the most fashionable music teachers in Vienna.

She also learned foreign languages, history, and geography. Baron Wolfgang von Kempelen, an inventor and mechanician, taught Paradis to read with cardboard letters and gave her a small manual printing press so that she could keep up with her many correspondents. Beyond these educational accomplishments, Paradis ingratiated herself to the wigged and corseted gentlemen and ladies of the eighteenth century with her social graces, which included dancing, private theatrical performances, and good taste in clothing.[18]

In 1777, she attracted the attention of Dr. Franz Anton Mesmer, whose name gave us the word "mesmerize," thanks to his controversial work in "curing" all kinds of ailments with magnets and perhaps a kind of proto-hypnosis—"animal magnetism" was the name of his game. His house was the meeting place of all Viennese musicians. It was also the place where he performed his famous magnetic cures.

"In Vienna the intelligentsia discussed it, debated it, and even practiced it," explains Ishbel Ross in *Journey into Light,* "but the medical profession as a whole regarded his operations with the utmost distaste. He maintained that an invisible magnetic fluid flowed through all living things. In strong bodies the fluid was abundant; in the weak it was deficient. Mesmer insisted that the magnetic fluid could be passed from one body to another by grasping iron bars."[19]

Already renowned as a singer and musician in a city resplendent with musical talent, the eighteen-year-old Maria Theresia von Paradis with her mysterious blindness must have been a tantalizing patient for Mesmer. He installed her in the nursing part of his house and gave her magnetic treatments. The "cure" apparently took place when Mesmer waved his "magnetized wand" over her in front of a mirror, causing the nervous twitching of her eyes to cease. She felt a pain in her head and was at first extremely sensitive to light, but this decreased over time.

Initially her parents were delighted and sang Mesmer's praises to Vienna, but the doctors remained unconvinced: if she was sighted now, she must not have been blind before. In most accounts of Paradis's "cure" there is some speculation that she fell in love with Mesmer—perhaps there was even an affair— but nobody knows for sure. What seems fairly certain is that if Paradis was cured, it was short-lived and riddled with adverse consequences. Here's how her father described what happened after the cure with regard to her musical virtuosity: "Whereas formerly she played long concertos with great accuracy and was able to carry on a conversation at the same time, now—with open eyes—it is difficult for her even to play one piece. She watches her fingers move over the keyboard and misses most of the chords."[20]

Whether it was due to the fact that she had lost her ability to perform or that her value as a performer would be lessened without the blindness factor, her animal magnetism treatment was cut short. Here's how Weygand sums up the infamous event: "The patient became subject to attacks of nerves, and her virtuosity suffered as a result. Alarmed by her state, her parents wanted to take their daughter back from her therapist. Paradis resisted. The affair degenerated into a scandal that Mesmer's enemies hastened to exploit. He had to interrupt the cure and return the girl to her family. He soon left Vienna for Paris, where animal magnetism created the same craze, followed by the same condemnations."[21]

Paradis is mentioned in books about the history of the education of the blind just as Mesmer is mentioned in histories of psychology because of his (perhaps unwitting) use of autohypnosis, and the possible romantic connection makes for a good story that has been exploited in numerous novels and films. I have seen one of these films and it was quite terrible—far too much in the way of temper tantrums and fainting spells. What I've always been most interested in when it comes to Paradis's story is how her talents were intertwined with her blindness.

If we believe that Mesmer provided her with a cure, it's clear that this cure did not work in her favor, at least in terms of her potential to generate fame and fortune for herself and her family. After some initial emotional outbursts (she apparently did not want to leave Mesmer's care), she seems to have accepted both her vision loss and the loss of Mesmer as the necessary sacrifices to assume her destiny as a brilliant blind musician, dubbed "the blind magician" by the end of her European tour. She would go on to enjoy a long life as first a performer and later a composer and teacher. I will indulge in a flourish from Borges and venture to say, as he does of Milton in his autobiographical essay "Blindness," that Paradis's blindness was voluntary.

In a letter to the *Journal de Paris* in April 1784, the "General Officer of Correspondence for the Sciences and the Arts" announced Paradis's arrival in Paris. After the performances, spectators were invited to see her tactile tools of education and amusement such as maps and playing cards at her home at the Hôtel de Paris, where she was staying with her mother. The performances and demonstrations were such a success that the pair remained in Paris for six months.

Weygand explains the enthusiastic reception: "Parisian polite society—ever eager for novelty and perhaps tired of observing the reactions of those born blind and operated on for cataracts by renowned surgeons—doubtless rushed to Mademoiselle Paradis's for the spectacle of a distinguished blind person offering proof of the benefits of tactile pedagogy."[22]

Thanks to his visit to Paradis's performance and demonstration, Haüy picked up practical methods—particularly the use of carved block letters to teach the alphabet by touch—that was the final impetus he needed to put his teaching-the-blind plan into action. Now he went out in search of his first student, whom he found begging on the steps of the Church of Saint-Germain-des-Prés. François Lesueur was seventeen years old and had been blind since the age of six weeks. His family was extremely poor, and he had never had any education. Lesueur did not exactly jump at the opportunity for education offered by Haüy, as he was not ready to give up his profitable post on the church steps during the Pentecostal season. But then Haüy promised to pay him for his time.

Haüy first taught Lesueur to recognize letters using carved wooden tablets, but this was a labor-intensive method, as each new page had to be carved. As it turned out, the student rather than the teacher hit upon the next important innovation. Sorting through some papers on Haüy's desk one day, Lesueur found the back of an invitation card, and he was surprised by the feel of the letter "o." It was embossed type that had been impressed from front to back on the thick paper. He ran to his teacher to tell him what he'd found, and Haüy immediately recognized the usefulness of this discovery. He traced more letters in reverse, so that they could be read on the backside, and Lesueur named them all.

It did not take Haüy long to realize that the method was as old as the printing press. He merely had to reverse the block letters that ordinarily stamped ink onto paper from the top, and make them big enough that the fingers could feel from right to left on the reverse, the blocks with their embossed letters now stamping tactile impressions from beneath. Although the type would undergo many changes over the years, Haüy had initiated the art of embossing, which led to the creation of the first library for the blind.

After that, Lesueur's education moved more rapidly. In six months he could read and print characters in relief. Now that Haüy had his method, he set about getting support and more students. He turned to the Philanthropic Society for both financial assistance and help with gathering his first students—six blind children who were pensioners. They received free education, room, and board—these were not the special cases of wealthy and brilliant blind individuals (such as Saunderson and Paradis), who had always had more opportunities to learn, even if the methods were haphazard. The real innovation of Haüy's school had everything to do with the new, enlightened ideals that encouraged all children to have an education. Haüy was not the first to make a blind child literate, but he was the first to create a school that attempted to keep middle-class and poor children from ending up as beggars, to encourage these children to make a living. It did not work out perfectly—many of the children still wound up on the streets or back at Quinze-Vingts (as even Lesueur himself eventually did), but the endeavor was utterly novel and led to lasting results. Inspired by Haüy's ultimately short-lived success, schools for the blind sprang up around the world in the coming decades.

Haüy's school—the Royal Institute for Blind Youth—opened its doors in Paris in 1785, and soon it was one of the sights of the City of Light—attracting all the fashionable and intellectual people of Paris who were interested in seeing the blind children demonstrate their newfound literacy and their musical talents. Although he'd been offended by the spectacle at the Café of the Blind, it cannot be said that Haüy did not also indulge in exhibitionism himself. It could even be argued that the performers at the Café of the Blind had more agency than the children of Haüy's school, as there is nothing to suggest that the men were compelled or coerced to perform or leave the hospice of Quinze-Vingts. The same cannot be said for Haüy's students, who were, after all, beholden to the school for their livelihood as well as their education.

I am not here to pass judgment on what types of entertainment by the blind (for the sighted) are good or bad, right or wrong, as I think such judgments are part of the problem and do not speak to the fact that oftentimes in retrospect an idea is neither one thing nor the other but rather terribly mixed and confused.

Take, for example, Laura Bridgman (1829–89), who was the first deafblind person to be educated and who was in her day called the most famous woman in the world besides Queen Victoria. She lived nearly her entire life at the Perkins School for the Blind in Boston (the first such school in America, which was inspired by Haüy's school), where thousands came to visit her and see what she could do. One of the most famous of her visitors was Charles Dickens, who wrote about his encounter with Laura in his 1842 *American Notes:*

> Long before I looked upon her, the help had come.
> Her face was radiant with intelligence and pleasure.
> Her hair, braided by her own hands, was bound about
> a head, whose intellectual capacity and development
> were beautifully expressed in its graceful outline, and
> its broad open brow; her dress, arranged by herself,
> was a pattern of neatness and simplicity; the work she
> had knitted, lay beside her; her writing-book was on

the desk she leaned upon.—From the mournful ruin
of such bereavement, there had slowly risen up this
gentle, tender, guileless, grateful-hearted being.[23]

Besides the fact that it is very clear that Laura was a spectacle in her own right—drawing famous visitors such as Dickens
to see her perform her education, I personally find this description to be irritatingly saccharine. Yet, it was reading this very
passage more than forty years after its publication that gave
Helen Keller's mother her hope that something might be done
to educate her own daughter, also struck deafblind by illness
(likely scarlet fever).

Before we leave Laura Bridgman, I need to draw attention
to one more tidbit that Dickens offers about blind children in his
day: "Like other inmates of that house, she had a green ribbon
bound round her eyelids. A doll she had dressed lay near upon
the ground. I took it up, and saw that she had made a green fillet
such as she wore herself, and fastened it about its mimic eyes."[24]
Besides being a striking image, this indicates to me the fear or
loathing that sighted people often show at the sight of blind eyes,
and, more poignant perhaps, how easily those insecurities can be
internalized by a blind person living in a sighted world.

As you may have surmised, I personally believe that precious and inspiring depictions of blind people (such as Dickens's)
need to be balanced with the bawdy and burlesque (such as the
Café of the Blind). I'm not speaking here of sighted actors playing blind people (badly, as so often happens in movies and television), but of blind people playing themselves in all their sublime
and ridiculous variety. That said, I am not so cynical that I cannot also celebrate, with Ross, the glamorous exhibition of Haüy's
students at the court of the ill-fated Louis XVI and Marie
Antoinette (who would, in a few years, lose their royal heads).

In the winter of 1786, Haüy's students were invited to Versailles for the Christmas festivities. For eight days at court they were both entertainers and entertained. They wandered, as Ross so delightfully puts it, "through the gardens and parks, conscious of the scents of forced blooms, of the rippling sound of fountains, of the swishing silks and high laughter of the courtiers who fluttered around Louis XVI and Marie Antoinette in the last days of their splendor."[25]

Ross gives us a detailed description of the exhibition itself from the *Journal de Paris,* a review of sorts, published the following month: "A blind boy listened to and corrected the reading of one who could see. False orthography was recognized and re-written properly in raised print. Geographical relations were pointed out by Lesueur, the first blind professor, . . . Quite difficult fractions were reduced to the same common denominator with such a degree of exactitude that the Duc d'Angoulême, to the infinite amusement of the court, sat pen in hand and worked out the problems with them. The pupils presented to the King and Royal Family a book printed by themselves, . . . followed by models of all their little printed works, which had been executed under the careful instruction of M. Clousier, printer to His Majesty, who was second only to Haüy himself in his unselfish and disinterested zeal for the welfare of the blind."[26]

Haüy's school hardly had a moment to flourish before the French Revolution erupted. The benevolent aims of progress were nearly forgotten in all the bloodshed, and with so many of its rich patrons beheaded, the Paris school fell on hard times. It would struggle on without Haüy, who found himself on the wrong side of the new regime. Years after he was ousted from the school he had founded, a young Louis Braille would enter that school, be educated, and then invent a writing system that would eventually revolutionize blind education.

9

Braille and His Invention

Louis Braille was born in 1809 in Coupvray, a town twenty-five miles east of Paris. His childhood home is now a museum (La Maison Natale de Louis Braille), located very near Disneyland Paris. I'm ashamed to say that I've been to the latter and not the former. My only excuse is that during the two summers that I lived in Paris trying hard to learn French for grad school studies, I had a lot more vision, but far less access to the incredible array of information and tools I now have at my fingertips on my iPhone, including an almost limitless number of books, travel guides, GPS apps, and so forth. Thus, I have been to Space Mountain: De la Terre à la Lune, but I have not been to the house where Braille was born nor the re-created workshop of his father. I'm guessing that if I had had access to all that information back then, I surely would have known that Braille's birthplace was right there.

Perhaps I could be forgiven also because I was not much of a braille reader then. Sadly, I am not alone. According to most estimates, only about 10 percent of the blind people in the United States read braille. The reasons for this are complex and disheartening, as we'll see. However, for me, and many younger blind people I know, the trend seems to be shifting, in large part thanks to technology, specifically the braille display, which we'll spend some time with shortly. But before all that, let's get to know Louis, the boy genius.

In the first histories of blind education that I read in my padded cell in the basement of NYU's library, including my favorite, the lively *Journey into Light,* I first read about Braille's childhood home: "It had only two rooms—one upstairs and one downstairs, where the Brailles lived, ate, and created their simple pattern of family life. Part of the downstairs room was partitioned off as a workshop."[1]

The workshop belonged to Braille's father, whom Ross calls a saddler, but it turns out that he was actually a harness maker, which is (who knew?) not the same thing. In *Louis Braille: A Touch of Genius* (an impressive coffee-table book with many photographs),[2] Michael Mellor explains the difference: "The former makes equipment for those who ride horses, while the latter makes equipment for those who use horses as a source of power,"[3] i.e., farmers who use horses to pull ploughs. The distinction may seem trivial, but since Braille blinded himself in his father's workshop—attempting to mimic his father's movements—it has been the point of more than a little scrutiny.

I had always thought that Braille blinded himself with an awl—a tool that eerily presaged the tool he would use to invent his alphabet, but that also turns out to be not quite correct. The most reliable account (according to Mellor) of Braille's blinding, in the summer of 1812, comes from Hippolyte Coltat, Braille's schoolmate and lifelong friend: "One day, at the age of three, sitting beside his father, . . . the boy wanted to work too, and imitate the movements he saw his father make. In one of his little hands he seized a leather strap, and in the other a serpette (a slender, curved knife rather like a small pruning hook) and there he was at work."[4]

Little Braille lost control of the knife and stabbed himself in the eye. As happened in the days before antibiotics, the injured eye grew infected and the infection spread to the other eye, leaving Braille quite blind. Though the guilty tool was actually a little knife, not an awl, the accident arose out of an effort of industry. That impulse was perhaps part of Braille's DNA. Besides the harness-making business, Braille's family ran a small vineyard, and was, it seems, thrifty and hardworking. Braille inherited these familial traits, as demonstrated by his modest will, included in Mellor's book. Upon his death at age forty-three, Braille had a little something to give to his nieces and nephews (he never married), his friends, a few charities, and to forgive the debts owed him as well.

Braille's family, though not rich, was not illiterate. According to Mellor, a friend of the family reported that "Louis learned the alphabet at an early age, at home, by feeling the shapes of letters made with upholstery nails that had been hammered into a wooden board."[5] Braille was allowed to go to school, and proved himself intelligent. The local priest managed to secure a place for him at the Institute for Blind Youth in Paris. This was in 1819, when Braille was ten years old and Haüy had years since been ousted from the school he'd founded. Haüy would visit the institute in his old age, when, after many adventures—including a protracted and ultimately fruitless visit to Russia (by invitation of the Czar) to found a school there—he was himself quite blind, but there is no record of the man who first systematized the education of the blind meeting the boy who created the now-universal writing system for the blind.

As it turned out, it was neither Haüy nor Braille who came up with the idea of using embossed dots rather than lines to create a tactile writing system. That invention is generally credited to Charles Barbier de la Serre, a former artillery officer in Napoleon's army who had an interest in cryptography. Barbier invented a system that he called *écriture nocturne* (night writing), a means by which military intelligence could be read in the dark—without lighting a torch, without alerting the enemy. His system was never employed in Napoleon's (or any other army's) warfare toolkit, but he thought it might be useful to the blind. He first brought his night writing to the Institute for Blind Youth in 1820, when Braille was eleven. But it was met with resistance from the director (who would soon be forced out due to a scandalous affair with the head music instructress). Barbier returned in 1821, when his system was greeted more favorably by the new director, Alexandre François-René Pignier, Braille's friend and mentor through the many years of his directorship, until he too was forced out—not by romantic affairs but by finding himself on the wrong side of the governing powers in those volatile decades after the French Revolution, reminding us once again that blind education does not exist in a vacuum, political or otherwise.

At the time of Barbier's visits, the students still learned how to read using the embossed books with Latin characters that Haüy had pioneered decades earlier. These letters were very bulky, hard to read, and nearly impossible to write. Barbier's system was also pretty bulky, but the improvement of dots over lines was obvious, as they were more readily comprehended by touch. Not only were dots easier to read, they were also easier to write by using a few simple tools—which would develop into what's now known as a slate and stylus.

However, Barbier's system did have some drawbacks, one of which was the fact that it was sonographic, based on assigning symbols to sounds rather than letters. Another problem was its size. Night writing was based on a combination of twelve dots, which was too big for the finger to glide over from left to right and required some vertical exploration as well, slowing the overall reading experience.

Barbier left some samples of his punctiform writing and the

tools he used at the institute, and Braille began to tinker and improve the system. Although he would continue to augment and perfect it for years, by the ripe old age of fifteen he had invented the writing system named for him. His two great innovations were to cut the cell in half—from a twelve-dot cell to a six-dot cell—and to assign dot formations to letters of the alphabet. Braille's system, simple and elegant, which he also developed into a musical notation system (Braille was a professional church organist), is still the alphabet that we learn today.[6]

My first attempts at learning braille began thirty years ago. Jewel was the name of the woman who first taught me. She was in her sixties and I in my late teens. We had the same kind of eye disease, a degenerative one. She was nearly completely blind, and I was mostly sighted. Jewel's apartment featured exotic knick-knacks from her world travels as an advocate for blind rights. I remember small sculptures as black silhouettes against pristine white walls. The shapes of my first braille characters were similarly black on white. Jewel had me draw dot formations with a Sharpie on a large white sketchpad.

"The braille cell consists of six dots," she told me at my first lesson. She had me draw a full braille cell and number the dots: dots one, two, three run down the left side of the rectangle, and dots four, five, six down the right side. Dot one is the letter "a," dots one and two are "b," dots one and four are "c," and so on. All the dots raised together form a full cell (also the word "for").

I did not know then that the size and shape had been the particular innovation of Louis Braille, nor anything about Barbier and his night writing. I discovered all this a decade or so later when I was in graduate school. Then I took *Écriture Nocturne* as the title of my master's thesis, a beast of a paper that

explored the many connections between blindness and enlightenment. I even typed out the title on a plastic protective folder
on my manual braille typewriter. Because even years after Jewel,
after feeling like I'd never be fluent and had failed at braille, I
never forgot my alphabet, and sprinkled it around my world for
aesthetic purposes, and some practical ones too—for example,
labeling my lipsticks.

A manual braille typewriter is most often called a Perkins
brailler, named for the man who endowed the Perkins School
for the Blind in Boston. It is similar to the classic typewriters
that many young writers fetishize these days. Just as with an
Olivetti or Remington, the working bits are partially visible
and readily understandable. In my mind's eye I can clearly see
my mother's clunky fifties typewriter on which I learned to
touch-type when I was a teenager. With its metal arms—each
embossed with a letter of the alphabet—that strike the ribbon
overhand being similar to the mechanics of the Perkins brailler
in which six metal dots—one for each dot of the braille cell—
strike the paper from beneath, popping up the embossed letter or word sign. There is something very satisfying about the
Perkins brailler with its heavy metal construction and clanking
sound effects.

Just as with that old typewriter of my mother's, I feed the
paper—of cardstock weight to make the dots more durable—
into the back of the Perkins brailler, clamp it down, and roll it
in using wheels on either side to bring it to the top of the page
to start typing. Unlike the slate and stylus that Braille invented,
where one must actually poke holes from the backside—thus
from right to left—in order to read the letters from left to right
on the reverse (which I just can't get my brain around), the typewriter is simply a matter of placing one's fingers on the keys that
correspond to the dots of the braille cell.

The left first three fingers rest on dots one, two, three, and the right on dots four, five, six. If you push all six fingers at the same time, you have a full braille cell (the word sign "for"). There is also a spacebar under the thumbs, right where you'd expect it to be. Each time you strike you are creating a braille cell, which often represents a letter in the alphabet, but can also represent a word: dots two, three, four, and six make the word "the" when it appears alone, but also stand for the letters *t-h-e* in words such as "other."

I've always found braille to be cool and beautiful, and, in my artsy phases, I've been known to make jewelry, cards for sighted friends, wall art, and more with it. I find that the beauty of the system rests in the patterns the dots make when words or signs are repeated. I do not particularly like it when sighted artists appropriate braille for installations or T-shirts using giant dots. To me, this is not braille. Braille is dependent upon the dots being a certain size to glide under the finger smoothly from left to right. That was, after all, Braille's great innovation.

What's generally called grade 1 braille includes the letters of the alphabet, numbers, and punctuation. Contractions such as the "the" sign and the "for" sign are used in grade 2 braille (the standard for most books) in order to save space and increase reading speed. Braille is about as small as it can be for our human fingers to comprehend, but it is still pretty bulky. For example, the first braille novel I ever finished was a four-volume set of *The Poisonwood Bible* with each hardcover volume measuring approximately twelve by twelve by four inches! The books came in soft crates with handles—one for each volume. Alabaster took a photo of me when we set out to lug them back to the post office to be sent as "Free Matter for the Blind." I am standing on our stoop weighed down by ten or fifteen pounds of literature—a far cry from *The Poisonwood Bible* paperback print edition (545 pages) that, according to Amazon, measures about eight by five by one inches and weighs approximately twelve ounces. Between the bulk and the dearth of titles, it's no wonder braille literacy struggles.

In 2009, on the anniversary of Louis Braille's birth, the National Federation of the Blind (NFB) published a report titled "The Braille Literacy Crisis in America," outlining the obstacles that blind children and adults encounter in learning braille and the disadvantages experienced by those who do not learn it. Two depressing statistics noted were that "fewer than 10 percent of the 1.3 million people who are legally blind in the United States are Braille readers" and "a mere 10 percent of blind children are learning it."[7] The report proposed steps to reverse the trend and double the braille literacy rate by 2015.

Ten years later, I thought I might check with the NFB for an update, and Chris Danielson at the national office in Baltimore was kind enough to speak with me over the phone. He explained that while the NFB does not gather statistics, it has brought "significant awareness to the issue." For example, he pointed me to a 2019 *New York Times* article about braille Lego:[8] "When Carlton Cook Walker's young daughter developed health problems that led to near-total blindness, [Ms. Cook Walker] knew she wanted her to learn Braille," the article reports. "But the family's school, in rural central Pennsylvania, was resistant. A teacher pointed out that the girl, then in preschool, could still read print—as long as it was in 72-point type and held inches from her face."

Cook Walker countered, "What about when she is in high school? How will she read Dickens like this?" to which the teacher responded, "Oh, she'll just use audio."[9]

As someone who went through college and graduate school using audio, I feel both gratitude for that option and frustration at having only that option for reading. Cook Walker had to fight to get braille instruction for her visually impaired daughter, which unfortunately is not an uncommon situation. It seems that today's low braille literacy rates are at least partly attributable to an unwillingness or a perceived inability among teachers and schools to provide instruction. The mostly sighted teachers of blind and visually impaired children are generally overworked. It is simply easier for them to teach what they know, and they often do not know braille. As Danielson puts it, "We shouldn't assume that educators are necessarily any more enlightened about braille than other people."

Sighted teachers' inability to read braille and their unwillingness to learn it cause them to underestimate its power and worth. This is a bias that goes right back to the days of Louis Braille. Mellor tells how in 1840 Braille (who was then a teacher at the school where he once was a student) "experienced a terrible setback." He had published his system in 1829, and he and the other blind teachers and students were using it to great benefit. But when Braille's friend and mentor Pignier was forced to retire, his deputy and successor, Pierre Armand Dufau, became the school's director. Dufau used his position to promote his own system of embossing Latin characters, and to ensure that it replaced the system that Haüy had pioneered, Dufau ordered the burning of all previously embossed books and, while he was at it, banned the use of Braille's dot system, too. As it had been relegated to personal (or individual instructional) use among the blind students and instructors—not something that the sighted instructors bothered with—there were, as far as I can tell, no braille books to burn.[10]

Like so many sighted people—then and now—Dufau believed that "blind people should use the same (or as close to the same) reading and writing techniques as those with eyesight in order to avoid erecting barriers between the two," writes Mellor.[11] In Braille's day that meant embossed Latin characters; in our day it means using standard Windows or Mac computers made accessible with text-to-speech programs such as Jaws, NVDA, or VoiceOver. In other words, technology that sighted instructors can use without having to work very hard to learn or adapt. How much of this belief system is rooted in a desire for convenience or flat-out prejudice on the part of sighted teachers, and how much is rooted in concerns about the integration of blind students, I will leave to you, dear reader, to decide for yourself. That said, I am not arguing that blind students do not experience problems in integrating with their sighted peers; feelings of otherness are certainly an issue, but this is not particular to using braille. Kids who use magnification or speech output also do things differently.

As my friend Laurie Rubin, an opera singer and educator, tells it in her 2012 memoir *Do You Dream in Color?,* her speech-output laptop also acted as a barrier between her and her teachers and fellow students. "My laptop, now plugged into an outlet in the very back corner of the classroom, had a synthesized voice telling me what was on the screen," Laurie explains. "In order to spare the others in my class the sound of its emotionless drone, I plugged a one-sided earphone into it, which allowed me to listen to the teacher and type notes at the same time."[12]

Laurie was born blind from Leber congenital amaurosis (LCA), which meant that her retinas developed only enough to detect light, and so she learned braille at an early age, but the speech-output laptop was also part of her equipment in school in the early nineties. In fact, she needed two lockers to hold all her stuff (which also included braille books).

In Laurie's first days in a new middle school, her teacher, Tasha, was perhaps flustered by the blind kid with the laptop and actually asked if she could hear her, to which Laurie quipped, "I'm blind, not deaf," a retort that every blind person I know has been forced to utter at least once. But the young teacher, unembarrassed by her own ignorance, barreled ahead with her insensitivity:

> "I'm glad you're able to hear me then," Tasha said with an awkward chuckle. "You just look like a robot all hooked up to your machine like that. I wanted to make sure you're with me."
> I blushed, suddenly feeling like the kid with the pocket protector again. It was no wonder the others around me were so uncomfortable in my presence. I was an alien from outer space, a foreigner with some curious customs, and now, Tasha had voiced out loud that I was a robot, unrelatable, inhuman.[13]

Though I unfortunately went to school before a laptop was a possibility, I have had similar experiences at work. During a brief but oddly enlightening stint of employment with New York's Children's Services, I helped run the facilities department in an outwardly gorgeous Art Deco building on Wall Street that on the inside was composed of eighteen floors of leaks and rats and broken air-conditioning units. I fielded complaints and fired off emails to my electricians and plumbers. One day, as I was studying a new computer system that was to be implemented the following week, I heard one of my superiors yell across the vast floor of cubicles, "Leona! Wake up!"

Because I was not staring intently into my screen, but rather listening intently to my screen reader through my earbud, he had decided I was sleeping on the job.

The point is that children (or adults) in school (or at work) using any kind of different equipment are likely to stand out, though the ubiquity of laptops in the classroom today probably mitigates that difference. As I often say, "Little blind kids are so damn lucky these days!"

It's not only that I feel sorry for my own young self who did not have access to the technology I have now, but also the world has gone digital, which means that everyone—not just the blind or visually impaired kid—is attached to electronic prostheses these days. It is my belief that this fact has gone a long way to reducing the gap between sighted people and blind people. I remember distinctly the evening that I taught my sighted uncle how to use his new iPhone. This simply wouldn't have been possible twenty years ago. And judging by some of the conversations I have with my blind friends, being useful is something that we often feel our lives sorely lack.

Beyond today's universal use of technology, it seems strange to me to think that braille would be stigmatizing, as whenever I use it in public, sighted people seem to be quite charmed and fascinated by it. After all, braille is cool. I mentioned this insightful observation to Chris Danielson at the NFB, who agreed, telling me how his friends in school wanted to learn it and that he taught one friend well enough to pass notes in class.

"So how is it that the stigma of braille persists?" I asked him.

"Look, there's a visual bias in our society," Danielson concluded, "and I think that extends to the way that blind and low-vision children are treated."

Even among ourselves, there's no consensus about the usefulness of braille. As I was working on this chapter, I saw that my friend Caitlin Hernandez, who, like Laurie, was born blind from LCA, posted a small rant on Facebook about "pompous, windbaggy blind people" who advise parents not to bother with braille for their blind kids because, they argue, blind people who use braille notetakers for most of their work are unemployable.

Although Caitlin, who has dubbed herself my pet millennial, is often mistaken for a child, which is partly due to circumstances beyond her control—namely, that she is petite—and partly her own doing—she tends to order from the kids' menu and covers her world (including her cane) in rainbows (although she's never seen colors)—she is very much employed. She teaches elementary school special education, and she is also a very talented published writer. Recently she delivered the keynote speech at a conference of braille transcribers and educators of the blind and visually impaired, in which she said, "I don't really remember learning braille. I feel as though I was always reading, writing, thinking in, and loving braille."[4]

Caitlin does the vast majority of her reading and writing on her BrailleNote Touch, a wildly expensive and utterly useful mobile device—commonly called a braille notetaker—which has a braille display and keyboard that allows her to download and read books, surf the Web, read and reply to email, etc. Unlike the Perkins keyboard, Caitlin's is virtual and disconcertingly untactile. You simply place all ten fingers on a screen that is as flat as that of an iPad and about the same size, in typing formation. The screen recognizes them, gives a little buzz, and then you begin typing. Easier said than done.

When we met, in my hometown of San Francisco, where Caitlin lives, she graciously let me try out her BrailleNote Touch. I placed my fingers on the smooth screen, waited for the slight buzz that told me it had registered them, and began typing. I managed to push out an occasional word amid the gobbledygook. "It takes some getting used to," she said, which did not dispel my frustration.

I became so annoyed and flustered with my inability to keep my hands straight enough to type out a simple sentence that, between sips of gin (we were sitting at a bar), I asked Alabaster, who was looking on, to verify the "English" on the screen. Caitlin duly chided me. "You sound like a sighty!"

Indeed, that braille is like a foreign language is a common misconception. Despite my barroom gaffe while struggling with Caitlin's fancy braille contraption, I am fully aware of the fact that braille is a writing system for any number of languages, including its original language of French! Thinking of braille as a foreign language contributes to its being thought harder to learn than it is. Or perhaps more to the point, braille's supposed foreignness contributes to the feeling that learning how to read visually is easier, just because everybody does it.

"Braille has been elevated to the realm of the occult by those who know nothing about it," wrote Robert Russell (who was a blind professor of English literature) in his 1962 memoir, *To Catch an Angel*. "People have always either marveled at or ignored things they don't understand, so it is really not surprising that they should dissolve in admiration before someone purporting to make sense out of a sheet of paper covered with pimples." However, reading and writing braille can be learned not only by the blind but by the sighted as well. Motivation is the key. "As soon as I went off to school," said Russell, "my mother learned it and wrote me letters long before I could read well enough to understand them."[5]

One of the biggest misconceptions people have about braille stems from their forgetfulness about how much trouble it takes to learn to be literate. We give sighted children years to perfect their reading and writing skills, and then suppose that blind children should be born reading braille, or never taught it. Braille is a writing system, it bears repeating, just like the Latin alphabet used by English, French, Spanish, German, etc., is a writing system. English is no more or less English because of the letters we use. An alphabet is merely an accepted writing system for recording and transmitting spoken language. Thus, braille is as good—as useful and arbitrary—as any other, and when practiced, it can be learned like any other. Too many people forget that alphabets were not handed to humans from on high, but developed through circumstances of war and conquest and adaptation and learning, just like all cultural artifacts.

In fact, when Louis Braille died in 1852, there was no guarantee that his writing system was going to dominate the blind literacy landscape. By the end of the nineteenth century, there were several other tactile systems in use, among them New York Point (a kind of dot system that laid the cells on their sides), Boston Line Type (a modified version of Haüy's system), and Moon Type (a kind of shorthand version of Latin characters consisting of minimal curves and lines, named for its inventor, William Moon). However, one hundred years later, on the anniversary of his death, braille was established and beloved around the world, and France finally decided to honor one of the most famous blind men who has ever lived by disinterring his remains (originally buried in his hometown of Coupvray) and placing them in the Panthéon in Paris alongside those of Victor Hugo and Jean-Jacques Rousseau.

Helen Keller was there to declare, "[W]e, the blind, are indebted to Louis Braille as mankind is to Gutenberg."[6] And the world was there to witness hundreds of white canes tapping along the streets of Paris with the coffin of Louis Braille in what the *New York Times* called "a strange, heroic procession."[7]

It may have taken Braille's invention a hundred years to receive the acclaim and accolades it deserved, but that does not mean his system is universally used or taught, or even considered necessary, which is a sad state. I admit that years ago, I was one of those people who thought that text-to-speech technology would supplant braille because embossed braille books are so bulky and expensive. But I feel now that I was wrong. It was the refreshable braille display that changed my mind.

As we've seen, braille is this beautiful system of six dots that create alphabetical characters, words, partial word signs, and punctuation within a prescribed cell that holds its shape whether or not there is one dot, two dots, or three dots occupying it. With electronic braille, little pins poke up into each cell of six holes and then pull back down as you scroll through text. Braille displays usually come in twenty- or forty-cell units that connect to computers and mobile devices for reading and writing. Now that ebooks are generally published at the same time as print, blind readers can access new books as soon as their sighted fellows.

Although braille displays are ludicrously expensive, they are not exactly state of the art and have been around for decades. As I recall, you may glimpse one in use in *Sneakers,* the 1992 movie about a bunch of hackers that include a blind guy who has a very nice braille display. The only thing that's really changed over the years is how the refreshable braille display interfaces with other technology—now you can get wireless braille displays that come with braille keyboards. I've recently discovered that you can even find them used on eBay, though I must say I find it rather annoying that they are often listed under "Health and Beauty" or "Mobility Aids" instead of "Technology"—because, of course, blind stuff must not be confused with actual technology—insert Face with Rolling Eyes emoji.

About ten years ago, I managed to secure a braille mobile device—basically a portable stand-alone braille computer similar to Caitlin's. However, I was afraid of having to write braille, so I stuck to my familiar standard qwerty keyboard instead of getting it with a braille keyboard—a mistake, I now realize, as writing helps to cement reading. At that time, once again, braille reading still didn't take. Instead of improving my braille skills, I detached the braille display and just used the audio output, and developed a method of reading aloud by bringing my writing onto the device and cutting the lines very short, putting my earbud in my right ear, and scrolling down, line by line, with my computer voice whispering in my ear like a passionless Cyrano de Bergerac.

Although that had not been my original intention, it proved to be liberating nonetheless. I was, for the first time, able to read my own writing—to perform it, as writers are so often urged to do. I remember perfectly the first time I read a poem of mine aloud onstage. In a basement theater open mic in New York City's East Village, in the spring of 2011, I read a poem I wrote called "A Pain Named Dog," inspired by a line in Nietzsche's *The Gay Science:* "I have given a name to my pain and call it dog."

Fast-forward a few years of performing my writing, and we still find me cutting my lines short and reading in this Cyrano-esque way that works if I really practice hard before a performance. However, it is generally awkward and makes it difficult to pull off a swift or smooth read. Not to mention, it is nowhere near as cool as reading braille.

A while back, I did a reading in Denver, with my electronic (de-brailled) device in my lap, my earbud in my ear, and the middle finger of my right hand scrolling through the spoken text of my story line by line, when I was suddenly distracted by the words of perceptual psychologist Lawrence Rosenblum echoing in my head: "Even blind individuals who have no Braille experience, and have been blind only two years show greater touch skills than the rest of us. In fact, a blind individual's touch sensitivity seems to counteract the natural decline of aging and is typically as great as that of a sighted person 25 years younger."[18]

Why then do so few of us learn braille? If we can develop the somatosensory parts of our brain in compensation for the loss of the visible world, what stops us from doing so? We saw some of the systemic problems above, but for me personally, I think it was simply that I thought I couldn't do it. Some part of me believed that I was too old—even at age eighteen—to learn to read in a new way, and it was only learning about the concept of neuroplasticity, that our brains are constantly capable of blossoming in new areas, that gave me the necessary framework to believe that learning braille is possible. Maybe I will never be as fluent as someone like Caitlin, who learned as a very young child, but putting the work in has made me a braille reader. I'm still pretty slow, but I do ask my baby braille brain (and fingers) to read fairly difficult material. I should probably spend more time reading children's books!

Most of us are so young when we begin to read, and our parents and teachers so forgiving, that the memory of the struggles of progressing from *See Spot Run* to *Great Expectations* hardly makes a lasting impression. We sometimes forget that we must learn to read, just as we must learn to use the technology that many of us now use daily but that once was so foreign to many of us.

Perhaps it is useful to reveal to you how I am writing these words right now. I am typing into a Word document using the touch-type method I taught myself on my mother's manual typewriter. As I write on my slick little Windows laptop I receive audio feedback from my text-to-speech software called JAWS (Job Access With Speech), made by Freedom Scientific. I find that listening to what I write, read aloud by my disinterested computer voice, tells me a lot about how my sentences sound. There is a distancing that happens when you hear your words read without benefit of bias or emotion that can be a very good indicator of the quality of your writing. And I think it's important to mention that I'm pretty quick at finding what I need on the Internet and can blow through pages of information at speeds comparable to my sighted companions because my speech output is set pretty fast—friends have told me it's incomprehensible—and sometimes I'm probably even quicker, since I'm not easily distracted by advertisements for vitamins or pictures of kitty-cats.

Although my braille reading and writing skills have improved tremendously over the past year or so—mostly because I finally got a wireless braille display with a Perkins-style keyboard that I use with my iPhone on a daily basis, I'm still slow. And so, although I love braille and feel that I will incorporate it more and more into my work as a reader and writer, I will likely not move away from text-to-speech technology anytime soon. I believe braille will augment rather than replace my audio methods.

I want to say here that although I do not feel illiterate, I do feel the lack of braille. I always have, and I am working very hard to recover what is missing. I do not know if every blind and visually impaired person needs to be fluent in braille, but I do feel that every blind and visually impaired person should be given the opportunity and encouragement to learn it. After all, we do not universally use the algebra or chemistry we learned in school, but it is assumed that a certain level of understanding in basic subjects will help us make informed decisions about our future endeavors.

I'm guessing that, as an inventor and tinkerer, Louis Braille would have been dazzled by the accessible technology that surrounds us, but I think he also would have been saddened to know how few of us are literate in the first writing system created by a blind person for blind people. Braille, thus far, is the only way a blind (or deafblind) person can read silently or aloud, at one's own pace and with one's own voice. I believe that integrating braille with current technology ought to be standard in educating blind children and adults. Expectations and learning systems need to be in place to demand that kids who can't read standard-size print (as well as those who are [because of progressive eye disease] likely to lose the ability to do so) integrate braille literacy at an early age. I'm guessing the only way this will really take hold is if we truly embrace diversity in all its guises, including literacy. Audio methods may be preferable for some, but that decision ought to arise from choice and opportunity, not be dictated by circumstance. As we've seen, blind education does not exist in a vacuum. It is, and always has been, part of the grand project of enlightenment and modernity, for better and for worse.

10

The Tap-Tapping of Blind Travelers

The image of the blind man (less often woman or child) traveling town streets and country roads with a staff, stick, or cane is as old as blindness itself. Yet until about the mid-twentieth century, when organizations for the blind codified orientation and mobility training (O&M), each blind individual had to figure out how to get around with only a slender bit of wood between them and the ocularcentric world. In the millennia before the standard-issue white cane came into existence, blind people used whatever was to hand. And for nineteenth-century gentlemen, what was to hand was the walking stick. James Holman, a.k.a. the "Blind Traveler," used his walking stick as both tactile and sonic tool, which helped to make him the most traveled individual of his day.

In 1810, as a young English naval officer, Holman was struck blind suddenly while on leave at Bath. He'd gone there to attempt relief from rheumatoid symptoms that he'd contracted during his service in the frigid Atlantic waters of Canada. He had entered the navy with dreams of seeing the world—dreams that would surely be curtailed by blindness? Instead, he fashioned a career as a renowned world traveler and as author of such books as *A Voyage Round the World, Including Travels in Africa, Asia, Australasia, America, etc., etc.* Besides his walking stick, another low-tech tool made this career possible.

Holman did not know braille. As we have seen, Braille's

system took some time to establish itself, and was not introduced into Britain until 1861—almost ten years after Braille's
death in 1852 and a handful of years after Holman's own death
in 1857. But Holman had an excellent middle-class education—
there was some talk in his youth that he would join the clergy, a
respectable occupation for a middle-class son of an apothecary.
Therefore he was literate at the time of his blindness and did not
need to learn to write, but rather needed the means of writing.
Enter the noctograph, which is basically a wooden frame strung
with wires—in effect tactile lined paper that one used with a
dull quill. The innovation really lay in the fact that the dried
printer's ink was on the underside of the paper (carbon paper),
so that as one wrote from left to right, pressing the ink onto the
sheet of paper beneath, the writing would not be smudged by
the hand, as would happen with the standard quill and ink of
the day.

I, like so many others, first learned about the Blind Traveler in a 2007 best-selling biography called *A Sense of the World*.
In it, Jason Roberts explains the limitations of the noctograph,
which left no tactile cues—Holman could use it to write, but he
could not read his own writing: "And, while legible, his script
bore no relation to the swoops and flourishes of his previous fine
hand. The letters were fat and rounded, with small ascenders
and, because of the wires, no true descenders at all—a child's
writing, but exactly straight across the page."[1]

Like Barbier's *écriture nocturne,* the noctograph was invented
as a means of writing military intelligence in the dark, for spying
or for relaying any kind of message that might require lighting
a torch and alerting the enemy to your whereabouts. According
to Roberts, Holman was one of the first to grasp its use for the
blind, and endorsed it in the pages of his books. But it would
never come into wide use, either for the military or for the blind.

Of course Holman could have employed an amanuensis—a secretarial freelancer not uncommonly employed by the sighted and blind alike, which he did when he returned home to compile and sort his notes and memories into books. Generally, however, a full-time secretary would have impinged on his self-reliance as well as his pocketbook, and it was useful for Holman to be able to take down notes whenever and wherever he liked.

In the opening lines of *A Voyage Round the World,* Holman explains the origins of his wanderlust: "The passion for travelling is, I believe, instinctive in some natures. For my own part, I have been conscious from my earliest youth of the existence of this desire to explore distant regions, to trace the varieties exhibited by mankind under the different influences of different climates, customs, and laws, and to investigate with unwearied solicitude the moral and physical distinctions that separate and diversify the various nations of the earth."[2]

Besides being his childhood dream, travel offered Holman compensation for his loss of sight: "I am bound to believe that this direction of my faculties and energies has been ordained by a wise and benevolent Providence, as a source of consolation under an affliction which closes upon me all the delights and charms of the visible world." Rather than highlighting what he could not see, travel provided stimulation and distraction: "The constant occupation of the mind, and the continual excitement of mental and bodily action, contribute to diminish, if not to overcome, the sense of deprivation which must otherwise have pressed upon me," he explains. Travel kept Holman from feeling sorry for himself, while it supplied him "with inexhaustible means of enjoyment."[3]

Although many praised Holman's lively descriptions, he was not without detractors: those who out of jealousy, skepticism, or malice, denigrated his "observations" as secondhand, and discounted what a blind man could tell of the world—just as they would doubt the veracity and authenticity of Helen Keller's words in the following century. And so Holman attempts to mitigate skepticism by explaining not only what he gets out of travel but what he can offer the presumably sighted armchair traveler: "I am constantly asked, and I may as well answer the question here once for all, what is the use of travelling to one who cannot see? I answer, Does every traveller see all that he describes?—and is not every traveller obliged to depend upon others for a great proportion of the information he collects?"[4]

In other words, without the investigating, the curiosity, the interest and study of another culture, another land, the traveler must be satisfied with eye candy. How many of us look down upon those tourists who rush from one "must-see" attraction to another with nothing but unspectacular photos to show for it? The superficial sighted traveler can neither describe nor know everything about the things he sees.

Holman addresses this superficiality. "The picturesque in nature, it is true, is shut out from me," he admits, "and works of art are to me mere outlines of beauty, accessible only to one sense; but perhaps this very circumstance affords a stronger zest to curiosity, which is thus impelled to a more close and searching examination of details than would be considered necessary to a traveller who might satisfy himself by the superficial view, and rest content with the first impressions conveyed through the eye."[5]

In order to understand anything as a traveler to unknown lands, one must have curiosity on the one hand, and a willingness to be surprised and astounded and even made a little foolish on the other. I mention this because as we continue to examine how blind travelers get about generally, and how Holman in particular traveled the world using his other four senses, there must be in the mind of the sighted reader a similar curiosity and openness to accepting a completely new paradigm for navigating and observing the world.

———

Although today it is difficult, perhaps, to envision the blind person's cane in a color other than white, it was only a hundred years ago that the age-old staff, stick, or cane received its modern face-lift. As the story goes, in 1921 James Biggs, a blinded photographer, hit upon the idea of painting his cane white in order to be better seen in his Bristol streets. It makes sense to me that the mental eye of the former visual artist would recognize the importance of contrast. From England the idea spread to the Continent and then to America, where the Lions Clubs began giving white canes to blind people throughout the 1930s.

Even so, the practice of sweeping the long cane from side to side did not become the norm until blinded vets began returning from World War II. According to the Perkins School for the Blind, a veteran rehabilitation specialist named Richard Hoover pioneered the standard technique for using a white cane. The method he taught was to hold the long cane in front of the body and sweep it back and forth with each step in order to detect objects and level changes. It's still what mobility instructors teach today, and is known as the "Hoover Method."[6]

When you are fitted out for a cane, ordinarily you will get one that, when stood upright, is about sternum height or taller. When you are walking, the cane's top end is held in your dominant hand at about the level of your solar plexus and the cane is swept to the right or left in opposition to your step. The motion is meant to tell you what's happening at a distance of about two paces. When you sweep left, your right foot steps out, when you sweep right, your left foot steps out. Some mobility instructors teach you to use a very low arc with a light tap at each end, and I have found this technique helpful when dealing with broken sidewalk or cobblestones, but mostly the cane should be in contact with the ground so that it can tell you when things like steps or curbs are coming, though there is a lot that must be done with your hearing as well. In the long years of my visual impairment—when I could still see sidewalks and buildings and cars and people perfectly well during the day, less so at night—I liked to walk and think. So it is not natural for me—now that I have virtually no sight left—to think so hard about walking. I can keep up my vigilance for about twenty minutes and then I start walking into traffic. But I've known many blind people who rock the white cane.[7]

Similar to the long white cane, Holman's walking stick was useful for giving warning by touch about objects and level changes in the micro environment—the environment reachable by the extended arm, so to speak. However, because the typical walking stick is quite short, heavy, and stiff, it is not great for sweeping from side to side in the style of the Hoover Method. As Roberts notes, "Hitting an object didn't send a gentle pressure to the user, but a solid jolt." Furthermore, its shortness made the field of warning quite small, and Holman apparently did not hold it out in front of him, but rather held it "balanced like a paintbrush in the crook of his thumb and forefinger," making it good only for "limited sweeping purposes."[8]

I should say that sometimes limited sweeping is exactly what's needed. My dad passed away in 2018, but in the decades before his final years of disability (due to a progressive neuropathy that crept from the bottoms of his feet to his knees and from the palms of his hands to his elbows, leaving his feet like blocks, his hands like mittens) and near-complete house-boundedness, he had been an avid traveler, visiting more than a hundred countries and all seven continents. In his travels he collected many beautiful knickknacks that neatly cluttered his North Beach apartment from floor to ceiling. This was not a place for swinging a cane. Of course I did not use my cane once I established myself in the house, but when I walked in with my suitcase trailing behind me for a visit, the delicate paintbrush grip on my cane, dabbing at the space in front of me as if poking daisies with my parasol, was precisely what was called for, even if my dad did make fun of me for looking like I was tiptoeing through the tulips, Charlie Chaplin style.

Although Holman probably did use his walking stick to detect obstacles directly in front of him, Roberts explains how the sturdy construction of this "standard strolling equipment for gentlemen of the day" also helped him to glean information about the macro environment. Specifically, it was the metal tip, called a ferrule, that made it so useful, producing as it did a series of sharp taps as Holman walked.[9] He learned to use those taps to tell him a great deal about the depth and dimension of his surroundings, not unlike the way a bat uses its clicks (and their reflecting echoes) to detect obstacles and prey. In other words, Holman used the taps of his walking stick to echolocate.

I'm no James Holman, but I have found that when I do venture out on my own, one of the most satisfying things to do is trail a wall by whacking my cane against it, producing wonderful echoes that bounce back at me, describing the space of a quiet street or cavernous university hallway. Holman figured out the usefulness of echolocation as many blind children do— often by emitting clicks with their mouths as soon as they begin walking in order to avoid walls. This active kind of echolocation has historically been downplayed by many blind organizations. In my many adventures with mobility instructors over the years, echolocation was never mentioned, and I've heard from friends who were born blind that they were dissuaded from using their own voices to echolocate. Similar to arguments against braille, the fear with regard to echolocation seems to be that the use of clicks or other sounds to help determine space is too different and potentially alienating, likely to erect barriers between the sighted and the blind. At least that has by and large been the prevailing ideology until very recently.

It's likely that I first learned about Daniel Kish—the real-life Batman, as he's been dubbed by the media—from Roberts, who calls him "a spiritual successor to James Holman."[10] Kish lost first his right and then his left eye to retinal cancer by the time he was thirteen months old. Thanks mostly to his parents, who allowed him freedom and encouraged his independence (unlike many parents of blind children), he was able to learn about the world in his own way, and in doing so, he discovered how emitting sound could help him get around. Since the 1990s Kish has established himself as the authority in echolocation as a mobility tool for blind people, and has garnered more than a little media attention in recent years.

In his very popular 2015 TED Talk called "How I Use Flash Sonar to Navigate the World," he delights his audience with his clicking, which he describes as "flashes of sound that go out and reflect from surfaces all around me, just like a bat's sonar, and return to me with patterns, with pieces of information, much as light does for you."[11]

This is not a mere analogy, as Kish explains: "My brain . . . has been activated to form images in my visual cortex, which we now call the imaging system, from those patterns of information, much as your brain does. I call this process flash sonar. It is how I have learned to see through my blindness, to navigate my journey through the dark unknowns of my own challenges."[12]

He assures his audience that although he will accept the

Batman moniker, he has never thought of himself as remarkable. "I have always regarded myself much like anyone else who navigates the dark unknowns of their own challenges. Is that so remarkable? I do not use my eyes, I use my brain."[13]

Importantly, Kish not only discusses his "flash sonar" in his TED Talk, but he also mentions his cane, something that is often downplayed in media attention—perhaps because it does not seem the accoutrement of a proper Batman. Nonetheless, his cane is onstage with him and acknowledged as an important tool: "Fortunately, I have my trusty long cane, longer than the canes used by most blind people. I call it my freedom staff. It will keep me, for example, from making an undignified departure from the stage."[14]

The audience obligingly laughs.

Kish founded World Access for the Blind, which teaches individuals and groups how to use "flash sonar" as well as doing a lot of outreach to reframe blindness as containing the possibility of freedom, self-efficacy, and empowerment. Kish and his colleagues are so good at using and teaching flash sonar that they even organize mountain-biking expeditions!

In fact, just such an impossible-sounding adventure as this opens *See What I'm Saying,* a 2010 popular science book about the wonders of cross-modal plasticity, by perceptual psychologist Lawrence Rosenblum. In the astounding chapter on echolocation, Rosenblum describes Kish and his fellow instructor, Brian Bushway (who is also blind), riding with their student through the streets to a trailhead: "As the three of them climb the hill and get closer to me, I start to hear sharp intermittent clicks—different from those of the bike wheels. These sharp clicks are emanating from the mouths of Kish and Bushway, who are using them to hear what I can see. They click with their tongues, about once every two seconds, so that they can hear the sounds reflect back from nearby curbs, shrubs, parked cars, and other obstacles. . . . They both click using the side of their tongues, as if coaxing a horse to gallop. And they often change the loudness of these clicks depending on their surroundings."[5]

As they move onto the trail, Rosenblum observes, "Here comes the hard part!" But Bushway feels the opposite: "I prefer riding around rocks, trees, and shrubs rather than the cars, running dogs, and kids in the streets. Mountain biking is more relaxing for me."[16]

It was not until the mid-twentieth century that scientists began to understand that bats used sound for navigating, but even then some scientists balked at this discovery. As Richard Dawkins relates in his 1986 book about evolution, *The Blind Watchmaker,* the zoologists (Donald Griffin and Robert Galambos) who discovered bat echolocation and presented it to their colleagues in 1940 met with something more than skepticism: "One distinguished scientist was so indignantly incredulous that he seized Galambos by the shoulders and shook him while complaining that we could not possibly mean such an outrageous suggestion. Radar and sonar were still highly classified developments in military technology, and the notion that bats might do anything even remotely analogous to the latest triumphs of electronic engineering struck most people as not only implausible but emotionally repugnant."[17]

"It is easy to sympathize with the distinguished sceptic," says Dawkins. "There is something very human in his reluctance to believe. And that, really, says it: human is precisely what it is. It is precisely because our own human senses are not capable of doing what bats do that we find it hard to believe."[18]

This skepticism seems to echo the crux of the disbelief that so many sighted people hurl at those who are blind: "I can't cross a street with my eyes closed," they say to themselves and conclude therefore that blind people must not be able to cross streets.

As Dawkins says, however, our lack of understanding about echolocation should not trouble us any more than our lack of understanding about vision does; we do not need to understand the mechanics or mathematics of a sense in order to use it: "The mathematical calculations that would be necessary to explain the principles of vision are just as complex and difficult, and nobody has ever had any difficulty in believing that little animals can see. The reason for this double standard in our scepticism is, quite simply, that we can see and we can't echolocate."[19]

Of course, our blind travelers and mountain bikers testify to the fact that humans *can* echolocate, which Dawkins acknowledges, albeit with a dismissive air: "Well, blind humans sometimes seem to have an uncanny sense of obstacles in their path. It has been given the name 'facial vision,' because blind people have reported that it feels a bit like the sense of touch, on the face. One report tells of a totally blind boy who could ride his tricycle at a good speed round the block near his home, using 'facial vision.' Experiments showed that, in fact, 'facial vision' is nothing to do with touch or the front of the face, . . . The sensation of 'facial vision,' it turns out, really goes in through the ears. The blind people, without even being aware of the fact, are actually using echoes, of their own footsteps and other sounds, to sense the presence of obstacles."[20]

Even if blind people possess extraordinary echolocation skills, Dawkins suggests, they are unconscious of it. Yet there were those who did realize the truth of "facial vision" within a decade or so of the discovery of animal echolocation. In his 1959 memoir, *The Sound of the Walls,* Jacob Twersky describes how he had developed "the obstacle sense of the blind," in the years after losing his sight to scarlet fever as a child:

> Near a large object I could sense its presence and steer out of the way of it. This obstacle sense depends on noticing subtle changes in air currents and temperature, but chiefly on hearing and interpreting tiny echoes as they rebound from obstructions. It is something like the bat's method for detecting obstacles, or like radar. The sound of a footstep, in fact the slightest sound, releases the echoes, yet it does not require acute hearing, but concentrated and trained hearing. Nor does it give any sort of auditory impression—the impression is of vague sight or of slight pressure on the face. It is often called facial vision. I certainly did not suspect that it had anything to do with my ears, though I usually did not bump into things except when confused by too much noise.[21]

What Twersky is referring to is a kind of passive or even unconscious echolocation. One does not have to click or tap in order to benefit from reflected sound. Unlike the deliberate use of flash sonar, one's footsteps or even sound reflected from else-where—a fan or car engine, for example—can tell the listener something about her surroundings whether or not she is fully conscious of it. In this way, as Rosenblum argues in his book, all hearing humans echolocate, even if they are often largely unconscious of it. However, when blind people are made aware of echolocation and trained to use it, they can make much of the faculty. Blind humans, like all humans, are the products of culture as well as genetics. Because of this, it is very helpful to have the concept of human echolocation in place in order to make the most of it.

As demonstrated by Holman and Kish and others—even me in my fledgling way—humans can and do echolocate. Maybe we are not quite so proficient as bats, but as we develop techniques, we will improve. And if we pay attention, we will hear the musicality in the acoustics of travel by echo.

———

It is James Joyce who, perhaps for the first time in literature, draws attention to the musicality of the blind cane with the "Tap. Tap. Tap. Tap" of the blind stripling in his 1922 modernist novel, *Ulysses.* The blind stripling is one of hundreds of minor characters who parade through the *Odyssey*-inspired book, crisscrossing the day's actions of the two protagonists, Leopold Bloom and Stephen Dedalus. His taps weave through the narrative like tiny veins of gold running through a vast and craggy cave. As so often happens with blind characters, the blind stripling is peripheral, but memorable. "Tap blind walked tapping by the tap the curbstone tapping, tap by tap," goes the blind stripling's cane as he moves through the Dublin streets.[22]

Despite all the tapping, sighted people, in the novel as in real life, often remain stubbornly or egotistically blind and deaf to the blind man walking: "God's curse on you," says the blind stripling sourly to the oblivious passerby who knocks his cane, "whoever you are! You're blinder nor I am, you bitch's bastard!"[23]

I'm pretty sure every blind person using a cane can relate to the blind stripling's sourness, as we often contend with sighted strangers who will kick aside a cane without a backward glance. I recall a horror story from a New York City friend who, while going down subway stairs, was cut off by some asshole whose rush to get to his destination was more important than everyone

else's, and crushed her cane, leaving my blind friend with a useless broken thing. He did not even stop to acknowledge, let alone
apologize. Luckily, there were others more kind who helped my
friend to get somewhere safe.

It seems that Joyce, who suffered from eye troubles all of his
adult life, may also have felt some kinship with the blind stripling and his frustrations. In *The Most Dangerous Book* (2014),
Kevin Birmingham tells us, "By the time he reached his late
forties, Joyce was already an old man. The ashplant cane that he
had used for swagger as a young bachelor in Dublin became a
blind man's cane in Paris. Strangers helped him cross the street,
and he bumped into furniture as he navigated through his own
apartment."[24]

It seems, then, that James Holman was not the only one
to repurpose the walking stick as a blind-person cane. The
ashplant, which is generally carved from a sapling, makes its
ambiguous appearance in *Ulysses,* as we'll soon see. Although
the above quote refers to a time after he had finished *Ulysses,*
Joyce began having eye trouble long before. Bouts of iritis (a
swelling of his iris, likely resulting from syphilis) began in 1907,
and through the years, despite and sometimes because of the
many harrowing surgeries to treat it, Joyce experienced periods
of partial or full blindness. In my very early years of graduate
school at NYU, I once visited the Irish House (one of the quaint
international buildings that line an old West Village lane called
the Muse) to get some piece of paper signed, I suppose for a Joyce
class I was taking, and met a Joyce scholar, who, when I told him
I was visually impaired, told me how Joyce spent much of his life
nearly blind. "He had to put his face right up to the paper to see
what he was writing."

Samuel Beckett famously took dictation from Joyce when
he was completely blinded after one of the iritis operations dur-

ing the long writing of *Finnegans Wake:* "And during the dictation, someone knocked at the door and I said something. I had to interrupt the dictation. But it had nothing to do with the text. And when I read it back with the phrase like 'Come in' in it, he said 'Let it stand.'"[25]

It is no surprise, then, that both of Joyce's main characters consider life without sight.

When we first meet Joyce's blind stripling, it is through the eyes of the older of the two protagonists of *Ulysses,* Leopold Bloom (the character loosely analogous to Odysseus in Joyce's reimagining of the Homeric epic). In the "Lestrygonians" episode, Bloom sees the blind stripling "tapping the curbstone with his slender cane" and offers to help him cross the street, giving Bloom the opportunity to observe his companion while they cross the busy intersection: "Stains on his coat. Slobbers his food, I suppose. Tastes all different for him. Have to be spoonfed first. Like a child's hand, his hand. . . . Wonder if he has a name. Van. Keep his cane clear of the horse's legs: tired drudge get his doze. That's right. Clear. Behind a bull: in front of a horse."[26]

There's so much to say about this passage that I'm not sure where to begin, but I suppose what I find most striking is how the goodness of Bloom's help is so intermingled with absurdities and genuine curiosity with insults. I feel it gives me insight into the mind of the sighted, particularly those, like Bloom, who are just trying in their bumbling way to be kind. I also feel that the blind stripling keeps the human connection at bay by remaining virtually silent. I've noticed that a lot of blind people develop good communication skills, which seems to me to be part of our survival toolkit: if we can make a verbal connection it can, to some extent, mitigate the lack of eye contact and such. But this blind stripling (who is a piano tuner) has other (musical) means of communicating.

After the crossing, the blind stripling "tapped the curbstone and went on his way, drawing his cane back, feeling again," and Bloom intuits the importance of that cane, as well as the use of facial vision (which we now know is actually echolocation): "Mr. Bloom walked behind the eyeless feet, a flatcut suit of herringbone tweed. Poor young fellow! How on earth did he know that van was there? Must have felt it. See things in their forehead perhaps: kind of sense of volume. Weight or size of it, something blacker than the dark. Wonder would he feel it if something was removed. Feel a gap. Queer idea of Dublin he must have, tapping his way round by the stones. Could he walk in a beeline if he hadn't that cane?"[27]

To his final question, I think the answer is obvious: no. The blind stripling needs that cane to tap through the bustling Dublin streets. Bloom's pity is strong, but his curiosity is perhaps even stronger. And it is this curiosity, this desire to explore the darkness for himself, that allows him to move beyond pity, at least a little bit. Bloom "slid his hand between his waistcoat and trousers and, pulling aside his shirt gently, felt a slack fold of his belly. But I know it's whitey yellow. Want to try in the dark to see."[28]

This yearning to see in the dark echoes the meandering thoughts of the younger of the two protagonists in an early scene in *Ulysses,* when Stephen Dedalus (analogous to Odysseus's son Telemachus as well as to Joyce himself) experiments with blindness while walking on the beach. In an attempt to circumnavigate the "ineluctable modality of the visible," he closes his eyes and uses his ashplant walking stick as a blind man's cane. "I am getting on nicely in the dark. My ash sword hangs at my side. Tap with it: they do."[29]

Even if Joyce felt some kinship with the blind stripling, he was still a sight-oriented person who might think, as Stephen does, of the blind as "they," as the other. Even so, Stephen notices that the moment he closes his eyes he hears things he'd not noticed before, namely the crunching of rocks under his feet: "Crush, crack, crick, crick." And then he finds himself contemplating "the ineluctable modality of the audible,"[30] reminding us that our perceptions are to some degree a matter of attention, and that the attention itself is gripping. That said, Stephen Dedalus (like so many scholars before him) puts on blindness in order to circumnavigate theoretical objects, not physical ones.

Sighted people tend to celebrate the quotidian skills in the blind people they encounter and, at the same time, discount the information a blind person might obtain by means incomprehensible to them as sighted people. This brings us to another of those strict dichotomies that epitomize considerations of blindness versus sight. Because blind people are understood to be so different from the sighted, their achievements are generally understood only as anomalies in an otherwise lamentable situation. That is, blind people are celebrated for what they accomplish despite their blindness, which tends to make their celebrity short-lived and sensational. They are often presented as novelty acts rather than purveyors of real and useful information. This is precisely what happened to James Holman.

By the time Holman died, his books were no longer being read. His last manuscript, a memoir, was lost, heralding the obscurity into which he fell until Jason Roberts resurrected him in his biography, *A Sense of the World*.

"I didn't set out to write this book," explains Roberts. "I set out to read it. After my first, brief encounter with James Holman . . . I sought out the 'H' shelves in the biography aisle of my local library. Two weeks later I was sitting in a research carrel in the University of California's Bancroft Library, shaking my head in sad amazement. Not only had such a book never been written, the paltry nature of Holman studies seemed to imply that it never could be written. . . . The last scholarly inquiries, as far as I could tell, had ended in frustration around 1890."[31]

Although Charles Darwin cites Holman as an authority in *The Voyage of the Beagle,* although Sir Richard Francis Burton (who spent years following in Holman's footsteps) pays tribute to him as "the Blind Traveler" in his commentary to the *Arabian Nights,* and although when at home in London, he was friendly with some of the great minds of the age—was, in fact, a member of the Royal Society, where so much new science was produced and disseminated—Holman was, in the minds of most, a novelty act. His blindness made him a curiosity rather than a man. His travels, notwithstanding his attention to detail, were largely discounted as secondhand. Roberts summarizes public scorn thus: "His sightlessness made genuine insight impossible. He might have been in Zanzibar, but how could the Blind Traveler claim to know Zanzibar?"[32]

This echoes the skepticism that is leveled at the blind time and time again: what can you know if you can't see? Nothing. It's a cultural bias that has been perhaps more detrimental to the self-esteem, and therefore the self-efficacy, of blind people than any other. As our sonar expert, Daniel Kish, puts it, "It's impressions about blindness that are far more threatening to blind people than the blindness itself." In his TED Talk, Kish asks his presumably sighted audience to take a moment and consider their impressions of blindness. "Think about your reactions when I first came onto the stage, or the prospect of your own blindness, or a loved one going blind," he urges. "The terror is incomprehensible to most of us, because blindness is thought to epitomize ignorance and unawareness, hapless exposure to the ravages of the dark unknown." As I've tried to do so many times in these pages, Kish makes the connection between the metaphors of blindness and the prevailing attitudes of so many sighted people. "How poetic," he concludes, and receives an uncertain laugh for his gentle barb, suggesting that the sighted audience, no matter how sympathetic, is entrenched in the ideology that insists that darkness can result only in stumbling helplessness, even when a real-life Batman reveals this to be untrue.[33]

11

Helen Keller in Vaudeville
and in Love

At some point during graduate school, I realized that academia was not for me. Despite my waffling, I managed to win a dissertation grant and found myself with too much time on my hands (because I didn't have to teach that year). So I started running around the East Village and the Lower East Side (with my guide dog), performing at open mics. Not long after I began moonlighting as a performance artist—dabbling in everything from storytelling and stand-up to the accordion and loop pedal—I stumbled upon a book called *The Radical Lives of Helen Keller,* which impelled me to make one of my rare forays outside the seventeenth and eighteenth centuries (my grad school and dissertation focus). This was around 2006, when obtaining ebooks was not yet so easy a thing (Kindle came into existence the following year), and so I was forced to scan the Helen Keller book page by page into OCR/text-to-speech software called Kurzweil.[1]

I stopped short when I got to this dismissive yet completely astounding statement concerning Keller and her teacher, Anne Sullivan: "Grasping for [financial] solutions, the two performed on the vaudeville circuit from 1920, when Keller was forty years old, until 1924. . . . This was not what Keller had anticipated for herself as she had basked in the glow of a Radcliffe degree."[2]

It was fascinating to find the almost palpable disdain in a book that itself sought to chip away at Keller's saintly blind edifice by revealing just how radical a thinker she really was. She was outspoken in the woman's suffrage movement, fought for workers' rights, was a card-carrying socialist, and was one of the founding members of the NAACP. Although *The Radical Lives of Helen Keller* paints a more nuanced and interesting portrait than any I'd read before, it seemed to want to distance Keller's vaudeville stint from her leftist politics—something Keller herself most certainly did not do. For Helen Keller, the vaudeville stages—where such stars as Charlie Chaplin and Buster Keaton got their start—allowed her the freedom to spout her socialist and civil-rights-oriented politics, particularly during the question-and-answer period, which was a standard component of lecture(ish) performances. Keller and Sullivan had prepared for that segment of the performance by drawing up a long list of possible questions and designing answers that ranged from serious to schtick. Here are some examples taken from Dorothy Herrmann's biography, *Helen Keller: A Life:*

Q: What do you think of capitalism?

A: I think it has outlived its usefulness.

Q: What do you think of Harvard College's discrimination against the Jews?

A: I think when any institution of learning applies any test other than scholarship, it has ceased to be a public service institution. Harvard, in discriminating against the Jew and the Negro on grounds other than intellectual qualifications, has proved unworthy of its traditions and covered itself with shame.

Q: Do you think women should hold office?

A: Yes, if they can get enough of their fellow citizens to vote for them.

Q: What is Miss Keller's age?

A: There is no age on the vaudeville stage.

Q: What is your conception of light?
A: It is like thought in the mind, a bright, amazing thing.[3]

The questions go on and on. Many have to do with the age-old relationship between blindness and prophecy, asking Keller to tell fortunes or give tips about the stock market.

It was not a stretch for me to imagine myself in Keller's place (as it was not a stretch to imagine myself in the place of the performers at the Café of the Blind that had so disturbed Valentin Haüy). However, many of Helen Keller's friends were very much alarmed by her vaudeville stint: "It had always been said that we went into public life only to attract attention," she writes in *Midstream* (her memoir about her middle years), "and I had letters from friends in Europe remonstrating with me about 'the deplorable theatrical exhibition' into which I had allowed myself to be dragged." She assures her readers that she went into vaudeville of her own free will and for very practical reasons—namely, financial ones that extended beyond herself to include her teacher: "The funds my friends had provided for my support would cease with my death, and if I died before my teacher, she would be left almost destitute. The income I had I could live on, but I could not save anything."[4]

Accusations of exploitation seem to me fraught with assumptions about what a blind person is supposed to do and be—assumptions that insist blind people be poets and prophets, saints or beggars, not lowbrow entertainers. Cries of exploitation also assume that the person being exploited is somehow incapable of making his or her own correct decisions. Keller was an accomplished, intelligent, full-grown woman of forty by the time she hit vaudeville, and she felt the pressure of making a living for herself as an adult whose childhood fame was finally beginning to wane.

———

Keller was born in 1880 in Tuscumbia, Alabama, the daughter of a Southern belle and a Confederate captain and plantation owner. The buildings and grounds where Keller was born and spent her first years running around playing with the dogs and servants are now a historic attraction called Ivy Green, named for the main house, which is covered (you guessed it) in ivy. At the age of nineteen months, she became gravely ill—some say it was scarlet fever, others that it was meningitis. In any case, the fever raged and then subsided, causing her family to rejoice, only to discover soon after that Helen Keller was left completely deaf and blind.

As I mentioned, it was in reading Charles Dickens's account of Laura Bridgman that Keller's mother first discovered the possibility of an education for her blind and deaf daughter, and this eventually led the Kellers to learn about and petition the Perkins School in Boston for help. The Perkins School agreed, and, in 1887, they sent a young woman to Alabama to teach Helen Keller. The young woman was Anne Sullivan, an orphan of Irish immigrants who herself was quite blind as a child but who had recovered much of her sight thanks to several success-ful operations, although her eyes would always be weak. Anne Sullivan became world famous as "Teacher," the woman who single-handedly brought Helen Keller into the world of the human by giving her language. Sullivan would continue to be Keller's companion, guide, and interpreter for decades until her health began to fail. Sullivan helped Keller attend and gradu-ate (summa cum laude) from Radcliffe College, and toured with her on first the lecture circuit and then the vaudeville circuits.

After the immense success of Keller's first autobiography, *The Story of My Life,* published in 1903, when she was barely into

ople clamored to get a look at her. For several
rld War I, Keller and Sullivan worked the lecture circuit, often called Chautauquas, named for Chautauqua
Lake in upstate New York where the educational assemblies
began.

Supposedly an edifying kind of performance that brought
important writers and thinkers to rural America, the lecture
circuit seems to have been grueling, with more than a dash of
Old West looseness about it. "In the nature of things a lecture
tour exposes one to many unpleasant experiences," explains
Keller. "Our lecture contract required that we collect the money
before we went on the platform, but that was seldom possible
and we disliked to imply distrust by demanding payment. In
Seattle we gave two lectures to appreciative Audiences, one in
the afternoon and the other in the evening. The local manager
told us he would not be able to pay us our share, which was a
thousand dollars, until after the evening performance. He did
not appear in the theatre after the evening lecture, and we had
no way of getting our money from him." Keller and Sullivan
experienced this kind of swindling many times in towns from
Dunkirk, New York, to Santa Rosa, California. Once when they
did demand payment before hitting the platform, "the audience
grew indignant," and the newspapers came out with a "great
headline" the following day: "Helen Keller refused to speak
unless she held the money in her hand."[5]

When such exploitation occurred, it was at the hands of the
supposedly genteel lecture circuit organizers, not those of vaudeville, even though vaudeville had a lowbrow reputation with its
variety shows that brought lecturers together with jugglers, singers, animal acts, and comedians. "Vaudeville offered us better
pay than either literary work or lecturing," Keller explains. The
vaudeville theaters, she writes: "protected us against the friendly

invasion of the crowds who used to swarm around to shake
hands with us at the lectures." Additionally, vaudeville allowed
performers to stay in one place for a week at a time and required
only two twenty-minute sets a day, whereas on the lecture circuit they were expected to travel constantly and often had to go
directly to the podium from the train, without any time to rest
or prepare.[6]

The instant I learned that Keller performed in vaudeville,
I knew I had to do something with it artistically. So, not long
after I finally finished my dissertation, I decided to use it as the
basis of "a one-woman, two-voice, three-act" play that centered
on Keller's time performing in vaudeville, which I called "The
Star of Happiness." I prefaced the play with comments about her
early life and education and bookended that material with my
own attempts to grapple with performance as a blind woman.
There were beautiful projections—many images of Keller that
my friend David Lowe (an artist and photo archivist at the New
York Public Library) put together. Projections also provided my
stage set—a virtual jewel-box salon complete with French windows and a piano (all based on Herrmann's description). There
were plenty of funny moments, and I packed in quite a bit of
historical information, but there was poignancy too, and some
audience members told me they cried. All in all, it was a strange,
beautiful little show that I worked very hard on with the help of
some dedicated friends. I marvel now at my bravery. I suppose
"The Star of Happiness" was a melding of all that had come
before: historical research collided with comedy, loop pedals
with Helen Keller's autobiographical writings.

The title of my play came from the title of Keller's vaudeville theme song, "The Star of Happiness," which was supposedly written by the same man who wrote "Yes! We Have No

Bananas." My friend David found the sheet music to it, and my friend Christina recorded it for me. The song is a bit schmaltzy, with lyrics that begin "Wonderful star of light / Out from the darkness of night."

According to Herrmann's biography of Keller, after her theme song played, Keller would deliver an opening speech, interpreted by Anne Sullivan, that included her oft-quoted line "Alone we can do so little. Together we can do so much."

I confess I felt compelled to add a bit of comedy when performing her speech myself, since it drips with sentimentality—a sentimentality that feels a little too saccharine and in line with how many people view Helen Keller from the many children's books that prime kids for the adult versions of inspiration porn. But Keller was a dynamic woman who did more than utter rousing statements about working together to overcome obstacles.

"I found the world of vaudeville much more amusing than the world I had always lived in, and I liked it," writes Keller. "I liked to feel the warm tide of human life pulsing round and round me." She describes how she was "often admitted to the dressing rooms of the other actors," and says that "many of them let me feel their costumes and even went through their acts for me."[7]

I love imagining Keller putting her hands on the bodies and faces of the other performers. It reminds me of how welcoming the Art Stars of the Lower East Side were when I first started frequenting the open mics with my guide dog. These were called open mics, but "open stages" would probably be the better term, taking place in black box theaters several nights a week. They were open to all kinds of performance—with and without mic—from comedy to dance, performance art to political rants, instrumental music of all kinds to monologues in the nude. I've since seen how rare is the stage that brings together so many kinds of performers, and realized how precious the experience was for someone who'd thought she could never be an artist.

There is something inclusive about performers—who often see themselves as outsiders and fellow freaks, rather than as able-bodied superiors. When so many come together to enact their dreams in the most sublime and ridiculous ways, there is little room for discrimination.

Keller became friendly enough with her fellow performers to see beyond the glamour to the sadness: "The thought often occurred to me that the parts the actors played was [*sic*] their real life, and all the rest was make-believe. I still think so, and hope it is true, for the sake of many to whom fate is unkind in the real world." Though she ends this part of her autobiography admitting that she can "conceive that in time the spectacle might have grown stale," she assures her readers, "I shall always be glad I went into vaudeville, not only for the excitement of it, but also for the opportunities it gave me to study life."[8]

I created one of my "Star of Happiness" monologues from this passage, but I'm afraid I never did Keller's words justice. I had not been the best actress I knew, merely the cheapest—or at least that's what I jokingly tell people. In fact, I was in a way picking up the thread of a dream that had been thwarted long ago. When I was a kid, I took a number of acting classes and had a little repertoire of monologues. I was maybe ten years old when I tried to pull off the opening pages of Poe's "The Tell-Tale Heart." My acting teacher attempted to dissuade me from a role that was so far from who I was. She was perhaps concerned with type, but I was excited about the darker emotions, about adult things. I also had a Dorothy Parker monologue that I thought was very witty—such a brave little drama nerd!—which I performed at summer camp, and people clapped politely.

The last monologue I performed as a kid was in high school. I plucked a speech from Chaim Potok's *The Promise,* one of the last novels I read with my eyes. It was a struggle by then. I needed strong light, I read very slowly, and could do so only for short periods. It was about a kid who was having a psychological meltdown. "You were scary," a friend told me.

So in some ways, it's no surprise that as I wound up my grad school days twenty years later, I decided to return to the stage. After decades of vision loss, it seemed high time to perform my disability, to give blindness a sexy-black-box treatment. As it turned out, I enjoyed creating "The Star of Happiness" more than performing it. Although its two short runs in NYC's East Village went well, I could not imagine performing the same play over and over again, or traveling from city to city on the theater fest circuit.

Yet, performance still pulls at me. I think it is an important vehicle for disability activism to create and enact roles that are of our own making. Furthermore, performance has always been a part of educating the public about the blind. And as we'll continue to witness, performance promotes education just as education promotes performance. In retrospect, some aspects of performance may appear silly and frivolous, others serious and sober, but I will continue to argue that the line of exploitation can never be easily or clearly determined.

However, if the performances are to be educational and authentic, the writers and actors must be blind. It does the world of inclusion and diversity no good to have sighted writers and sighted actors creating blind people in the theater and film, as has been almost exclusively the case historically and up until today. Consider how often able-bodied actors win the highest acting awards for their portrayals of disabled people. Take, for example, Jamie Foxx's portrayal of Ray Charles in the 2004 biopic *Ray*. He won every major best-acting award there is. That trend is just beginning to change, but it is taking a heroic effort on the part of disabled activists in the film and television industry—from casting directors to the actors themselves—to insist that we begin representing ourselves. A few decades ago, it was no big thing for the Russian American Yul Brynner to put on yellowface and play the King of Siam on Broadway and in Hollywood. I hope that the movement that made it important to see Asians playing Asians and other minorities playing themselves will take root with regard to representations of blindness and other disabilities.

Indeed, Hollywood is undergoing a period of transition regarding hiring actors with disabilities to represent themselves. In 2014 I was hired to play a blind woman in a national television commercial, and am proud to be part of a movement that believes that authentic representation is important. But this is all so new that the talent pool for blind actors is small. I get called for auditions because I am one of the few blind actors around, though I am hardly an actor. I gave up acting in high school and did not pick it up again until after grad school because I did not know how I would audition for parts if I could not read a script. And I was right to be concerned.

Marilee Talkington is one of the very few visually impaired people with an MFA in acting. In a *Forbes* piece she describes the unapologetic discrimination she experienced in her acting program from the start. She asked one professor to provide accessible materials for her, and was not only denied but unenrolled without her permission. "I can't teach you," the professor told her.[9]

Like me, Talkington has cone-rod dystrophy, which I'm guessing means that when she was pursuing her MFA, she did not "look" blind, although she needed materials in large print.

The resistance she experienced is almost unfathomable. "I had to fight to take my classes," she says, and things did not get a whole lot better after she graduated. When she requested large print at her first big audition, the director told her: "If you can't read the script, you don't belong on stage."[10]

After two decades of fighting for more blind actors and consulting to make blind characters more authentic, Talkington landed a role on *See*—an Apple+ TV show about a world in which, due to some mysterious disease, just about everyone is blind, and this circumstance seems to have caused civilization to crumble. Despite the show's premise, which I personally find a bit annoying—I mean, blind people are way more integrated with technology than a lot of sighted people are—Talkington is rightly impressed with the "diversity and complexity of the characters." She points out that blind characters in Hollywood have typically been very limited. "Normally when you have blind folks on screen, they're going to fit in one of four categories," she says, "the inspiration, somebody to pity, someone who needs to be fixed going after a cure, or someone who is newly disabled who wants to kill themselves."[11]

Although *See* has done a better job of trying to find blind talent than most shows and films, it must be said that the lead roles went to sighted actors. I had actually been called to audition for one of those lead roles, Paris. It was a bittersweet realization to find that I lost the part to a major actor. I certainly could not have competed with her experience. But that is kind of the point. How can we compete when it is still so rare even to be considered? Twenty years from now, there will surely be a larger pool of blind and visually impaired actors to fill the roles of so many blind characters. More important, perhaps, a new generation of blind actors will be able to go out for roles that do not call for blindness any more than they call for a specific ethnicity—

there are many of those. Then moviemakers and moviegoers will have to deal with the fact that blind people rarely look the way sighted directors have been depicting them since the beginning of film time.

In particular, blindface—the blank stare with no attempt to look in the direction of the other person's voice—should really be retired. We might not always nail the eye contact—indeed, I find it harder to fake it these days—but, honestly, there are few blind people who do not make an effort to turn in the direction of the voice that's speaking to them. We might lose someone if they move around without talking, but once their voice returns, it's pretty easy to judge where their head is.

The first major audition I had was in 2014 for the part of Reba McClane in the disturbingly graphic TV series *Hannibal,* based on Thomas Harris's novels. Because I was familiar with and loved that blind character, I worked very hard on my Reba audition and it was the first time I ever had the experience of acting blurring into real emotion—I felt real fear and almost began to weep when performing the scene.

The woman who got the part of Reba had become famous as one of the stars of the vampire series *True Blood.* I understand why the directors wanted to go with a big name, but until we have role models and opportunities, how can there be big-name blind actors? It's a catch-22 that is just beginning to be dismantled. When Alabaster and I watched the scene that I'd auditioned for, wherein Reba is being tortured by the Red Dragon and yet not even attempting to look in his direction, so focused is she on her blindface, I took it as a painful reminder of how far we have to go.

When we shot my television commercial, the director said, "You move so interestingly." I understood that to mean that I moved unlike anything he'd ever seen portrayed on film. Sighted directors have been creating and perpetuating stereotypes of blindness forever, and I think a big reason for that is that they don't want to deal with the real thing—we might knock over the lights or something.

The depictions multiply and exaggerate until they resemble no blind people in existence, and, worse, actual blind people fail to meet expectations. Thus, absurd situations arise like what happened to opera singer and memoirist Laurie Rubin when, years ago, she learned she did not get a part because she didn't "read as blind," although she has, in fact, been blind her whole life.

Not "looking blind" is a real problem in acting and in real life. My commercial inspired such remarks as "This is an actor! They need real blind people," as if the very notion of a blind actor does not compute. Others expressed doubt about how blind I was: "Her eyes are following the action. She at least has some vision."[12]

My friend and fellow blind writer Jim Knipfel (he has RP) mentioned in an email that having people accuse him of not really being blind makes him more angry than anything else about being blind: "It seems if we go to the store or cross the street or ride the subway by ourselves, then we must not really be blind. Few things these days dredge up the murderous rage quite like that."

Sighted people have very limited notions about what blind people look like—we all wear sunglasses or keep our eyes closed. A twelve-year-old kid recently told Jim that he wasn't blind because his eyes were open, "yet he's still alive because I'm a very forgiving fellow."

Faking blindness is a strange concept. Why would we want to pretend to put on such an act? For sympathy? For spare change? For the jokes? Because, let's face it, when sighted people are not accusing us of pretending to be blind, they are making jokes about our blindness.

———

My play about Helen Keller, "The Star of Happiness," did not shy away from the existence of Helen Keller jokes, which I am always amazed to learn have incredible staying power—young people whom I talk to have heard Helen Keller jokes even if they were born decades after her death in 1968. I thought it was important to acknowledge them because, for one thing, you can still hear comparable jokes flying out of the mouths of performers today with respect to Stevie Wonder, as we'll soon witness, and for another, because alongside the too-sweet and uplifting accounts of her life written for children, which most of us read in grade school, and perhaps *The Story of My Life* or *The Miracle Worker,* these jokes are a huge part of what people think of when they think of Helen Keller. Not incorporating them would have been, I thought, ignoring the elephant onstage with me. So I recorded an evil version of myself reciting some gems like: "What's Helen Keller's favorite color?" "Corduroy!" and "Why can't Helen Keller drive?" "Because she's a woman!" Obviously these jokes come from a place of not only ableism but also sexism, which I also exploited in my show because Helen Keller worked to get women the vote and allied herself with women who fought for women's reproductive rights (including abortion).

I also did not shy away from the sexuality that Keller struggled to tamp down in the face of so much opposition. The age in which she lived did not allow for the idea of a disabled woman fashioning herself as a wife and mother.

In *Midstream,* Helen Keller describes her relationship with Alexander Graham Bell in a chapter called "My Oldest

Friend." Bell had been a friend for many years and was the one who directed her parents to the Perkins School for the Blind in Massachusetts, from which Anne Sullivan was sent to teach little Helen. Bell had a particular interest in deaf education. His mother and wife were deaf, and he first conceived of his most famous invention, the telephone, as an instrument for the hard-of-hearing.[13]

One evening Bell and Keller found themselves alone on his porch. She was a young college student at Radcliffe, and he wanted to unburden himself regarding her future, particularly in the love and marriage department: "It seems to me, Helen, a day must come when love, which is more than friendship, will knock at the door of your heart and demand to be let in."[14]

She was surprised and asked what made him think of that. "Oh, I often think of your future. To me you are a sweet, desirable young girl, and it is natural to think about love and happiness when we are young."[15]

She told him that she did think of love sometimes, but "it is like a beautiful flower which I may not touch, but whose fragrance makes the garden a place of delight just the same."[16]

Bell argued that she should not think she was "debarred from the supreme happiness of woman." His reasoning is distasteful to modern ears: "Heredity is not involved in your case," which assumes that if her disability had been inheritable, they would not be having this conversation. Smacking of eugenics as his perspective was, it allowed for the possibility of Keller's participating in the "normalcy" of marriage and motherhood. However, for others in Keller's life, this argument would not be enough to believe in her fitness, and Bell suspected as much, encouraging her not to be cowed by naysayers if "a good man should desire to make you his wife."[17]

In fact, the love that came to Helen Keller a few years later would be brief and explosive, thanks to the adamant opposition of her mother and other family members. She writes of her brief affair with Peter Fagan in *Midstream,* though she does not name him.

On their second Chautauqua tour, when Helen was thirty-six, Fagan (a friend of Anne Sullivan's estranged husband, John Macy, and a socialist like Macy and Keller) accompanied Keller in order to help interpret, and he was "very much in earnest, and eager to have the people get my message. He returned to Wrentham with us in the autumn of 1916 after our disappointing and exhausting summer."[18]

Soon after, Anne Sullivan grew very ill, forcing Keller to confront the possibility of losing her lifelong companion. This lonely time in Keller's life provided the backdrop for Fagan's declaration.

She was sitting in her study one evening, "utterly despondent," when "the young man" entered and sat beside her. "For a long time he held my hand in silence, then he began talking to me tenderly. I was surprised that he cared so much about me. There was sweet comfort in his loving words. I listened all a-tremble. He was full of plans for my happiness. He said if I would marry him, he would always be near to help me in the difficulties of life. He would be there to read to me, look up material for my books and do as much as he could of the work my teacher had done for me."[19]

But their love had to be kept secret, for her mother did not like him and was, it seemed, adamantly opposed to her deafblind daughter being romantically involved. Herrmann describes how Keller's brothers ran Fagan off with guns when he and Keller tried to elope, but Keller is circumspect about the affair and seems to have internalized some shame about the whole situation. At the end of this small recollection, she concludes thus: "The brief love will remain in my life, a little island of joy surrounded by dark waters. I am glad that I have had the experience of being loved and desired. The fault was not in the loving, but in the circumstances. A lovely thing tried to express itself; but conditions were not right or adequate, and it never blossomed."[20]

A few years later, in 1922, when she was performing on vaudeville, Keller was prompted to express her relationship to sex, love, and marriage forthrightly, and with more candor, perhaps, than she allowed herself in her public, autobiographical writings: "All the primitive instincts and desires of the heart," she wrote in a letter to a suitor, "which neither physical disabilities nor suppression can subdue, leap up within me to meet your wishes. Since my youth I have desired the love of a man. Sometimes I have wondered rebelliously why Fate has trifled with me so strangely, why I was tantalized with bodily capabilities I could not fulfill. But Time, the great discipliner, has done his work well, so that I have learned not to reach out for the moon, and not to cry aloud for the spilled treasures of womanhood."[21]

Although she did not take the marriage proposal to which she was responding—made when she was forty-two, from a stranger with five children—very seriously, the opportunity to vent her heartfelt disappointments was. Bell's opinions notwithstanding, Keller had been discouraged by friends and family from the idea of marriage and children, so that, from the vantage point of middle age, she had little choice but to conclude, "I faced consciously the strong sex-urge of my nature and turned that life-energy into channels of satisfying sympathy and work."[22]

Helen Keller was often termed a saint, even if her socialist politics, her forthright liberal views regarding birth control, and her four years performing on the vaudeville circuit belied this notion. In order to combat the stereotype of the saintly blind, I closed out Act Two of "The Star of Happiness" with the candid and intimate words of Helen to her suitor. Although they end with resignation, it is important to notice that what Helen Keller presented as her public persona was itself largely a kind of act directed by the restrictive norms of the day: "You have read my books," she tells her suitor. "Perhaps you have received the wrong impression from them. One does not grumble in print, or hold up one's broken wings for the thoughtless and indifferent to gaze at. One hides as much as possible one's awkwardness and helplessness under a fine philosophy and a smiling face."[23]

Keller was a victim of the strict assertion that blind people—and really people with all kinds of disabilities—ought to be inspiring and saintly, rather than desiring and desirable. Hence, we have inspiration porn stars—countless people with disabilities who make a living doing inspirational talks—yet we rarely see blind people having sex in books or movies, let alone acknowledge the possibility of a disabled sex symbol. As more actual disabled people represent themselves, all that will continue to change.

Despite the changes on the horizon, people use the word "inspiring" when talking to me with alarming frequency. I try to accept it as the compliment they intend. I suppose sighted people would like to be inspiring too. However, as Haben Girma (the first deafblind person to graduate from Harvard Law) writes in her 2019 memoir: "People with disabilities get called inspiring so often, usually for the most insignificant things, that the word now feels like a euphemism for pity."[24] The problem is that in linking disability with inspiration we are subscribing to the idea that disability must *mean* something, rather than being just one aspect of our humanity with all its complex messiness.

As we continue to think about sex and blindness, I think it's important to note that in denying or dismissing sexuality, as well as political views, theatrical leanings, or any of the other things that make us human, human rights generally tend to fall away. Thus, not acknowledging our right to love and procreate often suggests more deeply entrenched denials of life and liberty, freedom of expression, and a reasonable right to privacy.

12

Sanctified by Affliction, or Not

Picture a blind person. Do they have boobs? A penis? Are they holding a tin cup, or simply swinging a white cane? How often have you seen a sexy, gorgeous blind person in real life? In a movie? Or described in a novel? Blind characters are so rarely depicted as sexy, sexual, or having a sex, that I suppose it seems a not unobvious conclusion that blind people are all saints and virgins. And yet blind people *do* have sex, although sighted people have not made it easy for us.[1]

In his 1953 novel, *The Face of the Deep,* Jacob Twersky describes the strict segregation of the sexes in the school for the blind that is the setting for the first part of the book, and how the kids learned to flout the rules and the teachers to get together. But these hookups do not always work out. Two of the characters whose lives the novel follows, Ken and Rosie, get busted during a clandestine rendezvous in the rubdown room behind the boys' locker room:

> We ought to get off the table and fix our clothes
> completely, but I can't move, and Rosie does not seem
> able to, either. The door opens—I hear it and feel the
> draught. I feel someone peering in at us.
> "All right," Rogers says.
> I get off the table, fixing my clothes. I want to grab

Rogers and choke the sneaky life out of him. Rosie
whimpers, shame and fear in the pitiful sounds she
makes.

"Make yourself decent, Miss Celli," Rogers says
sarcastically. "Pull your dress down," he shouts.
"Animals, plain animals."

Ken defends Rosie's honor, telling the teacher "You insult
Rosie again and I swear no one will ever recognize you." They
are expelled, even though Ken has already graduated (but has
no place to go) and Rosie is about to graduate, making them
about eighteen years old, though Twersky does not tell us their
ages directly. They will in fact get married soon and have a life
together with many ups and downs, but for now, the situation
looks bleak and Ken is bitter.[2]

Twersky was born in 1920 and went to school at the New
York Institute for the Blind in the Bronx during the 1930s. He
likely took inspiration from his own experiences to create his fictionalized school for the blind—the strict segregation between
the sexes is something that is iterated again and again in his own
memoir and others of the early and mid-twentieth century.

Ten years younger than Twersky but raised in the south,
Ray Charles confronted an even more intense segregation in his
school for the blind that divided students first into black and
white, then into deaf and blind, and finally into boys and girls.
However, the kids did their best to circumnavigate this last. In
his autobiography, *Brother Ray,* Charles explains how one girl
helped her boyfriend find his way to her room by constructing
an elaborate braille map: "This diagram was really somethin'
else—all detailed and precise and even included a contingency
option for dealing with the night watchman if he happened to

show up. It was a very hip strategy and an especially creative plan. You gotta remember that both these kids were blind. But then again, sex is a bitch of a motivator; it don't need no eyes."[3]

His frankness about sex has no doubt put off a lot of readers since *Brother Ray* was published in 1978. Charles, perhaps more than anyone, refutes notions of saintly blind folk when he says things like "Ever since I began singing and playing in public, I'd never had to ask for pussy. It was out there for the taking. All I needed to do was lightly suggest." He was a musician coming up in the forties and fifties and it was just like that, a "fringe benefit" of playing gigs constantly. "By the time I was eighteen, I could play the game like a pro."[4]

Ray Charles aside, it is rare to see sexually active blind people in the media, and when they appear, they are rarely the protagonists. As we've seen, the blind character is often there to flesh out the character—good or bad—of the main protagonist.

In Raymond Carver's famous 1983 short story "Cathedral," a blind man comes to visit the narrator and his wife, who had read for him ten years earlier. Besides the husband's comical (and all too painfully familiar) ableist insecurities about "the blind"—"My idea of blindness came from the movies. In the movies, the blind moved slowly and never laughed. Sometimes they were led by seeing-eye dogs. A blind man in my house was not something I looked forward to"[5]—the visit provokes marital insecurities of a more quotidian nature: "My wife finally took her eyes off the blind man and looked at me. I had the feeling she didn't like what she saw."[6]

The narrator does not seem to acknowledge the possibility that his wife did (or could) have an affair with the blind man. I think most nondisabled readers follow his assumptions. On the other hand, a disabled reader may more readily see in this story the possibility of a past love affair between the blind man and the wife/reader.

In fact, the notion is beautifully taken to the max by Jillian Weise, poet, novelist, and cyborg (she relies on a prosthetic leg with all the digital and electronic bells and whistles). In her poem "Cathedral by Raymond Carver," Weise imagines the audiotape exchange from the wife to the blind man about her first husband, whom she names Lenny:

> I miss driving you places and not just because
> of what you did while I was driving you places.
> Though you were very good at what you did.
> I never felt like you were doing it just to get
> the job done. Though your professionalism
> is commendable. You're an expert.
> Your hands were made for there, while Lenny's
> hands were made for, I guess, F-22 Raptors.[7]

As Weise writes in her introduction to this piece at Academia .edu: "The story is typically taught and discussed as if the blind man's relationship with the wife was entirely platonic and noble, even though the original story suggests otherwise."[8] (After all, the blind man marries his next reader.) Assuming a strict platonic relationship between the blind man and his reader reveals our ableist norms and expectations. Additionally, "Cathedral" has always bothered me because, while engaging and unique in many ways, it still falls into the old trap of depicting the blind man as sidekick to the protagonist's journey or epiphany.

As so often happens, the image of the blind in the hands of a deft sighted writer rises to the top of its class—"Cathedral" is often included in anthologies of great short stories—and thus the image of Carver's blind man and others like it become indelible in the mind of the sighted reader, and in the mind of the blind reader too. We are all shaped by these images, and I find it hard to shake them.

Unlike the blind man of Carver's story, blind female characters often magnify the distortions and fetishes of straight men within the metaphorics of stories and novels that have little or nothing to do with blindness, cementing the relationship between the helplessness of blind people and the attractiveness of a helpless woman.

For example, a glimpse of a blind dancing girl in an Algerian brothel is enough to send the protagonist of Paul Bowles's 1949 novel *The Sheltering Sky* into a fervent sexual fantasy that has everything to do with her blindness: "And in bed, without eyes to see beyond the bed, she would have been completely there, a prisoner. He thought of the little games he would have played with her, pretending to have disappeared when he was really still there; he thought of the countless ways he could have made her grateful to him. And always in conjunction with his fantasies, he saw the imperturbable, faintly questioning face in its masklike symmetry."[9]

When I first read *The Sheltering Sky* via audiocassette when I was in my early twenties, I was titillated by this portrayal of a sexualized blind woman. Perhaps this spoke to my own fears about going blind as a young woman who was a bit boy crazy. Two decades or so later, my young friend Caitlin Hernandez pointed out that the brief passage has more than a whiff of abuse about it, especially glaring in the wake of the #MeToo movement.

As a survivor of sexual assault herself, Caitlin feels strongly that there needs to be more consideration of the perils of being blind in a sexual context. The media might not like to think of young blind women as sexual, but that does not mean the people they like and trust do not. Disabled women are roughly three times as likely to be the victims of sexual assault,[10] even though they are rarely considered in such conversations, and thus often have a difficult time gaining access to services. Caitlin has written an as-yet-unpublished novel that seeks to redress the issue in a young-adult context. Her novel, which examines survival after sexual assault through a blind, lesbian lens, is a story that does not exist in the average sighted person's imagination. As she told me in a recent conversation, when she experienced her own sexual assault by a friend when they were freshmen at UC Santa Cruz, she did not know how to articulate the relationship between what he did and her blindness, and the authority figures in her life mostly brushed her off.

Of course, the desires or lack thereof on the part of the female love object have been problematic in literature written by men for ages, but blindness exaggerates the tendency. In *Waiting for the Barbarians* (1980), J. M. Coetzee manages to reveal the many metaphorical blindnesses of his male sighted protagonist despite the fact that he is our narrator. The characters of Coetzee's strange allegorical novel of empire and blindness do not have names but rather titles. The magistrate is the narrator and the barbarian girl—who was the first visually impaired character I met in literature—his almost-lover.

When I read *Waiting for the Barbarians* in my first year of grad school, the barbarian girl's central vision loss sounded similar to my own, except that for me, there was no blur: "Yes, I can see," she tells the magistrate. "When I look straight there is nothing." She struggles to find the word that expresses this nothingness, and the magistrate interprets her hand waving in front of her face as a blur. "There is a blur." She agrees. "But I can see out of the sides of my eyes. The left eye is better than the right. How could I find my way if I didn't see?"[11]

This blind, or rather visually impaired, girl helps our narrator, an old magistrate of the empire, relax. He can dawdle nude while she is in the room. He feels her vision loss keeps her from judging him, and yet, until he leaves the town, he cannot penetrate her: "I have not entered her. From the beginning my desire has not taken on that direction, that directedness."[12]

When the barbarian girl tells the magistrate what he thought he wanted to know—what her torturers did to her eyes—that does not penetrate either. Instead of wrestling with the strangeness of her story or listening to her assurance that "now it is getting better" he instead takes her face in his hands and stares "into the dead centres of her eyes, from which twin reflections of myself stare solemnly back."[13]

And there's the rub: when the sighted look into blind eyes they very often see nothing but themselves. This perhaps helps to explain why blind characters are so often depicted as portals to understanding for the sighted protagonists they encounter. They are rarely treated as individuals with their own complex inner lives. The magistrate cannot even see the barbarian girl's affections and jealousy, her incomprehension at his not having sex with her. "You visit other girls . . . You think I do not know?"[14] She breaks down and cries, and still the magistrate cannot see her or her desires.

As I mentioned, one of my favorite blind characters—even years before I was called in to audition for the role in the television adaptation—is Reba McClane in *Red Dragon,* the first of the Thomas Harris novels to feature Hannibal Lecter. I admit I first saw the movie and then read the novel, because I was on a Ralph Fiennes kick. At that time I was still visually impaired rather than blind, and I was delighted by Emily Watson's performance as Reba.

I like Reba because she is a smart, self-aware, and sexually confident woman, who makes the first move on Francis Dol-arhyde. Granted, he, a serial killer, may not have been the best pick, but her attraction to him, despite his own disability—a harelip and speech impediment—is precisely why he likes her too, and even, for a hot minute, considers giving up the murder game. And why not? She gives him head and then some great sex: "Oh, wait, I'll get them off. Oh, now it's torn. I don't care. Come on. My God, man. That's so sweeeet. Don't please hold me down, let me come up to you and take it."[5]

Reba asserts her desire for Dolarhyde, and demonstrates to him and the reader that people's misconceptions about the blind being "sanctified by their affliction," as she puts it, are unjustified.[16]

But Reba and the other few exceptions prove the rule that sighted people tend to think that blind people are less sexual, more spiritual than they are. It can be annoying when you walk into your local grocery store day after day with your partner (holding hands and paying together) and are asked by the clerk if you are brother and sister. Besides the fact that Alabaster and I in most respects don't look anything alike, it seems that a couple in their forties would be assumed to be just that, unless one of them happens to be blind, and then we must rather be siblings.

I wrote about that in my column for *Catapult,* and I remember having misgivings: Was I exaggerating the virginal blind effect? Had others experienced such a thing? I decided that it was enough that it was my experience, and the column was published. It provoked a greater response than usual. I received an outpouring of outrageous stories that mirrored and magnified my own.

Caitlin Hernandez posted a link to the article on her Facebook feed and, because she is active in the LGBT community, I learned from her friends that same-sex couples have an even harder time convincing the world they are lovers rather than siblings when one of the couple is blind. Skin color inflected the stories as well—an African American woman was assumed to be a personal care attendant (PCA) rather than a spouse. Perhaps the most ludicrous response came from a pregnant woman, who had to explain to a curious sighted person on a public bus how she'd gotten pregnant. Her wry joke that "many people have sex in the dark" was not enough to stave off follow-up questions about how blind people go about doing it.

But blindness does not change the fact that we are human, with all the drives and incentives to mate and procreate (or not) that those with full vision have. The complexities of blindness, personality, and sense of self are wrapped up in those of being human. There is not a blind personality or a blind way of being. Rather, being blind, or visually impaired, is a mode of being that twists and shapes our way in the world and is twisted and shaped by how we are treated in the world. Blindisms are cultural even if being blind is physical. And yet the attitude that sexuality (or lack thereof) is tied to sight (or lack thereof) impacts sex lives.

In *Red Dragon* Reba announces to the reader that "[s]he enjoyed sex very much." But Harris, an ostensibly nondisabled novelist, is surprisingly adept at getting at a fundamental issue about sex and disability—that a nondisabled person may not want to give in to desire for fear of "entailing a burden." Reba "did not like for a man to creep in and out of her bed as though he were stealing chickens."[7]

The notion that blind people need to be taken care of by their life partners or lovers seems to run deep, and yet is complicated by sexual orientation and tied to deep-seated gender norms and expectations. In particular, dating can sometimes be frustrating for a straight guy who is blind. Darren Harbour is an actor and founding director of Imagine Blind Players, a theater group in Louisville that defies stereotypes with an all visually impaired and blind cast that does not shy away from such things as dance choreography and fight scenes.[18] I interviewed him and a few other friends for an article I wrote for *Playboy* in 2018 about (literal) blind dating. At that time, he often ran into the problem of women who wanted to date him because "they want someone to take care of."

On the other hand, he also met women who just wanted to be friends in order to enjoy his attractiveness without bothering about his feelings. Darren has found himself in the downright insulting position of being on a date with a girl and her boyfriend, as if he did not pose a threat. Sitting at a cozy table for three, one woman said to her boyfriend, "You should get muscles like Darren." Clearly, she thought she could use this sexy blind guy to make her boyfriend jealous—but not too jealous.[19]

Of course it's hard to say where society's norms and expectations end and our own insecurities about those norms and expectations begin. Traditional gender roles might suggest inevitable impotence for some blind men. "Rather than risk being foolish, a failure, a blind bungler, I had started to withdraw from the contest, especially the sexual contest," writes painter-turned-writer Andrew Potok in his outrageous 1980 memoir *Ordinary Daylight,* as he toys with the idea of being a recluse while going blind. "At times, sacrifice seemed easy, particularly when the alternative was humiliating, even crushing. And sacrifice had its nobility. It had been quite foreign to me in my previous life, but it was considered characteristic, even expected, of the blind."[20]

Perhaps Potok is thinking of Helen Keller, who was so often depicted as a saint, but who, as we have seen, experienced sexual impulses, just like most of us. In any case, he doesn't have to consider renunciation or sacrifice for long. Ironically, this line of thought leads him directly into the arms of a new lover, who declares her attraction to him, and chides him for whining about his lack of manliness without sight:

"It's not true," she said. "From the moment I met you I wanted to sleep with you. You must have sensed that. It doesn't happen to me often. I'm very choosy. You've been a part of my fantasies ever since. I don't even understand why your eyes matter. You don't need your eyes for this."[21]

As a lover of art and artists, this woman expresses an idiosyncratic, yet not unheard of, perspective. Just after I turned thirty, I got myself partnered with my guide dog, Millennium, a sleek black Lab. Having never wanted the stigma of using the white cane, I somehow thought the dog would mitigate pity. Nonetheless, this act turned me from looking, in the eyes of the world, like a sighted person, to looking like a blind person. Cane or dog did not seem to matter, I was suddenly treated differently.

Admittedly, I met a lot of boys in those early days with Millennium. It seemed, with my visual impairment that allowed me still to move about with a certain amount of ease and to fake eye contact (if I could not see their eyes, I could at least see where their heads were), and my guide dog who pronounced me blind, that I was attractively different. On New York's Lower East Side, where difference had currency, I did pretty well. But when I left the comforting land of freaks and ventured, for example, to the Upper East Side, where difference had little power, I would encounter people who grabbed my arm and shuffled me across the street, as if I were an old person. This made me so angry. I yelled more than once, "Let go of me! I know karate!" (And I did. Blind karate is a thing.)[22]

Because many sighted people do not take well to having their assumed helpfulness denied, I was called a blind bitch more than once. Maybe I was being difficult or impossible. I know now that my lack of patience regarding their yearning to be helpful did not help the cause of blind people generally, many of whom benefit from the kindness of strangers.

In my first incarnation as a blind person in the eyes of the sighted, I felt a lot of anger and frustration. Those feelings were, I believe, what drove me to hit the open mics in order to express what I felt but had never witnessed in any representations. My sudden appearance as a helpless person drove me to try my hand at comedy when I was supposed to be writing my dissertation. My act quickly became "the somewhat slutty, almost always drunken, angry blind chick schtick." I felt compelled to shout to the rafters about aspects of blindness that are everywhere denied.

Once, when I went with a friend to visit another friend in Rhode Island, the three of us, after having loads of fun in a bar, walked to his car, I with my guide dog, and I heard some guy say to his friend, "Yeah, but would you really date a blind chick?" I yelled back something like, "Well, I wouldn't date you!" but my heart was not in it. Later, I would cry, knowing that in the end, the prejudices and biases are real.

"I have noticed that people think I am gay because I feel more taken care of by women," opera singer and memoirist Laurie Rubin told me for the blind dating article I wrote for *Playboy*. "I once had a girl say that it made sense to her why I'd be gay. She felt that because I was blind, I'd also be gender blind." It would be as astounding to find that seeing or not-seeing determined our sexual orientation as it would be to discover that our height or hair color did.[23] The idea seems to me insulting on three counts: (1) by assuming women are better caregivers; (2) by assuming blind people need to be taken care of (more than other humans); and (3) by assuming that gayness is a choice determined by practical needs and logistics rather than attraction and desire.

"One particular jewel that came out of the mouth of a singer friend of mine," Laurie told me, was that "because humans are animals, we always instinctively look for the fittest mate. But then I realize that even though you're blind, you have a vagina, and of course you'd want sex."[24]

We are often so programmed to think about sexuality as being conveyed through the eyes, that depictions of blind people acting out their desires become stereotyped—so stereotyped that sighted people take them as gospel. "May I touch your face?" asks Reba in her first meeting alone with Dolarhyde in *Red Dragon*. She fears she may have offended him and says by way of explanation, "I want to know if you are smiling or frowning."

It is one of the few blind moments in the novel that does not ring true for me. I have never asked to feel anyone's face, though I have had many sighted people ask if I *want* to feel their face. It always makes me laugh. I would prefer not to feel any faces out of the contexts in which most sighted people feel faces: intimate moments with loved ones such as spouses or children.

Am I just a misanthrope? A prude? I decided to reach out to others to gauge my feelings about face touching—specifically: Caitlin Hernandez, Laurie Rubin, and Michelle Kleinberg. At the time, the four of us communicated regularly in order to discuss our writing and our lives as blind women. I sent an email to them with the subject line "Face Touching," and asked them what they thought of it. All agreed that, with rare exceptions, this is not something we do. Caitlin, who admits to being a very touchy-feely person, and who has been blind since birth, agreed: "I never touch faces, unless I'm making out with someone and/or unless I'm very drunk and have a crush on that person and use my blind drunkenness as an excuse to hang all over them."

Now, perhaps you, sighted reader, are more circumspect and have never asked a blind person "Do you want to touch my face?" and are amazed that we must actually have responses for such a question prepared because it is so common. But all are not like you.

Laurie, our opera singer in Hawaii who has also been blind since birth, mentioned a time she sang in a master class that was open to the public. After the concert, a woman "around my mom's age came up to me, and asked if I had any interest in touching her face so that I would know what the person I was talking to looked like." Instead of waiting for an answer, the woman "took my hand and placed it all over her oily face. I tell you, all I remember from that encounter was a very long nose." Laurie hastily told her that she does not usually touch faces, and concluded, "It was funny to actually have someone placing my hand on her face while simultaneously asking me if I would find that helpful."

Laurie added that "truth be told," she doesn't even touch her wife's face very much. "I'll stroke her cheek or nuzzle my face against hers, but I'm really not much of a face toucher, and prefer cuddles and hugs over face interaction."

We had this conversation over a series of emails, and the stories kept coming—invitations to touch beards seemed to evoke some particularly gross memories! However, Caitlin mentioned that she has a friend who does feel that she gets something from face touching. The friend had once had vision, and Caitlin wondered if this made the difference, but Michelle and I disabused her of that idea.

Michelle is the mother of an eleven-year-old and is working on a memoir about parenting while going blind. She had this to say about face touching: "I hate when people ask me. I don't want to touch your face! And, as for one who did see previously, I do not get an image from it—I think it is because I am too busy wigging out at touching a face. The only time I actually loved touching a face was my baby's just after she was born."

I can only assume, then, that sighted authors and filmmakers are largely responsible for promoting the myth of face touching. Perhaps I need a larger sample? I'm guessing, however, that my guy friends would be even more disinclined to face touching, preferring to touch elsewhere instead.

In his memoir *The Sound of the Walls,* Twersky describes his first date with his future wife, during which she says, "Touch my face, . . . Do you think you could tell then if I'm really pretty?" Instead of touching her face, he took the opportunity for a first kiss.[25]

Another thing fictional representations don't often show when it comes to blindness is how it can make a person paranoid in the love department. Or at least that has been my experience: Is he looking at some other girl? Is she prettier than me? Is he looking at me with love? Such are the questions that have fueled my jealousy, which, with the help of booze, could easily get out of hand.[26] These experiences and struggles to commit to a relationship without destroying it with accusations and violent rages are not something I've seen represented—especially in considering women who are blind, although a similar kind of paranoia is illustrated in the 1991 Australian film *Proof,* starring Hugo Weaving and a young Russell Crowe, in which the blind character feels doubt regarding the world described to him by sighted people, and denies himself the possibility of love with his housekeeper, who is obsessed with him, because then he will not know if she loves him or feels pity for him.

Alabaster and I had many fights in our early days, resulting, almost exclusively, from my paranoia and jealousy. I had felt gnawing insecurities with other boyfriends, but my anger grew with my blindness.

Jacob Twersky also alludes to this blind paranoia in his memoir when he describes his feelings surrounding the woman he wishes to marry. He doubts what she could possibly see in him: "I was continually amazed that Esther wanted to keep seeing me. I told myself that it could not just be pity or kindness. But what else could it be?"[27]

The result of these insecurities was a tendency to peevishly push disagreements. In a restaurant, he and Esther are approached by a fortune-teller who gives them a happy future together, but assumes that Twersky had been blinded in the war, which angers him: "The old fool!" I said. "Of course a girl like you wouldn't go out with a blind guy unless she had been more or less engaged to him before he lost his sight in the war."[28]

This causes him to launch into a tipsy tirade that boils down to: "Why do you go out with a guy like me and let yourself in for such nonsense?"[29]

It's so painfully familiar, from the insecurity to the booze to the feeling of hopelessness, that the person you love cannot possibly say the right thing. That, in fact, they cannot know exactly why they are with you, why they love you—a blind person—or whether it is actually true that things would be better, easier, with someone sighted. Love is, after all, generally complicated.

I have finally mostly settled into my blindness and my relationship with Alabaster. And I think the coziness of feeling settled is directly related to a growing confidence in my own abilities and self-worth. Although I should say that growing a little older and drinking less is helpful. The small successes make the worries about prettiness and sight less important. In other words, feeling useful and capable has a lot to do with feeling worthy of love and vice versa. Unfortunately, however, as we'll soon see, the ocularcentric culture has not made it any easier for blind people to pursue our artistic and career goals than it has to encourage us in our relationship desires.

13

Portrait of the (Working) Writer
as Blind

Although we have the formidable image of the blind bard, blind writers—particularly novelists—are relatively rare. This is certainly changing and will continue to change, but I think it's fair to say that there exist nowhere close to the number of blind writers as there are blind characters in books. One problem is likely that disability is as yet hardly ever included in statements of diversity for major grants and fellowships. Another is that until the advent of digital culture, books, magazines, literary journals, and other writerly ephemera were, as we've seen, not easily accessible in a timely manner. Writing is not only about writing, but also about reading and being involved in a writerly community. It is also vital to have access to equal opportunity and working environments—professional and creative—that are open to difference and stripped of ableism.

Perhaps it is because of the relative dearth of professional blind writers that I keep returning to Jacob Twersky, whose 1953 novel, *The Face of the Deep,* follows the lives of the blind couple Ken and Rosie, as well as several others in their loose group of friends—from their moments of first blindness through their school days together to their adulthoods with marriages and careers, heartaches and failures. It is not an easy novel to read— painfully vivid in its stark depiction of the many trials blind people faced in the early to mid-twentieth century in negotiating the complex of government and philanthropic institutions, their limited prospects for work, and the ways in which the system could make them cruel to one another. Twersky's blind characters are full of variety and exhibit all the permutations of good and evil that exist in humans generally.

Some readers did not appreciate the rawness. As a review in the *New York Times* put it: "Mr. Twersky has seen fit to delineate only the worst phases of the schools and institutions, the worst workers, and certainly the most unsympathetic group of 'blinks' ever collected in print."[1]

The reviewer seems to feel that what is disturbing in the book overwhelms the inspiration that readers demand from blind authors, best presented as autobiography, not fiction: "He fell into a very deep pit when he wrote *The Face of the Deep* as a novel instead of following the autobiographical form used by many blind writers."[2]

Twersky perhaps took the demand for personal narrative to heart, and published his memoir (*The Sound of the Walls*) a few years later, which allows me the luxury of comparing the two. There seems to be much that is autobiographical in Twersky's novel. In particular, one of the main characters, Joe Berkowitz, shares with the author his Jewishness, his stubborn pride, and his ability to rise above the disconcerting slop of low expectations for blind people in midcentury America. He also tries to help his friends do so, with less success, and is frustrated by the prejudice of other successful blind people toward those less lucky. In a scene toward the end of the novel, Joe (a professor like Twersky himself) visits one of his former schoolmates, Fred, who (thanks to his own ingenuity and a leg up from his businessman father) is in a position to offer a job to their friend Ken, who has fallen on hard times. However, Fred refuses, saying, "Everything about him sickens me. I don't want him anywhere near me. I don't want him in any way associated with me."[3]

The sense is that Fred cannot see that Ken, orphaned after his blindness when he was just a toddler, never had the opportunities that Fred, with his wealthy family backing, had. As Joe pushes Ken's case, the anger between them escalates. Fred says, "He's a stinking slob. He gives people a bad impression about the blind. He hasn't any brains, hasn't any guts."

They are shouting now, and Joe counters, "I've known few people with as much intelligence and guts as Ken."

These two blind men, each successful in his own way, and yet so different in their sympathies, grow angrier still. Fred hurls a paper cup of whiskey at Joe, and they get into a fistfight. Joe leaves Fred's office with a bloody lip, feeling "foolish and futile."[4]

The upshot is that Ken—for the sake of Rosie and their kids—will end up in the subway, begging with the dreaded tin cup. "Thank you," Ken must say to the passing strangers who drop a few paltry coins in his cup. "God bless you.'"

Inside he fumes and thinks, "I'd like to stay drunk all the time, but I have to do a good job at this." Because, "at night Rosie cries in her sleep sometimes. Sometimes I cry myself." He worries, "Our kids will find out our shame one day," and others "who know us may find out one day." But, Ken concludes, "there's nothing to do."[5]

Perhaps it was this bleak ending that the *New York Times* reviewer did not appreciate. Other readers perhaps felt the same, as the novel has been out of print for some time.

There is so much to say about *The Face of the Deep,* which was recommended to me by a blind Facebook friend when she learned that I was writing this book. I'm so glad she did, and I hope I can help to renew some interest in Twersky, because we need more blind authors to tell our stories. He died in 2014 (at age ninety-four), so he will not benefit from my celebration of him. I think that in following his endeavors to "write with growing insight into people and blindness,"[6] we get a pretty good picture of how the blind writer can be pushed to the sidelines by the many insistent portrayals of blind people by sighted authors.

Laurie Alice Eakes is a blind author with twenty-five traditionally published novels in print and three more under contract in what might generally be called women's fiction. "That's a kind of code for I write romance," she told me.[7] "Except romance tends to conjure half-dressed men and women on steamy covers and the term 'bodice ripper,' which is offensive to most romance authors. Nowadays, they're more likely to be the lady doing the ripping off of clothing."

I discovered Laurie Alice Eakes (who goes by Alice) from her 2018 *HuffPost* opinion piece called "Yes, Blind People Read Books. We Write Them, Too," a delightfully snarky and poignant look at pervasive ocularcentrism in the publishing world. When I read it, I knew I had to get to know her, and so I reached out with some questions and found a new blind writer friend.

Although she now has a solid career as a professional writer, as well as the support of agent and editor, getting here was not easy. Alice encountered mind-boggling, unapologetic discrimination along the way. "My first encounter with an agent was shocking. She called to say she would take me on, then proceeded to mention how vivid my writing is. I disclosed . . . and never heard from her again." When Alice felt brave enough to try again, she found another agent and did not disclose—until they met for lunch at a conference, where she could not hide her blindness or her guide dog. It didn't help that this agent was terrified of dogs—even sweet golden retrievers. After that, the agent stopped sending out Alice's work to publishers.

Finally Alice met an agent who knew about her blindness and worked hard for her. Then editors became the problem.

"One flat-out said she didn't think a blind woman could go through the publishing process. I was already published." When Alice dared to write a contemporary suspense novel with a blind heroine who decides to give up her baby for adoption because of her blindness, "the editor rejected the manuscript because she said no blind woman would ever do such a thing." She knew this because of what she'd seen in the media.

In other words, what the media presents to the sighted becomes gospel and the multiplicity of lived blind experience flattened. But the stories of blind women giving up their babies for adoption are real and prejudice regarding blind parents' abilities to care for their children is also real. Besides the news articles Alice had read that inspired her character's backstory, she had personally wrestled with the issue: "As a blind woman, I had so many doubts about being a mother I chose not to be one." Regarding this painful episode, Alice said, "That the editor didn't know of the prejudice against blind women being mothers existed commends her. That she assumed I didn't know what I was talking about made me so angry I told my agent I was quitting."

Alice did not quit writing, and the discrimination also did not quit. On one of her more recent books, her line edits came in, which was no problem—"I rather like being edited"—but the editor had given her two copies of the manuscript, one with all edits accepted and advised her to turn it in "due to my visual difficulties." The nerve of that editor makes me so angry that I can't quite imagine how I'd handle it, but Alice has some distance now and is able to joke: "What visual difficulties? The gray coming into my hair? The excess size of my posterior from sitting on it too much to write and deal with ableist editors?"

Ableism in the publishing industry extends beyond agents

and editors to conference organizers. Alice mentioned that the only time she's invited to speak on panels is when they specifically relate to diversity or disability. Once, when she was told she was welcome to speak at a conference, she was advised by the organizers not to because there would be steps. "Um, what? What does being blind have to do with steps, and why in the world were they having a conference with steps anyway? They may as well have put in their brochure: 'No disabled people welcome.'"

And if we get past the blithely ableist organizers, we still must contend with our colleagues, who cannot quite believe that we belong in their midst. As Alice explains in her *HuffPost* piece, at one conference where she was nominated for the highest award in the romance genre (the RITA), and was wearing her pin that proclaimed she had twenty-five books published, and was presenting at a workshop, her fellow writers could not imagine having books (or anything else) in common with her. Instead they talked to her guide dog, because "apparently a creature with a brain the size of a walnut is more intelligent than a woman with a master's degree who can't see."[8]

During a writers' retreat in the Catskills I faced a similar situation, and wrote about my feelings of not being seen in the context of being in a loving partnership for the *New York Times'* "Modern Love." I had been nominated to the Logan Nonfiction Program for writers and documentarians by my agent, and felt that five weeks would be best spent writing this book, rather than using my indifferent mobility skills to find my way around campus. So I asked them if I could bring Alabaster to help me get around, and they kindly agreed.

However, having another human there as my guide seemed to indicate to my fellow writers that I was less professionally capable. When I was talking about reading something in an email, one fellow said, "And by reading email, you mean Alabaster reads it to you?" It also felt as though they were more comfortable talking to him than to me, as if my blindness made me less approachable. Perhaps it was my own paranoia, but it seemed they were much more interested in Alabaster's music and his long-ago military service than in talking books and writing with me. I sometimes felt invisible, oftentimes less respected. I spent a lot of my five weeks feeling angry. After years of people talking to my companion instead of me—"What's her name? Does she want something to drink? Put her there"—it's hard to know where my insecurities end and others' discomforts and anxieties about disability begin.

Until we have more blind and disabled authors telling our own truths, stomping down discrimination is nearly impossible. Social anxieties surrounding blindness and disability will not fall away until we are able to have more control over our narratives. And in the publishing world, it is not just about us being authors presenting our myriad perspectives, but the industry itself that needs to shift. It's hard to imagine such a shift until people with disabilities occupy positions in every aspect of publishing—from editors and agents to publicists and marketers. Although about 20 percent of Americans are disabled, only 11 percent of people working in the publishing industry identify as disabled according to the 2019 Diversity Baseline Survey conducted by Lee & Low, with "the clear majority of disabilities" being "mental illness (45 percent), physical disability (22 percent), and chronic illness (20 percent)."[9]

Perhaps it is for this reason that Alice has not yet been able to publish a novel with the kind of blind character she'd like to see depicted in mainstream media. For the most part, she's not written blind characters. "I want to," she told me. "I've discussed one with my current editor and she is open to an idea I have. But this would be more of the romantic-suspense fluff I'm writing now. I want to write something more serious. More women's fiction than romance, something that can touch and maybe even change a few readers' hearts. Just not sure if I can convince my über-supportive agent it's got a place in the market."

Then again, the push for diversity in publishing includes a demand for #OwnVoices narratives, so Alice might yet be able to write the kind of blind character she would like. "Some black authors I love, Farrah Rochon and Kwana Jackson, to name two, have their black characters talk about the prejudices and racism they encounter, and I think it makes good stories great because it is so realistic and honest. But people fear blindness—for the wrong reasons. Maybe writing realistic lives of blind characters would help educate without a documentary."

Ah yes, novels seem to penetrate people's hearts and minds in a way that feels more real than real—ditto for the movies—so when the blind character is wrong, they, as Alice puts it, "get the wrong impression and perpetuate the myths and misconceptions that lead to ableism and downright bigotry against blind people."

There are so many things that sighted authors get wrong. Guide dogs are often romanticized beyond recognition. "So much research is available," Alice points out. "Authors have no excuse for talking about picking out the puppy and raising it to be a guide dog, as though all that entails is teaching it to sit." Her thoughts on the ubiquity of face touching also resonates: "If I read one more blind character who wants to feel someone's face, I'll tell the author it's sexual harassment and disgusting." And regarding the blind (particularly female) characters' romantic attachments, Alice notes that she "often ends up with the ugly partner."

Indeed! When I was performing a lot, I had a series of jokes that circled the all-too-common presumptions of unattractive men being delighted to meet me, a blind woman who will "finally appreciate him for who he is on the inside." The irony being, of course, that they themselves are not willing to see women for what they are on the inside, but feel somehow entitled to eye candy. It's the old Adam and Eve hypocrisy that demands Eve love Adam despite the fact that he is, as Milton puts it, "less fair / Less winning soft, less amiably mild." The blind woman, like Eve, must come to accept that "beauty is excelled by manly grace," and realize that wisdom "alone is truly fair."

The blind heroine never ends up with a hot guy unless she gets her sight back, which leads to what is arguably the most dangerous of blind plotlines: the miraculous healing at the end, because, as Alice puts it, "you can't have a happily ever after if one character is blind. Blind people aren't allowed happily ever afters."

As Alice's many novels suggest, blind writers do not necessarily want to write about blindness all the time. My friend Jim Knipfel is the author of three memoirs, eight books of fiction, and thousands of articles on everything from crime and restaurants to movies, music, politics, and art. In an article about how he came to acquire the personal library of the sociologist Erving Goffman (who literally wrote the book on stigma), Jim explains how once you come out as a blind person who writes, it's very difficult to then write about things other than blindness. Of his eleven books, only two mention blindness, but that seems not to matter. "If a cripple makes something of him or herself," writes Jim, "that cripple then becomes a lifelong representative of that entire class of stigmatized individuals, at least in mainstream eyes. From that point onward he or she will always be not only 'that Blind Writer' or 'that Legless Architect,' but a spokesperson on any issues pertaining to their particular disability."[10]

Jim's use of the word "cripple" may strike certain ears as distasteful—"disabled" is generally the accepted term these days. And yet, why limit our language? We sometimes need to appropriate the un-PC words for ourselves to jolt people out of their complacency. A perfect example of this impulse can be seen in the Cripple Punk movement, founded by a young artist and activist named Tai, whose principles reject "pity, inspiration porn, & all other forms of ableism": "cripple punk rejects the good cripple mythos"; "cripple punk is here for the bitter cripple, the uninspirational cripple, the smoking cripple, the drinking cripple, the addict cripple, the cripple who hasn't 'tried everything.'"[11]

To me, Jim Knipfel's use of the word "cripple" helps to articulate just how angry we blind people can get in an ocularcentric world that has a hard time conceptualizing (and hiring) blind writers for anything not blind-related. "I was published long before I developed that creepy blind stare," writes Jim, "but if I approach a mainstream publication nowadays, the only things they'll let me write about are cripple issues. Every now and again if I need the check, I'll, yes, put on the mask and play the role. But I'm bored to death with cripple issues, which is why whenever possible I neglect to mention to would-be editors that I'm blind."[12]

The stigma of blindness is something we'll continue to consider, but for now I want to point out how that stigma relates to employment not only for writers, but also for every blind person seeking gainful employment. When I was in grad school, I applied and was hired to help a visiting professor from Norway with his written English. I entered his department with Millennium and asked for him. The administrative assistant must have mentioned something about a blind woman with a dog, because two minutes later the Norwegian professor came running out, blustering and sputtering as if I were about to let Millennium poop on his precious manuscript. "No! No!" he exclaimed. "I cannot work with you, I'm sorry." This was not about the dog, "I love dogs. But I need to learn fast and you cannot help me."

So we stood there in the lobby next to the elevators arguing for a good fifteen minutes, with me telling him about the laptop I had in my bag, and how he could simply email me anything he wanted to work on either before or during our meetings, and we'd have no problems. I reminded him that I was a fourth-year graduate student in the English department, but he said, "I know, I know, but . . ." Finally I said, "Well, I'm here. Why not just meet today for two hours, and if it doesn't work for you, then you can find somebody else." He relented. I'm guessing it didn't hurt that after his initial excitement of being somewhere new, Millennium lay down and made himself comfortable while I stood my ground, cementing our right to be there.

During that first session, I helped the professor with something he had written in which he had confused "cooperation" with "corporation." I busted out my rusty Latin and told him that *opera* (work) was at the heart of the former, while *corpus* (body) was the etymological root of the latter. And so I have my classical training to thank, I think, for finally winning over the professor. We worked together several hours a week for the remainder of his time in New York.

I've heard nearly identical stories from other blind and visually impaired friends who show up for work (hired on the basis of their impressive résumés), only to be told, "I can't work with you." And then ushered right out the front door. These employers, righteous in their belief that a blind person could not possibly do the job, apparently worry not at all about calls to the authorities reporting discrimination, which suggests that many employers have not gotten the memo that discrimination against disabled people is, in fact, discrimination and unlawful.

The difficulty the blind working author faces is analogous to cultural biases that other minorities experience, and mirrors difficulties that blind (and disabled) people have in finding work. Historically, there have been a handful of manual labor jobs for the blind, collectively known as the "blind trades." We've encountered one of these already—piano tuning, the profession of the blind stripling in *Ulysses*.

My friend George Ashiotis, a musician and actor, trained as a "piano tech" after graduating high school in 1965. "I call it piano technology because it was more than tuning," he told me. In the two-year program "I learned how to tune, repair, and regulate pianos. We took them apart and put them back together." Piano tuning remains one of the oldest and most prestigious of the blind trades, which also include caning chairs and making mops. There weren't a lot of options for blind and visually impaired kids who did not have the inclination or ability to go to college. That is still largely true.

For George, who grew up in a working-class Greek household in Astoria, Queens, college was not a part of the conversation, though he told me that he probably would have gone if the technology had been in place. As a visually impaired kid, he had not been taught braille, and the text-to-speech software that so many of us rely on did not yet exist. Once it did become an option, George did eventually go to college. But that was after he spent a few years tuning pianos in a showroom as well as in private homes, including one fancy piano owned by a composer who lived in the Dakota (a historic apartment building on Central Park West, often remembered as the death place of John Lennon).

As an attractive young gay man, George was, it seemed, a popular visitor to the homes of some wealthy older gentlemen, and was invited from the piano room to the bedroom on one memorable occasion. Suffice to say, George provides a charming counterweight to the image of the sullen piano-tuning stripling in *Ulysses*. But this is a happy example of blind employment. In many cases, the prospects are bleak; many blind people who want to work end up on disability.

When Jim Knipfel lost his job in 2006, he sought employment with several New York City blind organizations and found that despite his long-running Slackjaw column (as well as having a memoir of the same name and several other books under his belt), despite his impressive résumé as a professional writer and years working at the *New York Press,* manual blind trade jobs were what these "employment services for the blind" had to offer him.

"For all the blather and platitudes about self-sufficiency and gainful employment," he wrote in a 2016 article, "nobody really seemed to be doing anything toward that end." Even so, he contacted all the NYC organizations, but heard back from only one—the only one in New York City, it seemed, that had job placement counselors on staff. He sent his résumé and explained his situation—"It all sounded very encouraging."[3]

Over the next three years they sent him on exactly two job interviews: the first was at a mop factory in a "desolate section" of NYC's outer boroughs. "The factory prided itself on hiring the disabled, particularly the blind, a point driven home when I noted all the streets leading to the sprawling factory building were lined with talking stoplights." Unfortunately, he was told by "the young and frighteningly energetic job placement specialist" that he was, in fact, "too blind" to make mops. "I was also informed (and this was a first) that I was not retarded enough to work there." Being a guy with a twisted sense of humor and a penchant for the absurd, Jim was disappointed. He had looked forward to telling people he worked in a mop factory.[14]

Next he went for an interview at a facility that made uniforms for the post office and military. It offered below-minimum-wage pay and was, in light of its use of industrial sewing machines, a rather surprising job for blind people. "In a massive windowless basement filled with what sounded to be a thousand pounding and whirring sewing machines, I was placed in front of a silent sewing machine to be interviewed by a middle-aged Asian woman. That interview, likewise, lasted five minutes or less. I was not told I was too blind, nor that I wasn't retarded enough. She simply changed the subject after a few preliminary questions, then walked me to the door."[15]

Funny enough, I think I spent some time with the very same interviewer a few years later. Having been an avid hand-sewer and designer of performance outfits, and having exhausted the string of adjunct job allotment for PhD hangers-on, I too did the blind employment parade. I too sat in front of one of these giant industrial sewing machines. And, despite the fact that I had a guide dog, I was allowed to actually give the sewing thing a whirl. I did my very best to aim a thread straight on a khaki bit of material, but as the woman kept asking if I could see the thread, and I had to admit "sort of," she thanked me and walked me to the door.

I wonder how many overeducated, undersighted blind people that woman has rejected through the years.

Shortly after his uniform factory interview, Jim was told by the organization that there was nothing more they could do for him, and his file was closed. But of course, as Jim recognizes, his experiences "were hardly unique among disabled Americans looking for work."[16]

So you see that the kind of troubles facing the characters in Jacob Twersky's novel in the forties did not change as much as we might like to think over the decades and into the ADA (Americans with Disabilities Act) era. I can't help but think that in denying Twersky's bleak depiction of blindness and blind people, our culture denied the stories that did not fit in with our happy notions of progress. They still don't. Ending his novel, as Twersky did, with one of the main characters begging for money in the subway in order to feed his family is not what we want out of our blind characters. I would argue that denying the multiplicity of lived blind experience—allowing only certain kinds of blind stories to be written by only certain kinds of blind authors—allows the real problems of employment and self-efficacy to be swept under the rug. As we've seen with so many societal ills—from child molestation to sexism in the workplace—not talking about something is a very good way of perpetuating it.

It might be useful here to consider poet and cyborg writer Jillian Weise's "triangulation theory" of disability and authorship. In a 2019 interview, she describes how some readers and editors seem to prefer a "triangulation" method when it comes to books about disability. In psychology, triangulation is a kind of manipulation tactic wherein one person will not speak directly to another, instead employing a third person to communicate with the second, thus forming a triangle. "In practice," says Weise, "this might be why books about disabled people garner far more reach than books by disabled people."

She offers as an example Ann Patchett's biography of Lucy

Grealy, the Irish American poet and memoirist who wrote *Autobiography of a Face*, about her battle with cancer and her resulting facial disfigurement: "We already had Grealy's autobiography. Why did we need Patchett's?"[7]

Weise's "triangulation" theory helps me to understand why there are so few professional blind writers in the world. This is not just about novelists, poets, or memoirists, but also about journalists. It seems to me crucial that blind and visually impaired journalists exist in order to help unravel stereotypes, biases, and discrimination.

It's stunning how many feel-good stories circulate on the Internet and in traditional media about blind people—little bursts of inspiration porn written and produced, almost exclusively, by sighted people. Similarly, stories about blind technology are almost always presented through rosy-tinted, uncritical lenses. As I hope I've shown in these pages, technology has been very good for blind people. However, a lot of ridiculous blind gadgets pop up around the Internet that strike my sighted friends as exciting, but get a skeptical "meh" from my blind friends. For example, a few months back, there was this "Smart Cane" that was getting a lot of media buzz; no fewer than five sighted friends posted links to articles about it on my feed. I clicked through and found pretty quickly that the device was basically a limited smartphone attached to a standard white cane. $499. Cane not included.[18]

Though I heard recently from a friend that the company is now including the cane, he also told me that you need a smartphone to take advantage of everything that the Smart Cane has to offer, like GPS. But in all the stories I read, there was just no critical thinking happening, so either you bought the cane and tried it out or you laughed and moved on. I feel very strongly that such articles should not be written by gullible sighted people, and therefore let me state plainly that we need more blind and visually impaired journalists. Full stop. Only when we are able to report our own stories can we hope to have evenhanded reporting on blindness and blind people.

I am not saying that all blind writers should write about blind stuff, but I do think sighted journalists should think twice about writing about blind people and our news and culture. As with acting, we might need a little affirmative action to ensure that blind writers gain the experience we need in order to tackle blind issues for major news outlets when they come around.

So allow me to direct news outlets to the resource DisabledWriters.com, which is "increasing disability diversity in journalism." There you will find blind and other writers with disabilities to write up your stories about disability. That would help things greatly. Perhaps it would mitigate the inspiration-porn impulse to put the singular disabled person on a pedestal to admire as something distinct from the rest. Perhaps having more blind journalists would also help stem the flow of stories about blind people who are otherworldly, astounding, unique, and nearly inhuman. The rallying cry of the disability movement says it perfectly: "Nothing about us without us!"

14.

The Secret Life of Art
and Accessibility

When it comes to the blind writer, artist, and musician, we see a trend that applauds with one hand while it crushes with the other: the spirit of art—that which transcends the senses—is beautifully symbolized by a lack of physical sight, but that very lack presents barriers for honing talent and for involvement in an artistic community. In other words, blind people's assumed ability to transcend the physical is often so revered that the technology and accommodations we need are neglected or denied, making it difficult for blind artists to have the same opportunities as our sighted peers.

One might think that the obvious artistic path for a person who cannot see would be music, and, of course, there have been extraordinary success stories in that field—Stevie Wonder and Ray Charles, to name just two. However, there are also many challenges to the life of a blind musical artist, especially one pursuing a classical career. In her memoir *Do You Dream in Color?,* Laurie Rubin writes about how she was denied the performance experience of her fellow graduate students at the Yale School of Music—"the only singer in the whole program in this position," and the whole reason for her being there in the first place: "If professionals were going to give a blind opera singer a chance, they would need proof that I had experience." She learned of the casting "oversight" in an email and confronted her instructor in studio class.

Laurie managed more reasonableness and eloquence than I can imagine mustering in this blood-boiling situation: "I'm not asking for your compliments or your admiration," she said, when the instructor patronizingly told her how they were all amazed by her. "I'm just asking for the one thing I came to this program to get, and that is opera experience. I think you're not giving the stage directors you hired enough credit." If they are the creative people they are supposed to be, Laurie argued, they can figure out together how to make her being onstage work. But her instructor wasn't having any part of this line of reason and stomped her down by bluntly replying, "Our director has been involved in the decision-making process, and he feels that he doesn't have the time or resources to work with you."[1]

This prejudice in the opera world creates yet another infuriating asymmetry. Opera loves melodrama, and so blindness as a trope fits in very nicely. Take, for example, the opera *Iolanta,* composed by Tchaikovsky and with a libretto based on a Danish story called "King René's Daughter." In it we meet a beautiful blind princess who has been walled away in a garden unaware that she is a princess or blind or beautiful. Of course a nice young man falls in love with her and teaches her that she is blind, and in learning that she is blind, she will be able to be "cured."

I asked Laurie about this opera in an email. She had performed a scene from it at one of her summers spent at the prestigious music camp Tanglewood years earlier. "The sad thing is that she gets her sight at the end of the opera," she said, knowing that I would join her in a virtual eyeroll—the old happy ending by way of cure—"and she lived happily ever after." But still, "the music is beautiful."

I mentioned that I'd heard a recent production at the Met

was supposed to be quite progressive, although a sighted soprano played the title role.

Laurie responded by saying, "Yeah, if the Met's version was so progressive, why not take the opportunity to hire a blind singer? I'm available."

As far as I can tell, professional companies have not exactly gone out of their way to find blind or visually impaired sopranos to play the part of Iolanta. As ever, blindness as a plot device seems agreeable, while the logistics of dealing with blind people is not. And if they won't even work to hire blind opera singers for the blind roles, when will they hire them at all?

Aside from the real or perceived difficulties of getting around the opera stage as a blind singer, much of the communication that makes playing in groups—from rock bands to orchestras—possible occurs through visual cues. If you're a blind musician you thus have a rather narrow playing field on which to succeed: you must be a brilliant solo performer or bandleader, and even if you can overcome the obstacles with your talent and drive, you must contend with the jokes.

Andrew Leland, a writer, editor, and radio producer, has RP. An episode of his podcast, *The Organist,*[2] alerted me to a 2018 clip from *Jimmy Kimmel Live* wherein the actor and director Donald Glover describes his interactions with Stevie Wonder regarding using a Wonder song for his TV show *Atlanta.* The freak-show aspect of communicating with a blind person begins with Glover relating the crazy notion of texting with Wonder, and when Wonder replies that he'd like to read the script, Glover puts emphasis on the word "read" to suggest that even this is surprising.

The ignorance regarding blind people and technology, coming from a relatively young guy like Glover—he's thirty-seven—is eye-opening. Judging by Kimmel's and the audience's responses, the energy that fuels their laughter seems to arise from the notion that Wonder, because of his blindness, must interact with the world in vastly different ways than they do.

Besides the fact that Wonder has been using cutting-age technology in his music for decades, he is also no stranger to scoring for film, as was brought to my attention by Leland in his podcast. "Journey Through the Secret Life of Plants" was created for the 1978 film *The Secret Life of Plants,* which itself was based on the best-selling and outlandish pop science book of the same name. I have to say that I love that book, full of pseudo-science and real science alike—some of which inspired amazing discoveries that have proved that plant communication, although largely chemical and between individuals of the same species, is real. That's a rabbit hole we, sadly, cannot go down here.

"Stevie Wonder's Journey Through the Secret Life of Plants" is a whimsical, outlandish, and worldly sonic extravaganza that was generally panned at the time, and has through the years been largely ignored or dismissed by critics and fans alike. In a 2019 retro-review of the double album sound track, the online music magazine *Pitchfork* put it this way: "In nearly any appreciation of Stevie Wonder's profound run of music, *Secret Life of Plants* serves as a page break, a bookend, the arid valley after the vertiginous peak of the beloved *Songs in the Key of Life.* In almost every assessment, it marks the end of the greatest run in pop music history."[3]

Yet the article points out that this wacky and misunderstood album was not a mistake or misstep on Wonder's part, but a deliberate attempt to do something really new and oddly personal—an endeavor that a lot of musicians with millions of expectant eyes on them would not have attempted.

There was nothing magic in the endeavor either, at least not when it came to the how. According to *Pitchfork,* Wonder would go in with a four-track recorder and headphones. In his left ear the producer explained what was happening on-screen, while in his right ear the engineer would count down the frames in the sequence, "leaving Wonder to sketch out the score."[4]

Also, the reviewer points out, "in exploring the neglected, ignored, seemingly inhuman aspects that society affixes to the plant kingdom, Wonder finds resonance between his botanical subject matter and the black experience."[5] The heart of the album seems to be contained in the title track's lyric, "What we see is insignificant."

In order to explore the unfathomable realms of the invisible, Wonder employed state-of-the-art musical equipment, including, according to *Pitchfork,* two $40,000 Yamaha GX-1 synthesizers, which underlines the point that if there was ever a person—blind or sighted—to embrace current and experimental technologies, it is Stevie Wonder. So it's not only infuriating but laughable to hear Donald Glover peddling jokes about texting with Stevie Wonder. Every blind person I know has a smartphone with speech and braille output technology built in. I got one in 2011, and I was definitely not among the first.

Beyond the texting and the reading, Glover gets further mileage out of jokes about Wonder's ability to "watch" television: "And I'm like, how'd he do that?" says Glover, speaking of Wonder's reaction to the first cut of the show. "It's like his album covers. They're so good. Who's telling him? Or what?"[6]

Contrary to popular belief, blind people do not live in a bubble. We are perfectly attuned to the visual aspects of the world we live in. That said, I think of Wonder's 1972 album, *Talking Book,* which featured his name and the title in braille on the front cover, and a secret braille message to his blind fans on the inside flap over the credits.

I asked my friend Frank Senior, a jazz vocalist, if he remembered buying that album as a blind young person, and he said, "Oh, yeah, man, that was my first year at NYU studying music education." He told me he would have bought the album no matter what, because Stevie was everything back then. But the braille message was his icebreaker with his sighted fellow students: "I'd say, hey, you know that's braille on that album, and they'd be like, damn, really?"

I picture Frank's coolness factor (which is considerable) rising exponentially when he read Stevie's secret message to sighted friends:

Here is my music,
it is all I have
to tell you how I
feel. Know that your
love keeps my
love strong.
Stevie[7]

The message, like the title and his name on the front cover, is in grade 2 braille, which means it employs all the contractions that make standard braille more compact. So this is for real braille readers! Unfortunately, the braille message was lost in the CD era, and I understand that the 2000 album pressing added an ink-print translation; the taste of inaccessibility must have been too much for certain sighted people to accept any longer.

Alongside braille, the talking book—a full-text audio recording for blind readers—was part of Stevie Wonder's literacy toolkit, as it was part of mine and those of just about every blind reader since the 1930s when the Library for the Blind began recording books onto vinyl for blinded World War I vets.[8]

Of course, Kimmel does not think of *Talking Book* or any of Wonder's album covers, but rather of his love interests. He continues with the inevitable, "Yeah you know you see him with these women that he's married to or dating where you're like 'wow, she's beautiful.'"[9] This reminds me of how people always like to inform me that Alabaster is handsome, as if I couldn't tell, or as if a blind person dating a good-looking sighted person is some kind of waste. But Kimmel and Glover are almost out of time, so Glover delivers the segment's punchline: "Yeah, or just like touching the TV screen, and being like this is funny."[10] If I were Stevie Wonder, I'd be like, "Dude, give me my music back."

It's unbelievable to me that jokes about Stevie Wonder's blindness still have so much currency. But there's the rub of being a blind person in the entertainment industry; there are countless talking star-heads that will throw you under the bus for a cheap laugh. I experienced the same thing when I was doing comedy. Comedians love busting out off-the-cuff jokes prompted by fellow performers.

Regarding this whole blind joke thing, it cannot be said that we are innocent. Before we leave the annoying Glover/Kimmel bit, I should point out that it begins with a reference to Stevie Wonder's birthday party where he calls out Glover (who's in the audience) to join him on "Superstition" by saying, "I see Donald Glover's here tonight."[11] That, of course, gets a big laugh, and I should admit that I have, in my years of performing, plucked more than one of these low-hanging fruits. It's hard to resist the impulse to capitalize on the sighted person's doubts and fears regarding our prophetic vision.

However, I would argue that these jokes need to stay with us. As a white person, I would never dare to make a racial joke, but someone like the wildly successful comedian Ali Wong can make all the hilarious jokes she likes about Asian Americans (albeit in the service of ultimately poking fun at the hypocrisies and silliness of white America regarding Asians), because she is Chinese Vietnamese American. That seems to me to be a good rule of thumb that needs to be carried over to blind people jokes. And it might serve to influence non-blind authors, actors, and producers to step off the blind-trope train for a while.

Returning to this crazy notion of texting with a blind person, I suppose we have not yet done a good enough job of getting the word out about how integral technology is to our success, and also how blind technology both benefits from and fuels new technology generally. As I've said before, many of us began relying on technology long before our sighted friends and colleagues did.

In 1976, Stevie Wonder saw a segment on NBC's *Today* show, in which a blind man demonstrated a reading machine invented by the futurist author and entrepreneur Ray Kurzweil that used an early version of optical character recognition (OCR) software. Wonder contacted Kurzweil, and became the reading machine's first official customer.[12]

I did not have access to the incredibly expensive Kurzweil reading machine until the mid-nineties, when I found one in the Bobst Library at NYU. It was one of the pieces of equipment in the little padded cell that I shared with the other blind and visually impaired students. A Kurzweil reading machine was, at the time, basically a very large stand-alone scanner (probably weighing twenty pounds or so) loaded with OCR software as well as text-to-speech software for reading and operating the device using a number keypad. I would go to the circulation desk to order books to be pulled from the shelves, and then bring them down to the little room to scan. I placed the books, page by page, onto the bed of the scanner, and prayed that there wasn't any underlining or marginalia, which would often make important passages unreadable. Besides the less-than-perfect abilities of OCR software back then, it took a long time to scan, and it was not easy at that time to integrate the result into a computer, where searching for passages and copying and pasting bits for note taking would be possible. This is why I'm so excited about clean, ready-to-read ebooks.

I still use Kurzweil on an almost daily basis, but now it is a powerful (and still relatively expensive) piece of software that I use with a sleek portable scanner. I use it to scan physical books and, more often, to download ebooks from Bookshare.org.

Through the years when I've mentioned Kurzweil to certain friends with an interest in electronic music, they immediately recognized the name. Once, when Kurzweil visited Stevie Wonder at his studio, Wonderland, Stevie challenged Kurzweil to "create a computerized instrument with the desired deep sounds of acoustic instruments, with the powerful controls of computerized instruments." Kurzweil employed "pattern recognition and machine learning" to accomplish the task, and the result was the Kurzweil 250 music synthesizer.[13]

Back to the reading machine—it seems that Stevie Wonder was a proselytizer as well as a user. In his afterword to the 2004 edition of *Brother Ray* (published shortly after Charles's death), its coauthor, David Ritz, mentions the gift in connection to the books he collaborated on with other musicians after the Ray Charles volume, which was his first. Over the years Ritz would hand Charles those books written with artists such as Marvin Gaye, Aretha Franklin, and BB King, and Charles would read them using the reading machine Wonder had given him.[14] In the days before ebooks, this was a blind person's best way of accessing books as soon as they were published, without waiting around for a sighted reader. It was also out of the range of most people's financial resources for decades.

The language that people use to describe both Stevie Wonder and Ray Charles seems always to be dripping with awe that is nearly always couched in terms of their blindness: On the one hand, how amazing they are despite the blindness, and on the other, how their blindness makes it possible for them to transcend the banality of the sighted world and get to the heart of music. Never mind all the hard work, endless practice, and especially in the case of Wonder, technology, that makes their art what it is. The idea that these blind musicians are set apart is so pervasive that it's difficult to read about them without cringing.

In his 2010 biography of Stevie Wonder, Mark Ribowsky writes that Wonder's music "could only have been made by eyes that 'saw' more than ours did, so far did it come from an 'inner vision' and so far did it carry into the universe."[5]

There's no doubt that Stevie Wonder is an amazing artist, but the overblown and pat metaphors of insight make it very difficult to have serious conversations about what blind people actually need, which Wonder made clear during the 2016 Grammys. He got a huge laugh by playfully taunting his fellow presenters with not being able to read what was in the envelope because it was in braille. But before he read the winner, he spoke plainly and distinctly: "We need to make every single thing accessible to every single person with a disability."[6]

_____

It would seem a no-brainer that blind people would have potential careers in other sound-oriented arts besides music. Yet, historically, sound recording and editing software (often referred to as DAWs [digital audio workstations]) has been largely, ironically, extremely visual, effectively barring access to a sound-arts career for most visually impaired and blind people. My friend Andy Slater has recognized the odd dearth of sound artists in the world, and is working on remedying that through the creation of the Society of Visually Impaired Sound Artists (SoVISA).

SoVISA's manifesto proclaims: "Through our efforts we will spawn new artists and composers and introduce the sonic arts to blind and visually impaired people," because "we find it curious that the number of sighted sound artists outweighs that of the blind ones dramatically." SoVISA demands that art education for the blind includes sound-based works and artists, that museums provide more funding for sound-based works, and that accessible audio and recording technology be more available to blind artists.[17]

Though Andy has exhibited his work in many prestigious museums and galleries around the country and beyond, he still faces challenges in his daily pursuit of new skills. At the beginning of his studies for a master's degree in sound arts and industry at Northwestern University, he encountered many administrative and technical difficulties. For example, the computer that he was supposed to use had not had the accessible software loaded, and so he spent his first two months unable to participate. He got plenty of "I'm sorrys" from the IT department, but no one could explain why this simple thing had not been done, especially since he'd made the request before the semester began.

Thus it is not surprising that Andy's work is not just really cool, but also often an in-your-face form of activism and disability justice. He calls it "radical blindness," and many of his soundscapes involve "activating" a space by banging his white cane around, as well as clapping, stomping, and using clickers (small boxes, often used in dog training, that make a rather loud, sharp sound). In 2019 Andy and two fellow blind sound artists put up a performance installation at the Art Institute of Chicago involving a cacophony of disabled voices (including mine) called "Is It Cool That We're Here?" The intelligibility of each voice surfaces out of the jumbled, pitch-shifted recorded and electronic soup, and then fades back under. One memorable sound bite seems to be addressed to a museum guard: "Are you afraid that my cane is going to knock something over?"

"That performance was totally punk and totally radical because the whole thing was a critique of museums and art," Andy told me in an interview I did with him for a *Catapult* piece called "The Brain-Smashing, Pity-Bashing Art of Blind Punk." Ironically, "Is It Cool That We're Here?" took place in a huge marble room (what used to be the Chicago Stock Exchange), in a building containing amazing works of art. "And they never ever have anything to do with sound."[18]

As someone who dabbles in sound art—I've created soundscapes for my own writing as well as sound tracks for half a dozen wacky art films with my longtime collaborator and former bandmate David Lowe—I am a member of SoVISA. I haven't done a lot of sound recording and editing recently, but when I did that kind of work I used Pro Tools. I learned this beast of a DAW, as well as how to use an Apple Mac (I'd always been a Windows person), with the help of Marc Wagnon, an instructor at what was then the Music School at Lighthouse International in New York City, which has since become an independent organization—the Filomen M. D'Agostino Greenberg Music School.

Marc is not blind, but he taught at the music school for many years in many capacities, from audio editing to percussion to running the jazz ensemble. I first met him when I decided to take drum lessons. I was never the greatest drummer, which was brought home to me one day when I went for my lesson and found this little kid whaling away. It was the five-year-old piano prodigy Matthew Whitaker, who draws inevitable comparisons to Stevie Wonder, and, at age ten, opened for Wonder's induction into the Apollo Theater Hall of Fame. As an adult, Whitaker tours the world playing jazz with his band, but when I met him in Marc's drum room around 2006, his feet could barely reach the pedals, and I said to Marc, "Damn, that little kid's better than me." Marc was noncommittal: "No . . . Not yet."

Marc helped to organize a petition asking Pro Tools to make its software accessible, and when they did, I began to learn it. I would probably have to relearn it now, but I got pretty good at it. Once I gave a demonstration of how I used VoiceOver (Apple's text-to-speech program that's built into all their products) to navigate a visually complex project with more than twenty tracks for a group of students at NYU's Tandon School of Engineering. They were impressed. Interacting with so many tracks and nested tools is daunting even for sighted people, but for a blind person, a lot more memorizing needs to happen—you can't simply see that a track is selected for recording, for example, but must remember or check by tapping around. But the added layers of difficulty are welcome, given the power that comes from accessibility.

With accessible technology, careers for blind and visually impaired sound artists (as well as sound engineers) are very possible, and yet there are still relatively few of us making careers in these fields. Things are changing rapidly, though. I'm personally excited to try out Reaper, a DAW that has been embraced and enhanced by blind programmers, making it accessible in novel ways. For example, being able to interact with each track using a braille display, which allows for a spatial reference that is more akin to the way the visual tracks are laid out, and being tactile, the information does not compete with the audio that's being recorded and played.[19]

Accessibility in the arts thus has two sides: access to the tools and resources for making the art, and access to the artworks themselves. "Accessibility is very important to me and frankly should be to all artists," Andy Slater explains in the exhibit program for a live performance of *Unseen Reheard,* which is a two-sided album of sonic spaces containing such tracks as "Tap and Roll," "Paralytic Transit," "Tunnel to Orlando," and "Hauntings (Shape of an Echo)."[20]

As a disabled artist, Andy not only is aware of access for himself and other blind people, but also thinks about access barriers to his own art: "How can I make my work accessible to those who cannot hear it?" The answer is a noble and extravagant attempt at translation. "I have written descriptions for every piece on the *Unseen Reheard* album," writes Andy: "poetic, onomatopoetic, metaphoric, or however you accept it. Since all of the sounds represented in this work were recorded out in a world full of referential material, there is no shortage of ways to describe the passage/narrative/composition of the sounds." Here are some examples:

Something watches the starlings and concludes they are in fact metallic.

Feet rush out the door into the passageway. Startled by the bang and the running shoes a group look away. The cane exceeds up the limestone to observe the cracks.

Fighting crabs dispense echoes throughout the courtyard the wind guiding their migration.

Regurgitated water clogged with static electrons.
The shadows of voices bubble beneath.[21]

As with all translations, there will always be something lost and something gained. Embracing the challenge of verbal description for audio beautifully illustrates how translation from one sense to another can push art into new realms. Accessibility does not always have to be a sterile box checked to be ADA compliant, but can and should provide the tools to expand the realms of art and accessibility for all.

15.

The Scylla and Charybdis of Stigma and Superpowers

When I first saw *Star Wars* as a kid, I could see normally. Besides dressing up like Princess Leia for Halloween and getting quite a bit of attention for my resemblance to her, I remember being fascinated by the Force, a power felt rather than seen. From his blindfolded lightsaber training to the final exciting Death Star blowup, Luke Skywalker did well when he couldn't see. As Obi-Wan Kenobi said, "Your eyes can deceive you. Don't trust them."

So perhaps it's no surprise that the director of *The Last Jedi,* Rian Johnson, played with the idea of making Luke blind. In a 2017 *Rolling Stone* cover story, he's quoted as saying, "What if Luke is blind? What if he's, like, the blind samurai?" adding that this was before the blind warrior Chirrut showed up kicking ass in *Rogue One.*[1]

Chirrut the blind warrior, Zatoichi the blind swordsman, and Daredevil the blind superhero all exploit a sighted person's suspicions that their eyes get in the way, and that, in combat, using other senses gives you an edge. "We allegedly possess an unfair advantage that we could use against the sighted, hearing the secrets in their sighs, smelling their fear," writes Georgina Kleege in *Sight Unseen.* "The blind are either supernatural or subhuman, alien or animal. We are not only different but dangerous."[2]

Through the centuries, the idea of poetic and prophetic compensation has been translated into the superhero realm, wherein the blind person's other senses become potentialities for strange supernatural powers that far outstrip those of sight. Thus the expectations placed on us are all about those superpowers, while the ordinary aspects of being human are forgotten. As Kleege argues, when sighted people's low expectations are defied by a singular (as they understand them) blind person, "they are compelled to reinvent the ancient myths about compensatory powers, supersensory perception. The sixth sense, second sight, third eye. We are supposed to have both extra-accurate hearing and perfect pitch, more numerous and more acute taste buds, a finer touch, a bloodhound's sense of smell."[3]

How often people say things to me like, "Your sense of smell must be so good." "Your hearing is amazing." "Do you want to feel my face?" On the other hand, it's so rare that people ask me what I do for work, that I can sometimes get a little over-excited, like a puppy whose owner's attention has finally turned back to him after a long conversation with another human. However, when I tell them I'm a writer, they often say, "Good for you," in a way that suggests not sarcasm, as it might if it were said to a sighted person, but rather "How cute! That's really neat that a blind person does stuff," and is often followed by an upper-arm pat.[4]

To hear the direction from which people's voices come (and if they are smiling or frowning), to distinguish objecthood by touch and the size and character of rooms and streets by sound, are such obvious phenomena when you are blind, that the surprise expressed by sighted people at such things is at once amusing and alarming. So I feel vindicated, excited, and inspired by perceptual psychologist Lawrence Rosenblum's *See What I'm Saying,* in which we find the seemingly fantastic feats of the superblind alongside related abilities of the general population.

As Rosenblum demonstrates in his book's many examples (including Daniel Kish and his sonar-using colleagues), what we often think of as "superpowers" are really just expansions of what humans do unconsciously all the time: "Our less-conscious brains are absorbing a profusion of sights, sounds, and smells using processes that seem superhuman."[5]

Due mainly to lack of incentive and practice, sighted people may not exploit their sense of smell or attune themselves to the possibilities of echolocation, but that does not mean they are not capable of learning. It also does not mean that a blind person is just born with these faculties; rather, the faculties, in either case, must be used, practiced, honed. Humans may be born with language regions in the brain ready for action, but if they never hear (or see, in the case of sign language) a single word, if they are not introduced to language by their parents or others when they are young, they will languish. Humans are products of their environment and expectations, which is why the idea of superpowers is so detrimental to blind people. A blind person has more reason to exploit her human echolocation skills, but that does not mean she does not benefit from learning and practice.

"We all have an onboard sonar system and a type of absolute pitch; and we all can perceive speech from seeing and even touching faces," writes Rosenblum. "What's more, we engage many of these skills all day long. What largely distinguishes the expert perceiver from the rest of us is the same thing that gets us from here to Carnegie Hall: practice."[6]

I find the idea that all of us have unconscious faculties ready to be exploited very comforting. It challenges the stereotype of the superblind by suggesting that, if given the chance, we can all develop extraordinary powers. This is particularly important for blind people, who often find themselves navigating between extremely low and extremely high expectations.

In his 2011 memoir, *Blind,* Belo Cipriani tells how, after being violently thrown into the world of the blind and while still adjusting to it, he found himself facing the superblind stereotype: "The 'Super Blind' make it challenging sometimes for one to mingle with the visual community, because people expect those abilities from the rest of the blind family. At one point, I even had some guy at the bus stop ask me if I could hear his heartbeat."[7]

Hearing heartbeats on city streets from a distance of a couple of feet notwithstanding, blind people can do amazing things with respect to sighted people's everyday experience, but so can concert violinists with respect to non-musicians. One does not need to be a Glenn Gould to be a proficient pianist; one needs only to work at it consistently.

In addition to being a research professor in the field of perceptual psychology, Rosenblum is a dedicated amateur classical guitarist, which perhaps makes him more attuned to the importance of practice than most. When I interviewed him for my magazine *Aromatica Poetica,* I asked him about a scent-tracking experiment in which students don blinders, noise-canceling headphones, and gloves in order to follow a scent trail on their hands and knees—specifically, a rope that had been soaked in peppermint oil. The participants were amazed to find that they could do it.

"That leads me to wonder," I said, "is that more about selective attention or is there kind of a rewiring? At what point does it turn from being attention to actually changing your brain?"

Like any good professor, he reworked my question to be a bit more precise: "Well, that's a deep philosophical question because, in theory, anything you do with your brain subtly changes your brain. But I understand what you're saying. So the question might be, is it a long-term change or a short-term change?"[8]

Our perceptions can change in a matter of seconds. For example, when you close your eyes in a crowded place, you are likely to sense things that had previously been out of your conscious reach. I mentioned this to a friend at a cocktail party recently and he tried it. "I'm closing my eyes right now," he told me, "and I can hear a conversation behind me very clearly that I'd not heard a moment ago!"

Obviously, in cases like this, you are not effecting long-term change in the brain, but if you continue to practice, things do begin to change. "It's like learning any new skill," Rosenblum told me, "whether you're learning a musical instrument or learning a sporting task. First, you need to do the basics of kind of getting yourself into the mode. It's the idea of warming up, right? So when you're first learning a musical instrument, you really have to warm up for a long time in order to get the sound you want out of the instrument, but then once you've gotten it, you don't really need to warm up anymore. And I think that's probably the most intuitive kind of phenomenology we have of short-term plasticity going into long-term plasticity."[9]

Thus, getting good at being blind takes practice. In *The Sound of the Walls* Jacob Twersky tells how, at his school for the blind (New York Institute in the Bronx, which still exists), many boys picked on other boys they called "blindish"—"those who had not learned to use well their other senses, who bumped into things, groped, shuffled."[10] I mentioned this to Alabaster recently, and he very astutely said, "Oh right, so being blind means you have a skill set."

I'm afraid I'm blindish—at least when it comes to mobility—but I'm working on it. A few years back, when I first began venturing out with my white cane, I would sometimes stop at a corner, to find out what that corner felt like without sight, alone, and just armed with my hearing and my prosthetic feeling arm. People would often say, "Do you need help crossing the street?" and I would respond, "Oh, no thank you. I'm just practicing."

I never got a reply from that except for maybe a "huh." I

take from their lack of response that the idea of practicing with a cane is foreign to sighted people. The assumption seems to be that we go blind, are handed a white stick, and either walk into traffic or not, as if the shift is as abrupt as Matt Murdock's transformation into Daredevil—lose sight, gain super senses, including radar, just like that!

I was trapped for a long time—I still am, to some extent—in that way of thinking and it crippled my ability to adapt. As I lost more and more of my vision, I became more and more self-conscious about how bad my mobility skills were. Why can't I zoom around like the blind kids I used to see at the Lighthouse in NYC? Why did I just walk into that wall? Why, if my hearing is so awesome, can I not perceive where the subway doors are opening? Why am I so scared to venture out by myself?

Because I did not realize, until recently, that all these things come with time and effort, I just told others and myself, "I suck at being blind." Only after reading countless memoirs, like Belo Cipriani's, in which I learned how much work he put into getting good at being blind after suddenly losing his sight, and through learning about neuroplasticity from people like Rosenblum, am I beginning to formulate a new attitude: I may be superblindish now, but I hope someday to be full-fledged blind.

———

The problem with being considered and compared to superheroes is that the quotidian becomes heroic and circumscribed by expectations at the same time. Getting out of bed is celebrated, walking to the store an achievement, but if the blind dare to speak out about social issues or have children, then sighted people from social workers to the press renege on the "super" status and find the words and deeds not impossible, not heroic, but dangerous, wrongheaded, misguided, misinformed, and so on.

During World War I, Helen Keller took a message of peace into America's heartland. It did not go well: "The attitude of the press was maddening. It seems to me difficult to imagine anything more fatuous and stupid than their comments on anything I say touching public affairs. So long as I confine my activities to social service and the blind, they compliment me extravagantly, calling me the 'archpriestess of the sightless,' 'wonder woman,' and 'modern miracle,' but when it comes to a discussion of a burning social or political issue, especially if I happen to be, as I so often am, on the unpopular side, the tone changes completely. They are grieved because they imagine I am in the hands of unscrupulous persons who take advantage of my afflictions to make me a mouthpiece for their own ideas."[11]

Thus, the paradox of the superblind has been felt for quite some time. We feel the social expectations to be very low, while those for super-sensing abilities are ridiculously high. We are citizens, it seems, of another country, planet, universe of the blind, and to venture out of the imposed bubble and participate in our society fully and with critical eyes is supposed to be quite beyond our capacities. In denying us opinions regarding the world's many and great problems, sighted people often extend their doubts and mistrust of our abilities to the most natural aspects of humanity.

With so many superblind in the media, and so few normals, it is very difficult for blind people to have granted to them the same sort of expectations granted the sighted—expectations that a majority of people have for their lives: a good job, a happy family, and healthy kids with promising futures of their own. How often have you seen or read about a blind character who is also a mother? Or, to put it more strongly, a mother who just happens to be blind?

The dearth of such representations leads to doubts in the

minds of our society and unfair pressures on blind parents. And the lack of blind parents in our collective consciousness is perhaps responsible for such nightmares as blind women being confronted by social workers in the hospital just after giving birth. My friend Michelle Kleinberg had just this experience, as she writes in her memoir-in-progress. "I was taken aback," she said of the moment when a social worker waltzed into her room, announced herself as being from Children's Services, and proceeded to interrogate her about how she planned to care for her new baby: "Did I have anyone to help me? Am I in a good relationship with my husband? And what was my support system? Naïve me, I thought they did this for all the patients—not knowing they only did this for patients they were unsure could properly care for their children."

Michelle's experience of discrimination is not uncommon, and unfortunately, it is sometimes factions within the blind community that bolster such misleading stereotypes. In 2016, the Foundation Fighting Blindness (FFB), an organization that works to raise huge sums of money for retinal disease research, initiated its #HowEyeSeeIt campaign, which encouraged sighted people to don blindfolds and make videos of themselves doing simple tasks. These videos were no doubt hilarious—people trying to clean their houses blindfolded, drive, care for their children, and so on, without using their eyes. While their underlying motivation to get the message out about the urgent need for funding to find cures for some types of blindness is undeniably important (and could even benefit me someday), the result was upsetting to many blind people, who felt that it fueled fears of blindness and exacerbated skepticism about the abilities of blind people.

"In particular, suggesting that it is difficult or impossible for blind parents to care for their children is false and irresponsible," said Mark A. Riccobono, president of the National Federation of the Blind (NFB). "As a blind father of three children who also happens to be married to a blind person, I can say unequivocally that, with nonvisual techniques, we can, and do, capably parent thriving children every day. Yet children have been removed from the custody of blind parents solely because of misconceptions about their ability to care for them, without any actual proof of abuse or neglect, and the #HowEyeSeeIt campaign threatens to worsen this already grave problem."[12]

It cannot be stated too strongly that if we can be superheroes, we can also be parents.

———

Considering the ocularcentrism of our culture, which denies us many basic human rights and undermines our abilities, it is no wonder that so many of us fear the look of being blind more than blindness itself. Like me and so many others, Jacob Twersky wanted to pass as sighted: "I did not want any kind of guide. I wanted to pass as much as possible as one of the seeing— without a dog, without a cane, with my head held normally, with my eyes open."[13]

I can certainly relate. Throughout my twenties, before I got paired with my first guide dog, I refused to use a cane. Even though walking around at night was scary and dangerous, I still refused the cane. Even when I knew that it was stupid and that I should really use the cane, which I even began to carry in my bag, I would not pull out that stigmatized object. I'd just hold my breath and do my best to avoid bumping into people and to follow the street lamps in as near to a straight line as I could.

It's so glaring to me now that so many of us fear the look of blindness more than we fear for our lives; I think that is a huge part of why I felt the need to write this book. Being blind offers challenges, no doubt, but I believe I do not exaggerate when I say that one of the biggest challenges is throwing off the shackles of stigma.

Ray Charles summed up his refusal to look blind thus: "Now it's important that you understand that there were three things I never wanted to own when I was a kid: a dog, a cane, and a guitar. In my brain, they each meant blindness and help-lessness. (Seems like every blind blues singer I'd heard about was playing the guitar.)"[4]

So instead of carrying a cane or getting a guide dog, he worked to memorize the streets like he would a braille score: "You memorize five bars first . . . then another five . . . then maybe ten, until you have the entire thing straight in your head."[5]

Yet, much as he ignores the subject, Charles did use help throughout his performing life, though you wouldn't know it from how he talks. In the afterword to his autobiography, writ-ten by his coauthor, David Ritz, we learn that Charles received help entering and exiting the stage: "From the back door I see them leading him out. He is shaking. From afar, his sunglasses look like a bandage hiding some mysterious pain. When he comes closer, the glasses appear to be sewn into his face."[6]

I must admit I find this very comforting, as I always prefer a helping arm to get to the mic these days. I guess I don't like looking blind when it comes to performing except on my own terms—I mean, I fear the discomfort of banging around with my cane in front of pitying sighted spectators. I'm not proud of this anxiety and I hope one day to disarm it, but I acknowledge its existence as a holdover from the old "I don't want to look blind" mentality.

Speaking of "looking blind," let's talk about those sun-glasses for a moment. "We are dependent on eye contact," writes Ritz; "we seek approval in visual expression. . . . With Ray, there are only his sunglasses. And they tell you nothing. If you are uncertain to begin with, his mere physical presence will make you doubly nervous."[7]

Even people who worked with Ray Charles on a daily basis were intimidated. One employee said, "I always write down what I'm going to say or else I'm speechless. When he looks at me, I freeze. It's like he can see through me."[8]

Yes, I like this effect that sunglasses have on sighted people. I know a lot of blind people don't like to wear sunglasses because it feeds into stereotypes, but in recent years I have taken to wearing them in many social situations and for virtually all performances. Sometimes they are small and purple with silver frames; other times they are big and mirrored with flower frames. It's pretty easy to fake eye contact with sunglasses on, as I demonstrated before an audience once by swiveling my head in the direction of each nervous titter.

Returning to the other accoutrement of blindness, the white cane—its adoption seems particularly treacherous for those whose vision loss is incomplete, spotty, or degenerating. As Stephen Kuusisto tells it in his first memoir, *Planet of the Blind,* he inherited his horror of the white cane and dread of the stigma of blindness from his mother: "Raised to know I was blind but taught to disavow it, I grew bent over like the dry tinder grass. I couldn't stand up proudly, nor could I retreat. I reflected my mother's complex bravery and denial and marched everywhere at dizzying speeds without a cane. Still, I remained ashamed of my blind self, that blackened dolmen. The very words blind and blindness were scarcely to be spoken around me. I would see to this by my exemplary performance. My mother would avoid the word, relegating it to the province of cancer."[9]

It never helps that the complex of social workers, mobility

instructors, and aids for blind people increased so quickly to be an outgrowth of unattractive, uncool state systems. "A black sedan stops in front of our house," writes Kuusisto, "and a heavy woman climbs out with the help of the driver. Then she unfolds her white cane and makes her way to our door. My mother is roused both by a horror of blindness and incipient hostility for bureaucracy. Who are they to say her son is blind? He mustn't be seen in the company of a blind social worker—the stigma might be impossible to erase."[20]

In the case of so many with RP, the degeneration is so slow as to cause one to doubt, at each stage, if one really is blind enough to need any part of the organizational blind complex. In her memoir *Now I See You* (2014), Nicole Kear begins her tale with her reluctant acceptance to train with the dreaded white cane. On a virtually deserted street in Brooklyn, she fusses with a disguise, as her mobility instructor patiently waits. "I'd suited up with hat, hood, and glasses," writes Kear, "and at her direction, I'd taken the package she'd given me earlier out of my bag, rooting through boxes of animal crackers, broken crayons, and wet wipes. It was a tight white bundle roughly the size and shape of a microphone, though it weighed less, its five tubular pieces made from ultralight aluminum and held together with a black rubber band. I clutched it tightly in my right palm, as if it might come to life at any moment and attack me."[21]

She was still, after twelve years of almost complete denial as her RP worsened, not ready, but as a new mother, she would do it "for the kids." "Vanity, pride, and fear were formidable opponents but my sense of maternal duty was stronger."[22]

Kear finally unfurled her cane, and after peering at it with her sunglasses raised, she returned the shades to her face and said to Esperanza, her mobility instructor, "It makes this more authentic, right? Makes me seem more blind," to which she received a silent rebuke: "You are blind. You're only pretending not to be."[23]

Although I have not always felt this way, I now love my white cane, which, you should know, is named Moses! While it's true that I don't like banging around onstage, Moses is usually with me in the limelight and figures in many favorite photos. Alabaster and I never agreed who came up with this moniker, both of us wanting to take credit for coining the name that magically transforms the lowly government-issue red-and-white-reflector-taped object into a staff of power that conjures the parting of the endless seas of New York City pedestrians. I was probably the one who suggested it, but that was only because I'd gleaned the idea elsewhere. In his 1999 memoir, *Slackjaw,* Jim Knipfel reluctantly admits the usefulness of the white cane, telling a friend, "Everybody parts in front of me like the fucking Red Sea, that's for damn sure."[24]

Jim also took his time learning to accept the white cane. Before he embraced it as useful and inevitable, he was groping his way home one night and kicked an old man's dog. Naturally, thinking the careless passerby wasn't paying attention, the old man started yelling at Jim, who, feeling guilty, pulled the folded-up cane out of his bag. Jim explained, "I'm blind, sir. I didn't see the dog, and it was my fault."[25]

The old man began to cry, and Jim felt like a jerk. But I get it. People automatically think so little of you when they see the white cane, that it is not easy, having been a sighted person with all the stupid prejudices that come along with that state of being, to embrace the stigma.

For many years, I felt that whipping out the white cane would irrevocably launch me into the realm of the blind, and I did not want to go there. Even if my movements were limited, even if I avoided going out at night alone, even if I recognized that my life would have been better and easier with it, the look of being blind was just too terrible to support. Blind organizations did such a wonderful job of getting the word out about the white cane that over the course of the twentieth century, it quickly became not only a means of safe travel for the blind but also, ironically, a powerful symbol of helplessness in the eyes of many sighted people. Though it is incredibly useful, the white cane is also incredibly stigmatic.

Erving Goffman's influential 1963 sociological study, *Stigma,* opens with an explanation of how the word "stigma" comes to us from the Greeks, "who were apparently strong on visual aids." The stigma was a sign cut or burnt into the flesh of an individual in order to expose that person as "a slave, a criminal, or a traitor—a blemished person, ritually polluted, to be avoided, especially in public places."[26] Later, Goffman describes how the stigma, especially regarding disability, is the only thing that "normals" are able to see of an individual, so that "we believe the person with a stigma is not quite human."[27]

When it comes to blindness in particular, Goffman recognizes how "the perceived failure to see may be generalized into a gestalt of disability, so that the individual shouts at the blind as if they were deaf or attempts to lift them as if they were crippled. Those confronting the blind may have a whole range of belief that is anchored in the stereotype."[28]

The white cane is a stigmatized emblem with such universal recognition and power that simply holding it can make you blind. My dear friends David Lowe and Caroline Kasnakian are a couple not unlike Alabaster and myself—sighted guy, blind/visually impaired girl (with doctoral degree).[29] Once, while visiting the Eiffel Tower in Paris, Caroline handed David her white cane in order to button up her overcoat. Standing there, perfectly sighted, David witnessed another tourist walk up to him with his phone and proceed to take a video of him, the ostensible blind person, by unsubtly running his lens up and down his body. We'll never know for sure what attracted that tourist to the image, but what can be said with certainty is that, for him, the sight of a blind guy holding a white cane atop the Eiffel Tower was at least as film-worthy as the view.

Alabaster tells me that rather often when we are walking swiftly down the street, I holding Moses, both of us wearing mirrored sunglasses, looking straight ahead, people will jump out of our way, often with terrified looks on their faces because apparently one white cane can signify blindness for two!

Yet, strangely, Alabaster has also witnessed the opposite, wherein gaggles of young people standing outside bars and restaurants will look at us coming, look at the cane, look at us, and stand completely still, forcing Alabaster to do a little jostling and me to use Moses as a weapon, smacking ankles and shins as we barrel through.

Jim Knipfel, who has experienced the same phenomenon, suggests that this "stubborn new militancy" may have something to do with the ubiquity of the superblind in the imaginations of younger people—the blind characters we have now are superheroes or martial artists, and have no use for the white mobility cane. Indeed, in recent years, members of the Harry Potter generation have asked me if my cane is a magic wand or a sorcerer's staff. I have encouraged this line of thinking by adorning Moses with a jewel and a Chinese dragon scrunchie, but it does seem clear that the lack of recognition with regard to the cane's true (practical) powers is problematic. As Jim puts it: "If fewer and fewer people recognize the meaning, what use does the cane maintain as a symbol directed at the sighted? It seems the cane, and with it the blind themselves are once again becoming invisible."[30]

Of course, the mobility cane serves two main purposes in our modern society: to warn sighted people of a blind person coming and to warn a blind person of objects and level changes in front of her. Yet strangely there seems to be a reluctance to include white canes in depictions of blind characters, another kind of erasure. Even books that have the clout of greatness about them belittle the idea of the cane by basically not referring to it at all, or by dismissing it. I'm thinking here of José Saramago's *Blindness*. I just finished reading it again—largely by touch on my relatively new braille display that connects wirelessly to my iPhone, and am amazed all over again how dismissive the book is of actual blind people.

Besides the fact that the hero remains sighted, which lends her a superpower-like air in the midst of so many blind people, she also comes up with all the bright ideas, as if the mental capacity to think and problem-solve is extinguished along with the loss of sight. This is perhaps the most insulting part of the novel. Fans may argue that it's meant to be allegorical, and that is true, as far as it goes. But the narrative voice constantly reminds the reader of "real" blind people, and what real blind people can and cannot do.

"The blind are not interested where east and west lie, or north or south, all they want is that their groping hands tell them that they are on the right road," proclaims the breathless narrator, "formerly, when they were still few, they used to carry white sticks, the sound of the continuous taps on the ground and the walls was a sort of code which allowed them to identify and recognize their route, but today, since everybody is blind, a white stick, in the middle of the general clamour, is less than helpful, quite apart from the fact that, immersed in his own whiteness, the blind man may come to doubt whether he is actually carrying anything in his hand."[31]

It's always dangerous to conflate the speaker of a novel with the author (and I can't ask Saramago what he really thinks, as he's no longer with us), but it seems to me from this moment and others like it that Saramago does not understand that the groping hand naturally reaches for something longer: a stick, a cane, or even the handle of a broom or mop to tell where he might next put his foot. This appears to me, as a blind person, to be just plain lazy sighted thinking. I often use my empty water bottle when I'm just walking through the house in order to have a little extra warning for hip-level desks and tables, and my friend the sound artist Andy Slater once misplaced his cane in the confusion of a move from one apartment to another and resorted to using his son's six-foot-long fishing-rod case to make his way to his new home by bus.

So you see, the idea of all those blind people bumbling about Saramago's novel and not one of them thinking a long stick—a broom, a curtain rod, a fishing pole—would be useful in giving warning of objects a pace or two ahead strikes me as an implausible and obnoxious removal of blind ingenuity—an ingenuity that is just now beginning to be recognized as a kind of "life hacking" in the popular press. Disabled people are so good at doing things differently that we might actually be able to help nondisabled (or not-yet-disabled) people figure out creative solutions to thorny problems.

But perhaps you, sighted reader, still feel skeptical? Perhaps you believe that Saramago's blind people are too stunned by their sudden blindness to figure anything out in such a short time? Well, in fact, neurological research shows that the brain of a sighted person under blindfold can undergo quite profound change in a startlingly short period of time. In one experiment, the visual cortices of sighted people under blindfold for five days and taught braille during that time were activated by tactile input, as reported by *ScienceDaily:* "The researchers found that the subjects who were blindfolded were superior at learning Braille than their non-blindfolded counterparts." More extraordinarily, brain scans of the blindfolded participants "showed that the brain's visual cortex had become extremely active in response to touch (in contrast to the initial scan in which there was little or no activity)."[32]

After only five days the visual cortex deprived of visual stimuli can be rewired for touch input. However, these changes were temporary. After twenty-four hours without a blindfold, the visual cortices of sighted participants no longer responded to tactile stimulation. "In other words, reading Braille no longer activated 'sight' regions of the brain among the study subjects."[33] But of course, if the blindfolds had never come off, the participants' brains would have continued to change.

Countless memoirs by people who suddenly or gradually lost their sight testify to the fact that humans are adaptable. And we are much more likely to change in the course of finding new ways of doing ordinary activities than in the course of fighting crime or battling an evil empire. Even if the media does not think much of portraying blind people as normal but only as supernatural, most of us live in the quotidian realm where defying expectations necessitates shopping for groceries, obtaining work and showing up every day, having and caring for children, and so on. It is undoubtedly true that being blind affects the way we move through and perceive the world. However, it is essential to realize that the differences are not due to mysterious, godlike superpowers, but are rather natural outcrops of our very human capacities to learn, adapt, and change.

16

The Invisible Gorilla and
Other Inattentions

We tend to think that humans rely on sight more than any other sense, and it is therefore often regarded as the most important. So I searched for a number to put to this theory and, thanks to Google, I found an answer, reiterated on many websites (used by many eye clinics urging you to get your child's eyes tested), proclaiming that 80–85 percent of learning and cognition comes through the sense of sight, leaving only 15–20 percent to the other four senses combined. And though it is certainly true that my question about how much humans rely on sight as compared to their other senses furnished me with what seemed to be an obvious answer—that humans rely on sight much more than any other sense—that answer quickly revealed itself to be suspicious. As so often happens in our search for facts, my own preconceived notions and desire for clear-cut answers seem to have determined the kind of apparently scientific information I found.

For example, a blog called *Velvet Chainsaw* breaks down the numbers as to "how much information each of our senses processes," giving it an authoritative feel: 83.0 percent—Sight; 11.0 percent—Hearing; 03.5 percent—Smell; 01.5 percent—Touch; 01.0 percent—Taste.[1]

The article even cites three researchers as sources, including our old friend perceptual psychologist Lawrence Rosenblum, and this gave me pause. After all, his book *See What I'm Say-*

ing is all about cross-modal plasticity and how our brains are constantly perceiving our environment through multiple senses, often at an unconscious level. So I emailed him at his office at the University of California, Riverside, where he runs a lab, and he responded with some mystification of his own: "It has been incorrectly attributed to me and I've been asked about it a number of times."

Furthermore, he wrote, "I am unaware of any research that has addressed this question and I'm not even sure how something like that could be tested! I do believe that our non-sight senses play a bigger role in our perceptual world than we are consciously aware. But this belief is based on research showing that cross-sensory influences are much more common than once thought (despite our awareness), and that the perceptual brain seems designed around multisensory principles. I really don't know how one could conduct research to quantify the relative importance of the senses."

That said, until we create a world in which hearing, smelling, touching, and tasting are as ubiquitously used and entertained as sight, vision and its absence will continue to occupy a place of primacy among the senses, laden with metaphors that reach far beyond a physical ability or the lack thereof. I believe these metaphors combine with ocularcentric science to create an environment inhospitable to blind people generally and blind scientists in particular.

Hoby Wedler, a blind organic chemist, opens his TEDx Talk, "Sensory Literacy," with a story of traveling into nature with sighted friends, who all tried very hard to explain what they were seeing of the foggy field of Sonoma County, California. They even tried to describe the color green to him. "Frankly," he says, "I didn't really care what the color green looked like because of all the sensory information I was getting non-visually." Later, he tried to explain to them his own sensory impressions of birds and cows and the viscosity of the air and the "symphony" of smells from trees and grass and manure. But his friends had noticed none of that. "They were so focused on the visual that they were incapable of looking beyond eyesight." I believe that this common attitude among the sighted keeps the information that blind people can offer relegated to the novel or the absurd, the easily dismissed or the downright trivial (unless, of course, we are discussing blindness as a metaphor), and these biases have made it very hard for blind people interested in pursuing scientific careers.

Wedler, who received his PhD from the University of California at Davis in 2017, has been blind (no light perception) his entire life. His experience in the Sonoma field and others like it set him on a mission to expand people's appreciation and vocabulary for senses other than sight, senses that so often go unnoticed for many sighted people. Smell, in particular: "We're always smelling things that we recognize but being able to describe them and put words to those senses is a huge challenge," he told me in an interview for my magazine, *Aromatica Poetica*.[2]

Through his company, Senspoint, Wedler helps businesses market to senses other than sight. Besides talking about how you get wine grapes to release their flavors and the delicious smell of wet pavement, he and I also talked about how he got into chemistry and why he left the hard sciences to become an entrepreneur.

It all started with a great high school teacher who was persuasive in her claims that chemistry is the basis of everything. Wedler bit, but his teacher was skeptical that he could pursue chemistry professionally because the discipline is so visual, and she reminded him: "It's not practical, and you said you want to be practical."

Wedler embraced the challenge of convincing her that there were ways of doing chemistry nonvisually. But as he made his way through college and graduate school, he began to understand how his research and contributions might be limited by convention, rather than pure science. "No one needs to see to do chemistry," he told me, "because we can't see atoms anyway. We look at changes (which I can hire someone to describe to me), but really understanding the chemistry is cerebral."

However, Wedler did not pursue a postdoc position; instead he switched gears to his sensory literacy project because "while chemistry itself—doing the science—is cerebral and accessible and fun, the way that the world likes to present chemical information is extremely visual: getting things from the literature into my mind and getting things from my mind back out to the literature."

Perhaps once we have a critical mass of blind scientists, including chemists, we can encourage nonvisual means of communicating information: verbal, aural, tactile, even olfactory.

I've been aware of the ocularcentric bias in our culture for a long time—how could I, while going blind, not notice?—but as I've become more interested in the other senses, namely smell, I have become aware of the fact that the scientific community is just as biased as the rest of the population. When I interviewed Lawrence Rosenblum for *Aromatica Poetica,* he told me that for a long time his discipline had little interest in smell: "I should tell you, historically in perceptual psychology, professors kind of throw it to their teaching assistants to cover the scent material in their classes." I expressed my surprise, and he elaborated: "The big questions about perception are in sight and maybe in hearing to some degree, but scent isn't really all that important to humans, and it's really considered like, I don't know, the runt of the litter of the senses."[3]

He admitted that it wasn't until he was writing *See What I'm Saying* that he learned about the exciting work being done with smell. Interesting to note that in his acknowledgements, Rosenblum credits his parents for his early interest in the science of perception: "In the beginning, my mother and late father, Lenore and Milton Rosenblum, inspired the general topic of this book (and my career) through their work with sensory-impaired individuals."[4] In our interview he elaborated: "My dad ran a Lighthouse for the Blind in Syracuse, New York. And my mom worked with deaf children and their families. They were both old-school social workers; they provided services for folks. I used to go to their offices and learn about all the different devices and training they had designed. I think probably one of the aha moments was when I saw that schools for the blind had intramural sports teams—baseball, football, soccer—and were able to play through sound."[5]

Perhaps, then, it is no surprise that most of his research is "on audio-visual speech perception mostly, and also face perception and voice perception." He clarified: "We don't do neuroscience, we do behavioral science. . . . My research is very theoretically motivated, and so we spend most of our time—our exciting time—designing experiments to test theoretical ideas."[6]

As Rosenblum has helped to shape my own understanding of the possibilities of my brain to learn to perceive in new and multiple ways, I like that he began asking questions because of his encounters with people with sensory disabilities as a child. I think sometimes science believes itself to be cleansed of human personality, as if it works alone in the universe and is not theorized and made manifest by people, with all their experiences, flaws, and ingenuities.

Rosenblum alerted me to another researcher and author, Rachel Herz. She is one of the growing number of perceptual psychologists working in the field of smell. In her 2007 book *The Scent of Desire,* she mentions how the American Medical Association quantifies quality of life with regard to different sensory impairments: "The *American Medical Association Guides to the Evaluation of Permanent Impairment* currently gives the loss of smell and taste a value of only 1–5 percent of the total value of a person's life's worth, while loss of vision is given a value of 85 percent."[7]

While these numbers seem to align with the numbers regarding the information gathered through each of the senses, it's hard to imagine how such measurements are obtained and assessed. More importantly, these kinds of numbers flatten difference and create biases by suggesting that such things are biologically "human" and not largely determined by culture and individual circumstances. Loss of the sense of smell would be more traumatic for me than for someone who was not interested in scent, but probably not as devastating as for a perfumer or chef.

It seems to me that these numbers are problematic for all kinds of people with different sensory abilities and experiences, especially those at the extremes of the chart: people with visual impairment or anosmia. As Herz points out, the loss of the sense of smell turns out to be quite debilitating, although, unlike loss of sight, it seems generally to be progressively more so: "In one study that contrasted the trauma of being blinded or becoming anosmic after an accident, it was found that those who were blinded initially felt much more traumatized by their loss than those who had lost their sense of smell. But follow-up analyses on the emotional health of these patients one year later showed that the anosmics were faring much more poorly than the blind."[8]

I'm guessing that at least part of the difficulty that anosmics face stems from the fact that our culture thinks so little about smell that the loss of it is very often trivialized, and thus no infrastructure has developed to help them cope. Conversely, there are countless organizations out there to help the born-blind and the newly blinded to adapt. These organizational disparities do quite a bit to obscure the fact that the difficulties one faces in losing a sense have as much to do with anatomical differences as they do with societal assumptions about the relative importance of each sense. Furthermore, just because our ocularcentric culture believes sight to be the most important sense does not necessarily mean that it gives us an accurate, unbiased, or complete picture of the world.

So much about sight is taken for granted, in fact, that the blind perspective often reveals sighted people's insecurities. "One day I hear him ask everyone he meets about the configuration of the moon after it is full," says David Ritz of Ray Charles. "Does it go back to being a sliver, or does it get small gradually?'" Apparently, "no one can answer the question." His friends and colleagues are all tongue-tied, and so Charles scoffs, "'With all that twenty-twenty, y'all don't even look at the moon.'"[9]

Ain't that the truth. Sighted people don't use their eyes nearly as well as they believe they do, and even more than that, they do not use their vocabulary. I believe that the speechless aspect of dealing with a curious blind person has much to do with the fact that so many sighted people take it for granted that a picture speaks a thousand words. Well, maybe they should start attempting to use their words to describe the visual and realize that they can't. The frustration that sighted friends show when they are asked to put alternative text on their social-media images testifies to that. It's an impoverishment of education that, if rectified, could go a long way in translating those so-called valuable pictures into complex problems of language and thought.

We need blind and visually impaired scientists to push sight-centered questions in new directions. I think that most blind people have had the experience of different perfectly sighted friends telling them that the very same object is a different color. This was first brought home to me after a performance where a friend put little Matchbox cars under every audience member's seat. I got one that looked to my visually impaired eyes to be orange, but when I asked my friends what color it was, David said something, and Michele said something else. I laughed, and took my car to several others. The answer to my simple question: What color is it? proved to be controversial. Some said orange, some said pink, some said red, others said yellow, and many said some combination of these: "It's kind of a pinky-red, or it's sort of an orangey-yellow."

What's happening here? Are the discrepancies a matter of language? Of photoreceptors? Of aesthetics? In other words, are the differences in opinion a matter of eye anatomy or brain functioning or learning and experience or all of the above? Sometimes it seems to me that sighted people believe they are all seeing the world the same way and as it really exists, when, if they questioned one another more closely, and stretched to use their vocabulary, they might realize they are seeing only what they, as individuals with all their anomalies and attention biases, are able to see—a point made manifest by the famous "invisible gorilla."

The "invisible gorilla" experiment was first designed by Christopher Chabris and Daniel Simons in the late nineties at Harvard and has since been re-created in many places with many subjects around the world, with the same startling results: if distracted by a visual task, approximately 50 percent of perfectly sighted people will not notice a life-size gorilla when it is right in front of their eyes.

Here's a quick sketch of the psychological experiment: the two researchers divided their students into teams wearing black shirts and white shirts, respectively, and told them to pass a basketball around a gym. They filmed the game and then showed the video to volunteers and asked them to count the passes made by the players in white, while ignoring the passes made by the players in black.

Immediately after the video, the students asked the volunteer subjects a series of questions, at first about the players and the passes, and then more bizarre questions, including the all-important "Did you notice a gorilla?" To which about half responded, "A what?"

"The pass-counting task was intended to keep people engaged in doing something that demanded attention to the action on the screen," Chabris and Simons explain in their 2010 book, *The Invisible Gorilla,* "but we weren't really interested in pass-counting ability. We were actually testing something else: Halfway through the video, a female student wearing a full-body gorilla suit walked into the scene, stopped in the middle of the players, faced the camera, thumped her chest, and then walked off, spending about nine seconds onscreen."[10]

Although the experiment demonstrates how attention to one thing can lead to "cognitive blindness," it says even more about people's attitudes. Chabris and Simons describe how, after watching the video a second time without being given any task, all the participants saw the gorilla perfectly well, and some even accused the researchers of switching tapes on them. Confidence in their abilities, or rather skepticism about their inabilities, is really the interesting part. "The gorilla study illustrates, perhaps more dramatically than any other, the powerful and pervasive influence of the illusion of attention: We experience far less of our visual world than we think we do. If we were fully aware of the limits to attention, the illusion would vanish."[11]

As I mentioned in my consideration of blind spots, we are generally not able to see what we cannot see. As Chabris and Simons conclude: "Our vivid visual experience masks a striking mental blindness—we assume that visually distinctive or unusual objects will draw our attention, but in reality they often go completely unnoticed."[12]

I think Denis Diderot intuited the invisible gorilla by recognizing that sighted people nurture a grand hubris about the truth of what they see, and that they might do well to look to blind people to remind themselves just how limited and circumstantial are all our perceptions of the world, when he wrote: "I own I cannot conceive, what information we could expect from a blind man who had just undergone a painful operation upon a very delicate organ which is deranged by the smallest accident and which when sound is a very untrustworthy guide to those who have for a long time enjoyed its use."[13]

Unfortunately, however, when it comes to the rhetoric of "cure," not much has changed since the days of Diderot. The pervasive attitude of science toward blindness is its endeavors to put an end to it. Take, for example, the *National Geographic* September 2016 cover story: "Why There's New Hope about Curing Blindness" details with great glee promising cures, from stem cells to digital camera implants. It's a strange idea, this curing impulse. I personally have never thought much about it.

When I was younger and had to tell people that I was visually impaired (because it was not in any way visually apparent), they often asked if there was a cure. I usually shrugged and said something about stem cells and promising stuff done with mice. Now that I'm totally blind, no one ever asks about a cure, which is ironic, since science is much closer now to a cure than it was twenty years ago. And while I rarely think about it, I can certainly imagine getting excited about seeing again—it would be so different and a lot of fun to write about. And I've always said that if I could suddenly see well enough to drive, I'd get a motorcycle and ride across the country. Fantasies aside, I have no illusions about a cure—either that it will happen in my lifetime or that my life would automatically be better with sight restored. There are, after all, plenty of unhappy sighted people in the world.

Many people in the disability community find the rhetoric of "cure" problematic because it undermines perceptions about our ability to lead happy, fulfilling, meaningful, and impactful lives. And although the rhetoric of a cure is often driven more by the fears of nondisabled people than the needs and wants of disabled people, there's a self-fulfilling prophecy regarding quality of life: if nondisabled people assume that our lives are less worthwhile than theirs, then social barriers make that true. Feeling disabled has everything to do with environment and how people treat us. In this digital age, I can do the vast majority of my work as a writer without any kind of assistance, so that when I hit my desk every morning, I don't feel disabled in the least, I simply sit down and work as any other writer would. That was, as we have seen, not the case with Milton, who composed his poetry in the quiet of the night and then waited, patiently or not, for someone to come and "milk him," i.e., act as his amanuensis for the day. But of course Milton was also limited in his experience of disability, thanks to his already prominent position in the world of letters and his financial comfort. He could not have lain around reciting poetry if he'd had to shovel out stables or cook and wash dishes all day long.

It cannot be overstated how much family, finances, community, and society affect the level of disability we experience regardless of what's going on in our physical bodies.

Now, assuming the best-case scenario—that disabled people are getting all the technological, financial, and social help they need to do the work they love—what contributions can they make? Well, if a man like the theoretical physicist Stephen Hawking is any indication, we must say, a lot.

In *Enlightenment Now* (2018), the cognitive psychologist Steven Pinker celebrates the advancement of human rights, but he is strangely silent about disability rights. For Pinker, it seems that when it comes to disability and progress, what's important is ridding our world of disability by way of medical science. This is, as I mentioned above, problematic.

Even if everyone agreed that we should work to eliminate disability—an idea that is not without controversy (resistance to cochlear implants in the Deaf community being perhaps the most well-known but by no means the only locus of such disagreements)—unless a magic wand suddenly made all people able-bodied (whatever that may mean), we will need some human rights for those still waiting around for a "cure." Moreover, during this race to able-bodiedness, we are likely to negate the valuable experience of disabled people in hopes that such experiences will soon just go away.

I am no Democritus. I did not choose blindness, and I would consider sight restoration if it came my way. However, there is no doubt that my blindness has been an important piece in my own development, and may even provide some insight to my sighted readers. Like Diderot, I tend to write about the blind experience "for the use of those who see." But Pinker seems not to have read that particular Enlightenment treatise, and perhaps it is for this reason that he leaves ableism out of his list of -isms that Enlightenment progress has worked so hard to diminish.

His chapter "Equal Rights" opens with a rousing paragraph about how racism, sexism, and homophobia occur as a result of the fact that "humans are liable to treat entire categories of other humans as means to an end or nuisances to be cast aside." These injustices toward people of other races or creeds, women, non-binary, trans, queer folk of all stripes have been "rampant, to varying degrees, in most cultures throughout history," and "the disavowal of these evils is a large part of what we call civil rights or equal rights." Pinker calls the expansion of equal rights a "stirring chapter in the story of human progress," but he makes no mention of ableism—here or anywhere in his book.[14]

There is no doubt in my mind that Enlightenment ideals have improved the lives of blind people, but sometimes I think the progress is framed from a single point of view—that of the nondisabled, which is, in the end, not even a very useful category. Unlike many other categories of identity, disability may be fluid—we often move into it and sometimes move out of it. One of every five Americans has a disability, and most of us will experience some level of disability at some time in our lives.

Pinker is by no means alone in his inability to see ableism (rather than disability) as a blight on our pride of progress. It is still quite rare that I find disability included in statements of diversity. Yet I believe people are ready to hear the voices and opinions of disabled people.

"I'm proud to be part of a marginalized group on the rise," I said during a 2018 live taping in Denver of the RISK! podcast. To this, the two or three hundred people in the (largely millennial) audience spontaneously applauded. The story I told that night was about my dad's last years in a wheelchair—how his life as a military man and world traveler did not equip him to cope with disability. I think this is not uncommon. There is so much shame attached to being disabled and so much arrogance in the so-called able-bodied that we often assume the two states to be strict polarities, rather than simply precarious situations upheld by cultural as well as physical boundaries. Until we allow that disabled voices are as full of wisdom and folly as the rest of humanity, our enlightened perspective cannot help but be lopsided, false, and destructive to the once and future disabled of the world.

Just as women scientists, scientists of color, and others who were for so long shut out of the scientific establishment have done, I'm guessing that blind scientists will ask important questions that can push human understanding forward in new ways. Besides Hoby Wedler, in my far-flung blind community I can, off the top of my head, think of half a dozen people—mostly in their twenties and thirties—who pursued science as undergraduates and graduate students: cognitive science, rocket science, physics, computer science, and genetics.

Drew Hasley completed his PhD in genetics at the University of Wisconsin, Madison, in 2016. In a news story about his accomplishment, Hasley told the reporter: "I see an opportunity to improve biological education in a way that will get more people into it who are like me. There is no reason for me to be this rare." He continued, "The next generation of science students who are disabled should not have to be as passionate about science as I was. They should be able, like their peers, to dip a toe in and have fun. As it is now, you have to be committed, and that's not fair. If a school's version of accessible is assigning you to be the person who takes the notes, would you think a career in life science is possible?"[5]

Despite the challenges that blind people face in the scientific community, which has historically viewed them as subjects but rarely as colleagues, the very fact that blind scientists exist bodes well for the future of blind people and science alike. I find it so encouraging and exciting to think that in the future the big questions will be asked and answered not only by curious sighted people investigating blindness but also by curious blind people investigating sight.

To me, the best feminist criticism causes us to realize that men are as constrained by traditional gender roles as women are, just in different (generally more empowering) ways. I think something similar can be said for sighted and blind people. When we think of sight as a static and monolithic gift, a gift you either have or do not have, we deny ourselves the possibility of improvement. As recent findings in neuroplasticity indicate, our sense organs are not considered so distinct in our brains as to make the great historical divide between sighted and blind people necessary, useful, or even true. If we understand seeing and not-seeing for what they are—a vast interplay of physical, mental, metaphorical, and social situations—then our various ways of experiencing the world will be expanded and refined for all of us, the sighted and the blind alike.

17

Constructing Blind Pride out of Ancient and Evolutionary Blind Memes

Real or imagined, Homer is a kind of ground zero for a vast network of blind memes that dot our cultural landscape, but his image also literally gave rise to other blind bards; it's hard to imagine John Milton lying down in darkness night after night to compose *Paradise Lost* if he'd not had the image of Homer in his head. Likewise, armed with the blind seer Tiresias, Milton could take pride in his ability to plant eyes in that darkness and "see and tell of things invisible to mortal sight."

I employ the word "meme" as the evolutionary biologist Richard Dawkins originally intended: as "cultural replicator." We'll return to Dawkins and his coining of "meme" shortly, but for now, I'd like to suggest that the blind meme is a cultural replicator that—through image, text, and language—influences our understanding of actual blind people, so that realities blur with archetypes.

If the blind memes of ancient Greece have helped some, such as Milton, to construct careers out of blindness in an ocularcentric world, they can also be somewhat constraining. Once I went to an RP support group in San Francisco, where an older gentleman told us how he'd been sitting in the BART station with his guide dog reading the newspaper. A stranger came up to him and said, "You don't look blind!" So the man reached in his bag, pulled out his dark glasses, put them on, and continued reading the paper. We all had a good belly laugh.

We blind and visually impaired folk spend not a little virtual and in-person communal time laughing at the simple-mindedness of sighted people. We complain also, and gripe and grumble at the lack of sensitivity of those with perfectly functioning eyes who tend to think they rule the world, but we have jokes too, a whole class of which have to do with the "you don't look blind" line. I suppose we have a few thousand years of blind images with which we must contend, and reading the newspaper with a guide dog is not one of them.

The monolith of blindness tends not to allow for diversity, making the blind woman a less-common meme, and the blind child almost unheard of, although the blind youth is famous enough: remember the blind stripling, who taps his way through Joyce's *Ulysses,* trailing associations that are both an echo of, and a far cry from, the Homeric blind bard.

The average sighted person likely encounters many more blind memes than blind people. In *Blindness in Literature,* Jacob Twersky writes, "Considering how tiny a minority the blind have always formed—it is believed that they have rarely exceeded a small fraction of one percent of the population—they have decidedly received disproportionate attention in literature. Clearly, that in itself is significant, indicating that they have been found especially interesting or curious, stimulating to the imagination and the emotions."[1]

Even if recent estimates are more generous—approximately 2.4 percent of adults sixteen years and older in the United States, according to statistics at the National Federation of the Blind in 2016—blindness remains relatively rare in the under-sixty-five set.[2] Not long ago, we were having dinner with Alabaster's sister, Lisa, and her husband, Frank, and the subject of blindness came up. "I never knew a blind person before you," Frank said, and that launched me into my mini lecture on how "there are as many ways of being blind as there are of being sighted. The only difference is that there are more of you."

Because there are relatively few of us, blind people are often thought of as all being kind of alike. In fact we (as disabled people) are probably more different than other minority groups, since we often find ourselves the only ones in a family, a school, a neighborhood, and therefore have characteristics as diverse as the contexts in which we dwell. If we do happen to find ourselves in the same place, we are mistaken for one another.

I recently reconnected with a former colleague from NYU— Elizabeth Bearden, who is now a professor of Renaissance studies at the University of Wisconsin, Madison. We met toward the end of her PhD studies when I was still in the middle of mine. We quickly became friends as we discovered many shared experiences as visually impaired women who had stumbled through college trying to pass as sighted. She had a guide dog before I did, a golden retriever. Mine, later, was a black lab. In a recent conversation, she reminded me how the NYU community— from students to security guards—would often confuse us even though we didn't look at all alike—she and her guide dog, Shirley, were blond while Millennium and I had dark fur and hair, respectively.

Elizabeth and I did have things in common, including a group of friends who were all literature graduate students. However, sometimes it is just assumed that blind people must be friends with one another—perhaps even each other's only friend. In her 2019 memoir about her journey to become the first deafblind graduate of Harvard Law School, Haben Girma tells a story of how she was wandering around her college cafeteria trying to find an empty seat, when a stranger tapped her on her arm and asked if she was looking for her friend. Although she was not sure what friend the woman might be referring to, she agreed and was immediately led over to the other blind person in the room.

Haben is partially deaf and blind, so that when the woman found her "friend," she was able to see the long white cane and realized who it belonged to. She greeted her acquaintance, Bill, "a first-year student from New Mexico who is also blind. People here talk loudly to him, so he keeps trying to explain that he's not me." They laughed at the volunteer helper who presumed Haben was looking for her own kind because "all blind people must be friends, right?"[3]

Perhaps these confusions and assumptions stem from the idea that a sighted person cannot actually communicate in any ordinary sense with a blind person, as was so painfully illustrated in a 2014 *New York Times* opinion piece titled "Why Do We Fear the Blind?" In it, a teacher of blind children tells how she was prompted to write the essay by a woman at a party who asked, "How do you talk to your students?"

After explaining that the students were not deaf, the woman said, "Yes, I know they're not deaf. But what I really mean is, how do you actually talk to them?" The confusion seems startlingly ingrained. If we the blind live in a totally different perceptual universe, then ordinary communication is not possible, leaving room only for extraordinary platitudes.

In the introduction to *Monstrous Kinds,* which investigates how people with disabilities defined and were defined by early modern artistic representations, my former fellow grad-school blindie Elizabeth indulges in a rare personal anecdote in order to explain how ancient supernatural attitudes toward blind people coexist with more modern medical models: "As a blind woman navigating the streets of New York City, I have been told I am a blessed miracle as I emerge from the subway, am amazing as I buy a regular coffee, and am just like the girl the doorman saw on the news last night, whose vision was 'fixed' thanks to a miraculous medical procedure."[4]

In other words we are considered to be touched by God, endowed with superpowers, or in need of a cure. I think a majority of blind people experience these contradictory attitudes on an almost daily basis for no better reason than that we the blind parade through the theater of sighted people's lives as representations. Blindness must mean something, and therefore the blind individual must also mean something. We are regarded as signs and symbols, not people, which helps to explain why blind memes are so popular.

As noted above, the word "meme" was coined by Richard Dawkins, in his 1976 book *The Selfish Gene*. In that book, which is about gene-centered evolution, he identifies the lack of a word to designate the cultural replicator—and comes up with his own: "meme." Like so many of our important words in English, this one is consciously taken from Greek: " 'Mimeme' comes from a suitable Greek root," Dawkins writes, "but I want a monosyllable that sounds a bit like 'gene.' I hope my classicist friends will forgive me if I abbreviate mimeme to *meme*. If it is any consolation, it could alternatively be thought of as being related to 'memory,' or to the French word *même* [same]. It should be pronounced to rhyme with 'cream.' "[5]

While genes replicate themselves by leaping from body to body by sexual reproduction, memes "propagate themselves in the meme pool by leaping from brain to brain via a process which, in the broad sense, can be called imitation." Dawkins enumerates some examples: "tunes, ideas, catch-phrases, clothes fashions, ways of making pots or of building arches."[6]

Unfortunately, the very useful word "meme" has been crudely co-opted or—to use Dawkins's own term—"hijacked" by the Internet. At a recent family dinner, one of the youngsters—a twenty-something chef-in-training—asked me what I thought about (Internet) memes, and I found myself stuttering in an old-ladyish way about how stupid they are and how I don't feel particularly left out. (I'd had a bit of wine.)

When I read *The Selfish Gene* for the first time a couple of years ago and learned about the meme as cultural replicator, I felt shortchanged by the Internet and the sighted people who wield those (mostly) visual gags as if they were litmus tests for wit and cleverness. Memes have been distorted into (mostly) inaccessible social media image tidbits that seem so devoid of interest once they are translated into the spoken word by sighted friends that I, for one, feel a little cheap for even bothering to be curious about them when they come my way. But what can you do? Dawkins's brilliant conception of the meme is, for most people, nearly synonymous with the flotsam and jetsam of the Internet that streams in front of their overburdened eyeballs every day. But those are Internet memes, not to be confused with the meme itself, which can be so many things: a symbol like the cross, a character like Hamlet, an image like Botticelli's Venus, an idea like ocularcentrism. Interesting to note that after I used this term in a Facebook post, a friend created an Internet meme with image and text that explained what ocularcentrism is and gave me credit for turning people on to the term.

We have encountered many blind memes in this book: the blind bard, the blind seer, Helen Keller herself (with her attendant jokes and water-pump scene), the biblical-turned-hymn-lyric "I once was blind" (and the song in which it figures, "Amazing Grace," which is so recognizable that it is nearly a cliché), the confused blind man à la Gloucester, and the Molyneux Man (and all the instances of curing blindness ever since), and so many, many more. Thus I've been concerned with the blind meme network in all its paradoxical complexities from the start, but here I'm explicitly invoking Dawkins's terminology because he not only gave me this wonderfully useful way of conceptualizing the cultural replicator of blindness, he also presented me with "the blind watchmaker," a perfect foil for the blind bard and a painful reminder of how easily blindness is conflated with unconsciousness.

To be clear: my critique of *The Blind Watchmaker* (1986), in which Dawkins argues the case for evolution, is absolutely one of language, not science. I am all about evolution, and have been since I was a kid. In sixth grade we read *Inherit the Wind*, the play based on the Scopes "Monkey Trials" that fought for the legality of teaching Darwinism. I loved that book so much that for decades I'd been (mis)quoting it. I won't tell you how I mangled it, but the line I'd remembered (at least in spirit) was spoken by the lawyer on the right side of history and science to the lawyer on the wrong side: "All motion is relative. Perhaps it is you who have moved away—by standing still."[7]

This line still gives me chills. I think it's because the idea that change can occur in the very act of denying it seemed very profound to my young mind. As I would learn when I studied Latin, the idea of conservatism is not fundamentally about the particular ideology that one upholds, but rather the fearful desire to keep, or conserve, the belief system already in place. As most disabled people know, shifting perceptions is no easy task, and there are still a lot of unmoving "able-bodied" people out there, even if they are, as fragile humans, only precariously able.

The word "blind" in *The Blind Watchmaker* signifies, as it so often does, unconsciousness, thoughtlessness, a lack of foresight: "Natural selection is the blind watchmaker, blind because it does not see ahead, does not plan consequences, has no purpose in view."[8]

The word "poet" derives from the ancient Greek word *poiein* ("to make"), and so the blind watchmaker is perhaps less different from the blind bard than might be assumed at first glance. On the one hand, we have the poem-maker, who is capable of creating literary worlds and beautiful music—think Homer and Demodocus—and on the other hand, we have a watchmaker capable of designing the most intricate life-forms in the physical world. In the first case, blindness signifies a physical lack of sight that enables the poetic skills to blossom: musicality and an ear receptive to the voice of the Muse. In the second case, the word "blind" symbolizes purposelessness, making the blind watchmaker an unconscious creator: "In the case of living machinery," writes Dawkins in his consideration of the marvels of bats, "the 'designer' is unconscious natural selection, the blind watchmaker."[9]

At the risk of loading too much power or blame on Dawkins, it seems to me that he has helped to make "blind" and "evolution" an almost inevitable pair. Consider this moment in the brilliant and sweeping history of humankind, *Sapiens,* by Yuval Noah Harari: "Humans are the outcome of blind evolutionary processes that operate without goal or purpose."[10]

I recognize the danger of being called a politically correct whiner, but language is important. It shapes how we think and how we write. Language helps us conceptualize who we are, and can have grave consequences for our expectations and sense of power, as well as our political rights.

"It may look to you like it's only words," writes Michael Bérubé in his 1996 memoir, *Life as We Know It,* an account of raising a child with Down syndrome, "but perhaps the fragile neonates whose lives were impeded by the policies—and conditions—of institutionalization can testify in some celestial court to the power of mere language, to the intimate links between words and social policies."[11] The point holds for all disabilities.

We, the people who have disabilities, may not always agree on our terms, but we generally agree that the terms matter, and that, as societies change and grow, so does the terminology we use. Not too many people call themselves handicapped or crippled anymore, although "crip" has been adopted by many in the disability community (as in crip theory, crip time, and cripping the vote).

Interestingly, as sensitive and smart as Bérubé is on the relationship between our cultural construction of disability and its genetic realities, he is for just one instant pulled into Dawkins's rhetorical use of blindness after discussing *The Selfish Gene:* "Maybe the origins of the concept of justice, and the possibility of altruism that it entails, should be sought in provisional forms of conscious, linguistically mediated human agreement rather than in the blind workings of primordial ooze."[12]

Talk about the propagation of a meme! It's like a mental tic or a contagious yawn, this use of "blind." I almost want to deploy it myself: "Stop your blind use of the word 'blind'!" But what I mean is "Stop your thoughtless use of the word 'blind'!" I urge a dismantling of such broad rhetorical use, because when legions of sighted readers encounter these offhanded yet grandiose metaphors in works of true nonfiction brilliance, it seems to me inevitable that "blind" cannot help but signify something much more diabolical than lack of sight.

Of course, I do not pretend to speak for all blind people here or elsewhere. "Visual and blind metaphors have never bothered me," avers Canadian writer Ryan Knighton in *Cockeyed,* his 2006 memoir about grappling with vision loss due to RP. "You won't hear my fist slamming a podium about my victimization at the hands of metaphors or our tendency to assume sightedness."[13]

I take his point—that sight and blindness metaphors do not seem to directly affect his quality of life. They are metaphors, and most intelligent people recognize them as such. I'm guessing Knighton is not alone in not giving a damn about the ubiquity of the pejorative use of "blind" to indicate things like thoughtlessness, ignorance, or unconsciousness. However, I think metaphors matter because they shape and are shaped by our language, and there can be little doubt that language shapes our thought and, by extension, our assumptions, prejudices, and biases—all of which do in fact affect the quality of life of many blind and visually impaired people on a daily basis. The glaring problem with the ubiquitous use of "blind" as a pejorative epithet is that for those of us who have little or no sight, it makes it awfully hard to construe, let alone celebrate, any kind of blind pride alongside other pride movements.

I suppose I would argue that not all blind/sighted metaphors are created equal: "See you later" does not bother me, but "blind evolution" does.

The use of "blind" in *The Blind Watchmaker* is a particularly thorny case since, in that book, Dawkins is not interested solely in the metaphorical implications of seeing and not-seeing. He also makes much of the physical eye: "Without an eye you are totally blind. With half an eye you may at least be able to detect the general direction of a predator's movement, even if you can't focus a clear image. And this may make all the difference between life and death."[14]

As a person who spent the majority of her life visually impaired, I can testify to the truth of this. Partial sight was very useful. However, the problem with Dawkins's explicit and constant conflation of physical blindness with metaphorical blindness is that for most sighted readers, on almost every page one is being further indoctrinated into the misconception that blindness equals unconsciousness and an inability to have mastery over the world in which we live.

The blind poet and the blind watchmaker symbolize the wild oscillations of all the states and situations of blind people, ideas, and characters. While it's useful to think of these two constructs of blindness as different (though related) memes, there are still actual blind people living in the world who share the adjective with both, who are often even designated as simply "the blind," with all its fraught associations. I sometimes slip into calling my people "the blind," but usually it happens when I make a point of comparing "us" to "them": the blind versus the sighted. Otherwise, I personally prefer to write and say "blind people"—or even, when I'm trying to be comprehensive, "blind and visually impaired," though this distinction is by no means upheld by everyone in the blind community.

In *Sight Unseen,* Georgina Kleege tells us that although during the writing of her book she began "to use braille and started to carry a white cane," it was not these outward manifestations that caused her to make the shift from calling herself "visually impaired" or "partially sighted" to calling herself "blind." Rather, her research caused her to understand "how little I actually see. As a child I knew that I did not see what other people saw. I could not, for instance, read print without holding the text close to my eyes and using extreme magnification. But I knew I could see something—light, form, color, movement— and assumed that this was close enough to what other people saw. As I wrote this book and forced myself to compare my view of the world with what I imagine a normal eye sees, what I learned astounded me. I was shocked, for instance, to discover that a sighted person sitting in a lawn chair can look down and see individual blades of grass, weeds, and other plants, perhaps even crawling and hovering insects, while all I would see is an expanse of green." And so Kleege makes the startling assertion that "writing this book made me blind."[15] When compar-

282   M. LEONA GODIN

ing what she sees and does not see with the vision of a person with "normal" vision, she finds that blindness describes the lack, despite her remaining vision.

For myself, having traveled the long road from normal sight to blindness—still traveling, in fact, as I wake up every morning wondering if I will still be able to detect a glint of light from our bedroom window—I've found visual impairment to be a very different experience than either. (Oh, how I would love to have that expanse of green back!) Still, I agree with Kleege that blindness is a construct as well as an experience that derives meaning from what it's not, namely "normal sight."

During the writing of this book, I have lost most of the remainder of my vision. I would almost say that this past year marks the end of sight for me, but not quite. Still, in the far left periphery of my left eye, I can turn my head and put a light source there and be intermittently certain whether it is on or not. But it is such a tiny fraction of the overall light that constantly buzzes and scintillates and vibrates and undulates in front of my eyes that it hardly constitutes the kind of "light and shadow" that sighted people probably think of when they think of waning or very limited eyesight.

Besides that glimmer in the far periphery, when I turn on a lamp, I see a puff of light beyond the constant background hum of undulating scintillation, which sits on my retinas for several minutes, reminding me how I felt when I was very young and first noticed that when I entered the dark from the bright outdoors, my eyes did not adjust as quickly as those of my friends. Now I can have my face right up to a lamp and be unsure (after the initial switching on) whether the lamp is on or off. So I turn the ridged knob once, twice, thrice, and then there it is again, that puff of light—it's back on. So this time I count and get to where I believe it must be dark. And I lie back and watch the shimmering, glittery, pulsating lights that constitute my vision-scape at all times, but are particularly noticeable at night in the ostensible dark. Sometimes I wonder if I did in fact turn that light off because it still feels so light in my world, and so I'll take my iPhone (my iPhone that I, like many of you, keep within arm's length 24/7) and put my earbud in and flick around to an app called Seeing AI, then I double-tap (that's the same as a single tap for sighted users) and flick over to the mode selector: "short text, color, scene preview, light detector." I remain on light detector and a low hum starts up. Then I point it in the direction of the lamp in question, and if my suspicions were correct, the tone will rise sharply—perhaps an octave or two—then, holding the iPhone in one hand, I once again click the lamp until the tone drops, and I know that, in the world beyond my eyes at least, it's dark.

Another thing that has happened over the course of writing this book is the improvement of my braille skills. Now that I have a braille display, I can read any ebook, but when I first began practicing using braille to read books the available stock was limited. My braille-reading time was circumscribed not only by the fact that I was so slow, but also because the books available were not necessarily ones that I would have been reading had I all the choice in the world. There just aren't a lot of braille books being produced physically anymore. (There really never have been, compared to the number of books published in regular print each year, and even compared to the number of audiobooks produced, either commercially or through blind organizations.)

Ursula K. Le Guin's *The Left Hand of Darkness,* which was perhaps my third braille novel, stands out as one that I'd always meant to read and was delighted to find available from the Library for the Blind. One afternoon a violent thunderstorm started up. The summer thunderstorms in Denver, where we lived at the time, are intense. Huge, booming thunderclaps shook our building and the hail pummeled the windows. I reached a moment in the novel that made me cry. And for the first time since I was a little girl, the crying caused me to pause, a pause that did not involve scrambling for the Pause button. It was a memorable, nearly forgotten sensation, and I relished it. Since that afternoon, I've enjoyed other moments of the instantaneous pause, but that was the first.

To honor that moment I'll quote that marvelous book, published in 1969, which tells the story of a world where the sexes are divided not according to individuals—man and woman—but in phases within the cycle of life of each individual. The planet of Winter is a world where humans enter into sexual states periodically and exhibit the sexual traits that our world would call feminine or masculine. This state of sexual readiness is called kemmer, and in the following poem—an ancient alien lay—this mixed and intermittent duality is celebrated:

> Light is the left hand of darkness
> and darkness the right hand of light.
> Two are one, life and death, lying
> together like lovers in kemmer,
> like hands joined together,
> like the end and the way.[16]

The Left Hand of Darkness troubles the fixed polarities of male and female by invoking the equally fixed polarities of darkness and light. Perhaps this is why I love the book so much.

In complicating the simple dichotomies of blindness and sight, darkness and light, I follow the tradition set by other pride movements. It is a subtle yet powerful effect of such movements to create individuality and community at the same time. With a sense of community identity we, the blind and visually impaired, may be able to construe a bit of blind pride. This use of the word "pride" would not be (as it so often is) a rhetorical intensifier suggesting how pride may blind one to the frailness of one's humanity or to the dignity of others. This is not metaphorical blindness. I'd like to live in a world where blind pride might allow us—the blind and visually impaired—to celebrate our multitudinous points of view, instead of so often feeling bad about our poor vision. If sighted people constantly put so much stock in our idealized unique perspective (as demonstrated by their near obsession with us in literature and film), then we might as well do so ourselves. If there can be black pride, and gay pride, and more recently disability pride, then why not a little blind pride?

In her foundational text of disability studies, *Extraordinary Bodies* (1997), Rosemarie Garland-Thomson helped to nudge disability out of the medical model (which seeks to diagnose and cure) into a cultural model. As she says in her introductory pages, she wanted "to move disability from the realm of medicine into that of political minorities, to recast it from a form of pathology to a form of ethnicity. By asserting that disability is a reading of bodily particularities in the context of social power relations, I intend to counter the accepted notions of physical disability as an absolute, inferior state and a personal misfortune."[7]

As we've witnessed, disability is an experience of the body in the world, so that when the world is accessible to different physical, mental, and sensory modalities, disability is not likely to be stigmatized, not likely to impede one's relationship with other bodies. Garland-Thomson added to the conversation that destabilizes society's simple dichotomies—"male/female, white/black, straight/gay, or able-bodied/disabled"—so that "we can examine the subtle interrelations among social identities that are anchored to physical differences."[18]

No matter the diversity amongst individual blind people, there is something powerful in considering ourselves as a blind community. Solidarity is helpful in the world of disability just as it is for other marginalized groups. So if I tend to distinguish my long years of visual impairment from my relatively few years spent blind, it has as much to do with my personal experience as it does with my philosophical obsession with diversity in all its complicated and messy glory.

The huge network of blind memes influences, to a greater or lesser extent, those who consider themselves sighted, blind, in-between, and beyond—sight beyond sight being a wonderful compensation for the physical lack. I do not always find being blind a picnic, but the idea that there are things worth seeing that lie beyond the abilities of the physical eye helps me to retain a sense of power in an ocularcentric world. Thus the idea of the blind seer—the seemingly oxymoronic figure who dominates our metaphors—promotes the idea that blindness is actually useful for understanding. Although it has its trite and endless reiterations, as we've witnessed, I must admit that the blind seer meme helped me, especially in my early days of grappling with vision loss, to dredge up a bit of blind pride for myself.

I hope it is by now apparent that we must balance the metaphorical with the physical, the extraordinary with the ordinary, in order to address the still very real societal disparities between blind people and the sighted. According to the American Foundation for the Blind (AFB), in 2017 only about 39 percent of working-age blind and visually impaired people were in the labor force.[19] The low employment rate is painful to consider in terms of the self-worth of each blind or visually impaired person who would like to work but cannot find a job, but the low number also indicates just how impoverished our society is when it comes to the blind perspective.

Think how wonderful it will be when blind and visually impaired people work side by side with sighted people in all walks of life, from the arts to the sciences, business, academics, and the creation of media and information systems with mind-boggling diversity and power. We will all be forced to learn the differences and similarities of how we manipulate and understand the world. If we are vigilant and open, we may come to realize that if the left hand of darkness is light, and the right hand of light is darkness, then perhaps what stands between is all kinds of dappled that we have yet to exploit and enjoy.

Acknowledgments

My obsession with blindness and literature began when I was an undergrad at UC Santa Cruz: in my first Milton class with George Amis and then as a classics major, with John Lynch heading up a faculty that was welcoming to my half-blind earnest young self. At NYU, my interests took a postmodern turn with the help of Nico Israel, whose quiet and cozy seminar holds some of my fondest grad-school memories. There are so many professors to thank and apologize to in NYU's English department for supporting me as I sort of slipped off the academic rails, just barely squeaking out with my PhD. Gabrielle Starr and Ernest Gilman were friends as well as mentors, and teaching Conversations of the West with them shaped this book as much as did my eye disease.

Regarding that slippage, one Wednesday evening around 2003, my guide dog Millennium and I wandered into Reverend Jen's Anti-Slam and performed a monologue. I can honestly say my life's not been the same since. My heartfelt gratitude for the many musicians, comedians, storytellers, and performance artists who welcomed me into the wacky open-mic scene of the Lower East Side and helped shape my ideas of blindness and spectacle. And to Frigid New York, which gave my two plays a home; I thank you for a fantastic theatrical experience!

This book got its start with *Catapult,* which did exactly what the name suggests. Back in 2017, I was feeling a little lost and saw a "Don't Write Alone Weekend" advertised at a place called Catapult. I signed up and met the then director of writing programs, Julie Buntin. I was hooked. I took two more online fiction classes in which I made some virtual pen pals, including Wah-Ming Chang. When I noticed their online magazine, *Catapult,* was looking for columnists, I pitched A Blind Writer's Notebook. To my astonishment, Mensah Demary accepted it, and that column forms the basis of several of this book's chapters. After the first one was published in January 2018, Wah-Ming (who turned out to be an editor disguised as a student) wrote to congratulate me and asked if I had an agent. It just so happened that her boyfriend is an agent, which is how, Cinderella-like, I met the best agent in the world, Markus Hoffmann, without whom this book would not exist.

Giant thanks go out to my first editor, Catherine Tung, who took a chance on this project, and my second, Tom Pold, who guided this book through its ugly duckling phase into its swan-like adulthood—if there are still some funny-looking feathers sticking out, that is all on me. Special thanks also to Dan Frank, fearless leader of Pantheon, which is in all ways my dream publishing house.

Several friends read parts of this book and offered invaluable responses. My marvelous long-distance ladies' coterie—Caitlin Hernandez, Michelle Kleinberg, and Laurie Rubin—were among the first readers of drafts and offered so many gems. Jim Knipfel came to be a reader late in the game and was incredibly generous with his feedback and practical advice in boozy conspiratorial tones that resonated. Lawrence Rosenblum helped keep my sciency stuff on track, and my old grad school pal Elizabeth Bearden gave me confidence that I was not too far afield from literary facts (such as they are).

Countless conversations—formal and casual—with friends

and acquaintances—blind and honorary blind—helped shape the tone of the book and kept its rather sweeping history grounded in real-life experience. My thanks to Timothy Allen, George Ashiotis, Chris Danielson, Laurie Alice Eakes, Kira Grunenberg, Darren Harbour, Frank and Lisa Gail Hoins, Caroline Kasnakian and David Lowe, Andrew Leland, Lan Li and her students in the History of the Senses course, Sarah Pillow and Marc Wagnon, Rebecca Redmile-Blaevoet, Frank Senior, Andy Slater, Collin Watt, Hoby Wedler, Jillian Weise, and Lynn Zelvin. Thanks also to the Logan Nonfiction Program, which offered support at a critical point and gave me lasting friendships in my fellows of the fall of 2019—cheers to you, Loganistas!

My father, Lee Goodin, passed away just before this book found its publishing home, which makes me sad for many reasons, not least of which is because he was skeptical of a book about blindness, and I would have loved to make him toast me with a giant glass of Beefeater. To my mother, Evelyn Koupas, I owe my life and my excellent education. She sacrificed so much. And although she had her moments of doubt as to my methods, her love and great expectations for me never waned. To the Williamsons, Papa Bill and Mama Vel, who gave me a home and a family when mine was far away, I have so much gratitude, thanks, and love. Sadly, Mama Vel passed away in the late stages of editing, and we all miss her very much.

To my best friend and almost-sister Indigo Verton, thank you for always being there for cocktail conversations and unflappable moral support. Finally, to Alabaster Rhumb, my love, my life partner, I thank you for being here for me in all ways, especially being game to put your boundless talents to use in executing so many of my wacky ideas. I look forward to continuing this outlandish life with you, even should we be trapped forever in the eternal return.

Notes

Introduction: Seeing and Not-Seeing

1. Genetic testing in 2017 indicated that my blindness is caused by a mutation to the CERKL (pronounced like "circle") gene, which is short for ceramide kinase-like.

2. I first heard the idea that blindness is not only a subject but a perspective from Andrew Leland, who is a writer, editor, and podcast producer with RP, whom I met in November 2019. He had seen the documentary *Vision Portraits* by Rodney Evens (who also has RP), in which writer Ryan Knighton (who also has RP) explains how as a person and a writer without sight, he had come to find the idea of blindness as perspective (rather than subject) to be liberating. Since *Vision Portraits* was released in only a few cities, I did not see it until nearly a year later when the Whitney Museum screened it online (with audio description) in celebration of the thirtieth anniversary of the signing of the ADA (Americans with Disabilities Act). By that time, I was in the late stages of editing this book.

3. Milton, *Paradise Lost,* III.51–55.

4. Sontag, *Illness as Metaphor,* 3.

5. Sontag, *Illness as Metaphor,* 4.

6. Borges, "Blindness," 115.

7. Borges, "Blindness," 116.

8. Nor (though I don't discuss them in this book) either of his other late works: *Paradise Regained* and *Samson Agonistes*—about the biblical Samson in his blind-prisoner moments up to and including his destruction of the temple.

9. Keller, *The World I Live In,* xi–xii.

10. Keller, *The World I Live In,* 76–77.

11. Charles Bonnet syndrome, or visual release hallucinations, is not uncommon in those who lose their vision later in life. Oliver Sacks discusses the phenomenon at length in *Hallucinations.*

12. Borges, "Blindness," 107.

1. Homer's Blind Bard

1. West, "Proclus' *Life of Homer*," 423.
2. Homer, *The Odyssey,* 8.62–64.
3. Borges, "The Last Interview," 152.
4. Borges, "Blindness," 114.
5. Borges, "Blindness," 114.
6. Borges, "Original Mythology," 69.
7. *The Odyssey,* 8.65–71.
8. *The Odyssey,* 8.260–63.
9. I employ the word "literacy"—as being print-oriented—in order to distinguish it from the oral tradition, but I hope it will become clear that literacy can take many forms, including listening to books or reading with fingers. See, for example, Mara Mills, "What Should We Call Reading?":

    "The modern literacy imperative in the United States prompted the development of dozens of new formats—aural, tactile, olfactory, visual—by which blind and other print disabled people could read. 'Inkprint reading' became one among many possibilities, starting with raised print and Braille in the nineteenth century and joined in the twentieth by phonographic Talking Books, Radio Reading services, and a variety of electronic scanning devices for translating print into tones, Braille, vibrations, or speech."
10. *The Odyssey,* introduction, 12.
11. "List of Blind People," retrieved Nov. 19, 2020: https://en.wikipedia .org/wiki/List_of_blind_people.
12. With no hyphen, please, like email! Ebooks are generally accessible via text-to-speech and braille displays, so the snootiness some readers and writers exhibit toward them feels ableist to me.
13. Danielewski, *House of Leaves,* 423. The visual braille occupies about a third of the page of the opening of Chapter 20, and is in grade 2 braille (we checked the first few words to confirm that the note is in fact the translation of the dots): "The walls are endlessly bare. Nothing hangs on them, nothing defines them. They are without texture. Even to the keenest eye or most sentient fingertip, they remain unreadable. You will never find a mark there. No trace survives. The walls obliterate everything. They are permanently absolved of all record. Oblique, forever obscure and unwritten. Behold the perfect pantheon of absence."
14. Danielewski, *House of Leaves,* xxi.
15. *The Odyssey,* 8.486–88.
16. *The Odyssey,* 8.493–99.
17. Flynn, *Sharp Objects,* 150.
18. *The Odyssey,* 11.127.

2. The Tenacious Grip of the Blind Seer

1.   Sophocles, *Oedipus the King, The Three Theban Plays,* 179.
2.   Sophocles, *Oedipus the King,* 180.
3.   Sophocles, *Oedipus the King,* 181.
4.   Sophocles, *Oedipus the King,* 236.
5.   Kleege, *Sight Unseen,* 47–48.
6.   Tiresias's sexual and perceptual transformations are adapted from Charles Martin's translation of Ovid's *Metamorphoses,* 3.409–40.
7.   Daisy Johnson, *Everything Under,* Kindle loc. 453.
8.   Sophocles, *Antigone, The Three Theban Plays,* 110.
9.   Herbert, *Children of Dune,* 330–31.
10. Herbert, *Children of Dune,* 337.
11. Sophocles, *Oedipus the King,* 240.
12. King, "The Langoliers," *Four Past Midnight,* 268.
13. Sophocles, *Oedipus the King,* 242.
14. Sophocles, *Oedipus at Colonus, The Three Theban Plays,* 381.
15. "Now Let the Weeping Cease," song lyrics from *Gospel at Colonus.*
16. Burton, *The Anatomy of Melancholy,* from the introduction "Democritus Junior to the Reader."

3. I Once Was Blind, but Now I See

1.   Plato, *Phaedo,* 58.
2.   Plato, *Phaedo,* 79.
3.   Nelson, *The Art of Cruelty,* 110.
4.   Nelson, *The Art of Cruelty,* 110.
5.   Nelson, *The Art of Cruelty,* 111.
6.   Nelson, *The Art of Cruelty,* 111.
7.   John 9:1–25.
8.   John 9:32–33.
9.   John 9:34–39.
10. CBC Radio, Tapestry, "Punk Rock and Passion Plays."
11. Hull, *Touching the Rock,* xx.
12. Acts 9:3–4.
13. Acts 9:5–10.
14. Acts 9:17.
15. Brontë, *Jane Eyre,* 403–4.
16. Brontë, *Jane Eyre,* 421.
17. Brontë, *Jane Eyre,* 421.
18. Hull, *Touching the Rock,* 12.
19. Hull, *Touching the Rock,* 216.

4. Out, Vile Jelly!

1.   Orwell, "Lear, Tolstoy, and the Fool," 322–23.
2.   Bloom, *Lear,* 1.
3.   Bloom, *Lear,* 35.
4.   Shakespeare, *King Lear,* 1.1.8–16.
5.   Shakespeare, *King Lear,* 1.2.187–90.
6.   Milton, *Paradise Lost,* III.691. As Milton puts it: "goodness thinks no ill / Where no ill seems" (III.688–89).
7.   Shakespeare, *King Lear,* 1.1.60–62.
8.   Shakespeare, *King Lear,* 1.1.86–87.
9.   Bloom, *Lear,* 75.
10.   Shakespeare, *King Lear,* 3.7.6.
11.   Shakespeare, *King Lear,* 3.7.69–71.
12.   Shakespeare, *King Lear,* 3.7.81–82.
13.   Shakespeare, *King Lear,* 3.7.99–104.
14.   Bloom, *Lear,* 81.
15.   Sophocles, *Oedipus the King,* 236–37.
16.   Homer, *The Odyssey,* 9.388–94.
17.   Vendler, *The Art of Shakespeare's Sonnets,* 1.5–6.
18.   From AZQuotes.
19.   Shakespeare, *King Lear,* 4.1.19–20.
20.   Shakespeare, *King Lear,* 4.1.24–25.
21.   Shakespeare, *King Lear,* 4.1.54.
22.   Shakespeare, *King Lear,* 4.6.1–9.
23.   Twersky, *Blindness in Literature,* 23.
24.   Shakespeare, *King Lear,* 4.6.93–95.
25.   Twersky, *Blindness in Literature,* 24.
26.   Twersky, *Blindness in Literature,* 12.
27.   Twersky, *Blindness in Literature,* 12.
28.   Twersky, *Blindness in Literature,* 23.

5. Telescopes, Microscopes, Spectacles, and Speculations

1.   In Greek "prosthesis" simply means "addition" and here signifies how reliant modern science is on such devices—much more crucial to our perceptions as a society than a glass eye is to an individual, as the latter is merely aesthetic. As will be seen, glasses or contact lenses are to an individual what the telescope and microscope are to our society.
2.   Galileo, *Sidereus Nuncius,* 64–66.
3.   Galileo, *Sidereus Nuncius,* 12.
4.   These opening paragraphs on Galileo, as well as the passages on Hooke and Swift, are loosely based on portions of my 2009 dissertation, "The Spectator & the Blind Man."

5. Bacon, *New Organon,* 45.
6. Bacon, *New Organon,* 171.
7. Bacon, *New Organon,* 171.
8. Hooke, *Micrographia,* "Observation I: Of the Point of a small sharp Needle."
9. Hooke, *Micrographia,* "Observation V: Of watered Silks, or Stuffs."
10. Pope, *Essay on Man: Epistle I,* lines 153–56.
11. Dug is a term for a mammalian breast, similar to teat or udder, and thus Gulliver is making a brave attempt to dehumanize his giantess nanny.
12. Swift, *Gulliver's Travels,* Part II, Chapter I.
13. Swift, *Gulliver's Travels,* Part II, Chapter I.
14. Swift, *Gulliver's Travels,* Part II, Chapter I.
15. A long knife or short sword that hangs from the hip, like a cutlass worn by sailors and pirates.
16. Swift, *Gulliver's Travels,* Part II, Chapter II.
17. Eliot, "The Love Song of J. Alfred Prufrock," lines 55–61.
18. Johnson, "Life of Swift."
19. Galileo, *Sidereus Nuncius,* 2.
20. Galileo, *Sidereus Nuncius,* 2.
21. Jay, *Downcast Eyes,* 70.
22. Jay, *Downcast Eyes,* 69–70.
23. Jay, *Downcast Eyes,* Jay uses this as an epigraph to Chapter 1, and analyzes it on page 71.

6. Darkness Visible

1. "The Life of Mr. John Milton by John Phillips." In *Early Lives of Milton,* edited by Helen Darbishire. Note that she attributes this anonymous early life to Phillips, but it has since been ascribed to Cyriack Skinner.
2. Johnson, *Life of Milton.*
3. Milton, *Paradise Lost,* I.1–6.
4. Milton, *Paradise Lost,* I.61–64.
5. Kuusisto, *Eavesdropping,* 50.
6. Kuusisto, *Planet of the Blind,* 5.
7. Milton, "To Leonard Philaras," 780.
8. Magee and Milligan, *On Blindness,* 11.
9. Magee and Milligan, *On Blindness,* 11.
10. Magee and Milligan, *On Blindness,* 21.
11. Samuel Johnson, *Life of Milton.*
12. Eliot, "Milton I." Eliot prefaces this remark by saying: "The most important fact about Milton, for my purpose is his blindness. I do not mean that to go blind in middle life is itself enough to deter-

mine the whole nature of a man's poetry. Blindness must be considered in conjunction with Milton's personality and character, and the peculiar education which he received. It must also be considered in connexion with his devotion to, and expertise in the art of music. Had Milton been a man of very keen senses—I mean of all the five senses—his blindness would not have mattered so much. But for a man whose sensuousness, such as it was, had been withered early by book learning, and whose gifts were naturally aural, it mattered a great deal. It would seem, indeed, to have helped him to concentrate on what he could do best."

13.   Dobranski, *Milton's Visual Imagination*, 6–8.
14.   Milton, *Paradise Lost*, I.283–91.
15.   Milton, *Areopagitica*, 950.
16.   Milton, *Paradise Lost*, VIII.17–18.
17.   Milton, *Paradise Lost*, III.1.
18.   Milton, *Paradise Lost*, III.50–53.
19.   Milton, *Paradise Lost*, III.18–25.
20.   Brown, *Milton's Blindness*, 22.
21.   Milton, "Selections from Second Defense of the English People," 1079.
22.   Brown, *Milton's Blindness*, 1.
23.   Brown, *Milton's Blindness*, 61.
24.   Brown, *Corridors of Light*, Chapter 4.
25.   Milton, *Paradise Lost*, III.41–50.
26.   Eliot, "Milton I."
27.   Kuusisto, *Eavesdropping*, 59.
28.   Milton, *Paradise Lost*, IX.509–18.
29.   Milton, *Paradise Lost*, IV.505.
30.   Milton, *Paradise Lost*, IV.300–6.
31.   Milton, *Paradise Lost*, IV.466–91.
32.   Milton, *Paradise Lost*, IV.299.
33.   Milton, *Paradise Lost*, IV.358.
34.   Milton, *Paradise Lost*, IX.705–8.
35.   Milton, *Paradise Lost*, IX.865–66.

7. The Molyneux Man

1.   From Aristotle's *De Anima* (On the Soul).
2.   Locke, *An Essay Concerning Human Understanding*, II.I.2.
3.   Locke, *An Essay Concerning Human Understanding*, II.IX.8.
4.   Locke, *An Essay Concerning Human Understanding*, II.IX.8.
5.   Locke, *An Essay Concerning Human Understanding*, II.IX.8.
6.   Locke, *An Essay Concerning Human Understanding*, II.IX.8.

7.   Sacks, "A Man of Letters," Kindle loc. 984.
8.   Sacks, "A Man of Letters," Kindle loc. 997.
9.   Sacks, "A Man of Letters," Kindle loc. 997.
10.   Pollan, *How to Change Your Mind,* 261.
11.   Pollan, *How to Change Your Mind,* 263.
12.   Achromatopsia is the subject of Oliver Sacks's *The Island of the Colorblind.*
13.   Gregory, *Eye and Brain,* 57–58.
14.   Gregory, *Eye and Brain,* 5.
15.   Gregory, *Eye and Brain,* 5–6.
16.   I'll be referring to the essay "To See and Not See" in Sacks's collection *An Anthropologist on Mars.*
17.   Sacks, "To See and Not See," 108.
18.   Sacks, "To See and Not See," 109.
19.   Sacks, "To See and Not See," 109.
20.   Sacks, "To See and Not See," 109.
21.   Sacks, "To See and Not See," 109.
22.   Sacks, "To See and Not See," 110.
23.   Sacks, "To See and Not See," 139.
24.   Sacks, "To See and Not See," 121.
25.   Sacks, "To See and Not See," 121.
26.   Sacks, "To See and Not See," 121.
27.   Sacks, "To See and Not See," 122.
28.   Sacks, "To See and Not See," 140.
29.   Kurson, *Crashing Through,* 126–27.
30.   Kurson, *Crashing Through,* 223.
31.   Kurson, *Crashing Through,* 223.
32.   Kurson, *Crashing Through,* 258.
33.   Glenney and Silva, *The Senses and the History of Philosophy,* "General Introduction."
34.   Glenney and Silva, *The Senses and the History of Philosophy,* "General Introduction."
35.   Glenney and Silva, *The Senses and the History of Philosophy,* "General Introduction."

8. Performing Enlightenment

1.   Ross, *Journey into Light,* 97.
2.   Ross, *Journey into Light,* 97.
3.   Ross, *Journey into Light,* 97–98.
4.   Ross, *Journey into Light,* 96.
5.   Foucault, *The Birth of the Clinic,* 65.
6.   Diderot, "Letter on the Blind," 117.

7. Weygand, *The Blind in French Society from the Middle Ages to the Century of Louis Braille,* 63.

8. Diderot, "Letter on the Blind," 69.

9. Diderot, "Letter on the Blind," 69.

10. Diderot, "Letter on the Blind," 77.

11. Diderot, "Letter on the Blind," 90.

12. Diderot, "Letter on the Blind," 109.

13. Diderot, "Letter on the Blind," 109.

14. Diderot, "Letter on the Blind," 111.

15. Diderot, "Letter on the Blind," 112.

16. Vincennes was a medieval castle turned prison. Diderot was a prisoner from July 22 to November 3, 1749.

17. Curran, *Diderot and the Art of Thinking Freely,* 2–3.

18. Weygand, *The Blind in French Society from the Middle Ages to the Century of Louis Braille,* 74.

19. Ross, *Journey into Light,* 87.

20. Ross, *Journey into Light,* 89.

21. Weygand, *The Blind in French Society from the Middle Ages to the Century of Louis Braille,* 74.

22. Weygand, *The Blind in French Society from the Middle Ages to the Century of Louis Braille,* 75.

23. Dickens, *American Notes,* "Chapter III Boston."

24. Dickens, *American Notes,* "Chapter III Boston."

25. Ross, *Journey into Light,* 103.

26. Ross, *Journey into Light,* 104.

9. Braille and His Invention

1. Ross, *Journey into Light,* 122.

2. I'm referring here to the physical ink-print book; there was no ebook version when I bought it (I believe there still is not). It is available at NLS in braille and audio.

3. Mellor, *Louis Braille,* 14.

4. Mellor, *Louis Braille,* 16.

5. Mellor, *Louis Braille,* 24.

6. These paragraphs on Braille and Barbier, as well as the next section, on learning braille with Jewel, are adapted from my *Catapult* piece "Reading Blind."

7. National Federation of the Blind, "The Braille Literacy Crisis in America."

8. Mervosh, "Lego Is Making Braille Bricks. They May Give Braille Literacy a Needed Lift." Although the Lego Braille Bricks (which are very expensive and available only to educational institutions) can-

not alone dismantle the pervasive systemic problems facing braille literacy in our schools, they may help to mitigate the isolation that blind kids sometimes feel by offering an opportunity for blind and sighted kids to play with one another and learn from one another. As Danielson put it: "With these LEGO bricks, blind and sighted children will be able to play together, and that will sort of take away the sense of otherness, and the sense of being different."

9.   Mervosh, "Lego Is Making Braille Bricks."
10.   Mellor, *Louis Braille,* 97–99.
11.   Mellor, *Louis Braille,* 99.
12.   Rubin, *Do You Dream in Color?* 139.
13.   Rubin, *Do You Dream in Color?* 139.
14.   Caitlin Hernandez shared with me the text of her keynote speech that she read for the 2019 CTEBVI (California Transcribers and Educators for the Blind and Visually Impaired) annual conference.
15.   Russell, *To Catch an Angel,* 31.
16.   American Foundation for the Blind, "Movie Magic: Helen Keller in Paris to Honor Louis Braille, 1952." Quoted from the transcript, itself translated from the French.
17.   *New York Times,* "A Century of Louis Braille."
18.   Rosenblum, *See What I'm Saying,* 130.

10. The Tap-Tapping of Blind Travelers

1.   Roberts, *A Sense of the World,* Kindle loc. 1281.
2.   Holman, *A Voyage Round the World,* Chapter I.
3.   Holman, *A Voyage Round the World,* Chapter I.
4.   Holman, *A Voyage Round the World,* Chapter I.
5.   Holman, *A Voyage Round the World,* Chapter I.
6.   Winter, "10 Fascinating Facts about the White Cane."
7.   This and other bits on the white cane, Holman, and Joyce's blind stripling were adapted from "Parting the Sea, and Why the White Cane Is a Symbol of Power, Not Helplessness."
8.   Roberts, *A Sense of the World,* Kindle loc. 1233.
9.   Roberts, *A Sense of the World,* Kindle loc. 1233.
10.   Roberts, *A Sense of the World,* Kindle loc. 5312.
11.   Kish, "How I Use Flash Sonar to Navigate the World."
12.   Kish, "How I Use Flash Sonar to Navigate the World."
13.   Kish, "How I Use Flash Sonar to Navigate the World."
14.   Kish, "How I Use Flash Sonar to Navigate the World."
15.   Rosenblum, *See What I'm Saying,* 4.
16.   Rosenblum, *See What I'm Saying,* 4.
17.   Dawkins, *The Blind Watchmaker,* 35.

18. Dawkins, *The Blind Watchmaker,* 35.
19. Dawkins, *The Blind Watchmaker,* 35.
20. Dawkins, *The Blind Watchmaker,* 23.
21. Twersky, *The Sound of the Walls,* 18.
22. Joyce, *Ulysses,* Episode 11.
23. Joyce, *Ulysses,* Episode 10.
24. Birmingham, *The Most Dangerous Book,* 288.
25. Beckett, *Beckett Remembering / Remembering Beckett,* 45.
26. Joyce, *Ulysses,* Episode 8.
27. Joyce, *Ulysses,* Episode 8.
28. Joyce, *Ulysses,* Episode 8.
29. Joyce, *Ulysses,* Episode 3.
30. Joyce, *Ulysses,* Episode 3.
31. Roberts, "In the Realm of Blind Voices."
32. Roberts, *A Sense of the World,* Kindle loc. 81.
33. Kish, "How I Use Flash Sonar to Navigate the World."

11. Helen Keller in Vaudeville and in Love

1. Bits of this chapter were reworked from "How Helen Keller's Stint on Vaudeville Inspired Me as an Artist."
2. Nielsen, *The Radical Lives of Helen Keller,* 42.
3. Herrmann, *Helen Keller,* 227–28.
4. Keller, *Midstream,* 209–10.
5. Keller, *Midstream,* 211–12.
6. Keller, *Midstream,* 210.
7. Keller, *Midstream,* 210–11.
8. Keller, *Midstream,* 211.
9. Fitzgerald, "'See' Actress Marilee Talkington on What It's Like to Be Legally Blind in Hollywood."
10. Fitzgerald, "'See' Actress Marilee Talkington on What It's Like to Be Legally Blind in Hollywood."
11. Fitzgerald, "'See' Actress Marilee Talkington on What It's Like to Be Legally Blind in Hollywood."
12. I elaborated on this theme in a blog post on my website: "'She Doesn't Look Blind to Me': The Blind Actor Phenomenon."
13. For his views on promoting oral methods (over sign language) in deaf education and eugenics regarding intermarriage, Bell is widely reviled in the Deaf community. See, for example, "Alexander Graham Bell's Controversial Views on Deafness," at VeryWellHealth .com.
14. Keller, *Midstream,* 133.
15. Keller, *Midstream,* 133.
16. Keller, *Midstream,* 133.

17. Keller, *Midstream,* 134.
18. Keller, *Midstream,* 177.
19. Keller, *Midstream,* 178.
20. Keller, *Midstream,* 182.
21. Herrmann, *Helen Keller,* 134.
22. Herrmann, *Helen Keller,* 134.
23. Herrmann, *Helen Keller,* 134.
24. Girma, *Haben,* 210.

12. Sanctified by Affliction, or Not

1. This and a few other paragraphs in the chapter were reworked from my *Catapult* essay "Are Blind People Denied Their Sexuality?" which itself was inspired by my *Playboy* article "The Real Story Behind Blind Dating." There are also bits from my Modern Love essay "After Losing My Sight, Struggling to Be Seen."
2. Twersky, *The Face of the Deep,* 128.
3. Charles, *Brother Ray,* 53.
4. Charles, *Brother Ray,* 103.
5. Carver, "Cathedral," 209.
6. Carver, "Cathedral," 215.
7. Weise, "Cathedral by Raymond Carver."
8. Weise, "Cathedral by Raymond Carver."
9. Bowles, *The Sheltering Sky,* 140.
10. Disability Justice, "Sexual Abuse."
11. Coetzee, *Waiting for the Barbarians,* 29. I am not alone in feeling a kinship with this barbarian girl. In *Sight Unseen,* Georgina Kleege tells how she also experienced "a shock of recognition unlike any I'd known before" when she read about how the barbarian girl sees: "The girl's blindness is exactly like mine. That central blur that will not wipe clean is before my eyes, too. In fact, until I read *Waiting for the Barbarians* I had no language to describe my visual experience beyond saying that I didn't see well" (82).
12. Coetzee, *Waiting for the Barbarians,* 34.
13. Coetzee, *Waiting for the Barbarians,* 41.
14. Coetzee, *Waiting for the Barbarians,* 55.
15. Harris, *Red Dragon,* 330–31.
16. Harris, *Red Dragon,* 303.
17. Harris, *Red Dragon,* 302.
18. With the 2020 COVID-19 outbreak prohibiting live theatrical performances, Darren turned to pro wrestling and is now The Inspirer.
19. Godin, "The Real Story Behind Blind Dating."
20. Potok, *Ordinary Daylight,* 242.
21. Potok, *Ordinary Daylight,* 249.

22. World Seido Karate has a program for blind and visually impaired people. Their headquarters were on West Twenty-third Street in Manhattan. (Their move to a new facility has been halted by the 2020 COVID shutdown as of this writing.) I made it to brown belt. My blind training pal Collin Watt, who came up with me through the ranks till I quit, is now a fourth-degree black belt!

23. Godin, "The Real Story Behind Blind Dating."

24. Godin, "The Real Story Behind Blind Dating."

25. Twersky, *The Sound of the Walls,* 197.

26. Godin, "After Losing My Sight, Struggling to Be Seen."

27. Twersky, *The Sound of the Walls,* 200.

28. Twersky, *The Sound of the Walls,* 201.

29. Twersky, *The Sound of the Walls,* 202.

13. Portrait of the (Working) Writer as Blind

1. Kendrick, "Country of the Blind." This harsh review takes its title from H. G. Wells's story "The Country of the Blind," and begins: "My admiration for Jacob Twersky's mental and physical achievements against the crushing handicap of blindness is very high. I wish that I could honestly extend that admiration to any portion of 'The Face of the Deep.'"

2. Kendrick, "Country of the Blind."

3. Twersky, *The Face of the Deep,* 329.

4. Twersky, *The Face of the Deep,* 329–30.

5. Twersky, *The Face of the Deep,* 333.

6. Twersky, *The Sound of the Walls,* 233.

7. Laurie Alice Eakes, Interview with Leona Godin.

8. Eakes, "Blind People Read Books. We Write Them, Too."

9. Lee & Low, "Where Is the Diversity in Publishing? The 2019 Diversity Baseline Survey Results."

10. Knipfel, "All the World's a Stage."

11. Cripple Punk, "Principles of Cripple Punk." Sadly, the young artist who founded the Cripple Punk movement took their own life on November 9, 2017, as announced on the Cripple Punk Tumblr site in "Message from Tai's Family."

12. Knipfel, "All the World's a Stage."

13. Knipfel, "The Cliff."

14. Knipfel, "The Cliff." I recently heard from an NYC blind friend, who has no cognitive disability, that he works in a mop factory. They do pay above minimum wage and employ blind people with little or no vision. He told me that he does not use his eyes at all, in fact he closes them so that the dust does not get in them. When I

asked if they provided goggles, he said they had to bring them from home if they wanted to use them.

15. Knipfel, "The Cliff."
16. Knipfel, "The Cliff."
17. Young, "disabled queer poet Jillian Weise upends ableist assumptions in *cyborg detective*."
18. This smart cane is called the WeWALK, and was developed by a Turkish blind engineer. I think all the knee-jerk uncritical articles such as the Bored Panda one that so many friends posted on my timeline last September ("Blind Engineer Invents a 'Smart Cane' That Uses Google Maps to Help Blind People Navigate") actually hurt his cause, making the whole thing feel like a bit of a joke in the blind community. But the WeWALK is still going and perhaps I'll get a chance to try one out one of these days, and write about it, too.

14. The Secret Life of Art and Accessibility

1. Rubin, *Do You Dream in Color?*, 322–23.
2. Leland, "The Secret Life of Plants," *The Organist*. The episode also considers the conspiracy theorists called "Stevie truthers," who believe Wonder has been faking his blindness all these years, but I haven't the heart to go there.
3. Beta, "Stevie Wonder's Journey Through the Secret Life of Plants."
4. Beta, "Stevie Wonder's Journey Through the Secret Life of Plants."
5. Beta, "Stevie Wonder's Journey Through the Secret Life of Plants."
6. "Donald Glover on Singing with Stevie Wonder," *Jimmy Kimmel Live*.
7. Wonder, *Talking Book*.
8. The fascinating history of the talking book, a.k.a. the audiobook, is told by Matthew Rubery in *The Untold Story of the Talking Book* (2016).
9. "Donald Glover on Singing with Stevie Wonder," *Jimmy Kimmel Live*.
10. "Donald Glover on Singing with Stevie Wonder," *Jimmy Kimmel Live*.
11. "Donald Glover on Singing with Stevie Wonder," *Jimmy Kimmel Live*.
12. Kurzweil AI, "How Musician Stevie Wonder + Inventor Ray Kurzweil Made History."
13. Kurzweil AI, "How Musician Stevie Wonder + Inventor Ray Kurzweil Made History."
14. Charles, *Brother Ray*, 322–23.
15. Ribowsky, *Signed, Sealed, and Delivered*, 2.

16. I haven't watched the Grammys in years and was alerted to this fantastic moment by my friend Kira Grunenberg, who is a visually impaired music critic for *American Songwriter, Downbeat,* and other magazines. The clip can be found at *Slate:* "Stevie Wonder Reading the Envelope in Braille Might Be the Most Charming Moment of the 2016 Grammys" (video).

17. Slater, "The Society of Visually Impaired Sound Artists Manifesto."

18. Godin, "The Brain-Smashing, Pity-Bashing Art of Blind Punk." A live performance recording of "Is It Cool That We're Here?" at the Chicago Art Institute can be found at MixCloud.com.

19. I heard about Reaper Jaws scripts on Freedom Scientific's podcast called *FS Cast* (Episode 185). For my AudioBrailleHead friends out there here's a bit more (from the transcript): "You take your braille display and look at the routing buttons. And you can think of the length of your braille display as a ruler that represents the entire length of your project. So you can have it playing and just move around with the routing buttons and instantly jump to other positions in the project, hunting around for something that you know you want to focus on. . . . The braille display is formatted for compact and efficient display of what track you're on. Is it armed for recording? Is it muted? The time, the cursor time is on there, so I know I'm three minutes and 12 seconds into the project, and that advances as you move through."

20. Slater, *Unseen Reheard* (exhibit program).

21. Slater, *Unseen Reheard* (exhibit program).

15. The Scylla and Charybdis of Stigma and Superpowers

1. Hiatt, "Jedi Confidential: Inside the Dark New 'Star Wars' Movie."

2. Kleege, *Sight Unseen,* 28.

3. Kleege, *Sight Unseen,* 28.

4. These opening paragraphs and a few others in this chapter were reworked from "When People See Your Blindness as Superhuman, They Stop Seeing You as Human."

5. Rosenblum, *See What I'm Saying,* x.

6. Rosenblum, *See What I'm Saying,* x.

7. Cipriani, *Blind,* 98–99.

8. Rosenblum, "Scent Tracking, Dark Dining, & Other Sensations."

9. Rosenblum, "Scent Tracking, Dark Dining, & Other Sensations."

10. Twersky, *The Sound of the Walls,* 92.

11. Keller, *Midstream,* 172.

12. "National Federation of the Blind Comments on Foundation Fighting Blindness #HowEyeSeeIt Campaign."

13. Twersky, *The Sound of the Walls,* 113.

14. Charles, *Brother Ray,* 41.
15. Charles, *Brother Ray,* 41.
16. Charles, *Brother Ray,* 310.
17. Charles, *Brother Ray,* 314.
18. Charles, *Brother Ray,* 314.
19. Kuusisto, *Planet of the Blind,* 7.
20. Kuusisto, *Planet of the Blind,* 14.
21. Kear, *Now I See You,* 2.
22. Kear, *Now I See You,* 3.
23. Kear, *Now I See You,* 4.
24. Knipfel, *Slackjaw,* 226.
25. Knipfel, *Slackjaw,* 220.
26. Goffman, *Stigma,* 1.
27. Goffman, *Stigma,* 5.
28. Goffman, *Stigma,* 6. I was introduced to Goffman's ideas by way of this quote from Martha Nussbaum's *Frontiers of Justice:* "A central feature of the operation of stigma, especially toward people with impairments and disabilities, is the denial of individuality. The entire encounter with such a person is articulated in terms of the stigmatized trait, and we come to believe that the person with the stigma is not fully or really human."
29. Caroline Kasnakian has a Psy (doctorate in psychology) and is the director of the Counseling Center at the Pratt Institute.
30. Knipfel, "Hey, What's with the White Cane?"
31. Saramago, *Blindness,* 287. I must add that the only actual (pre-white-mist) blind person is a bad guy, who uses his braille skills to help the thugs keep track of their stolen booty in the hospital.
32. Beth Israel Deaconess Medical Center, "How the Brain Compensates for Vision Loss Shows Much More Versatility Than Previously Recognized."
33. Beth Israel Deaconess Medical Center, "How the Brain Compensates for Vision Loss Shows Much More Versatility Than Previously Recognized."

16. The Invisible Gorilla and Other Inattentions

1. Hurt, "Your Senses Are Your Raw Information Learning Portals."
2. The entire interview is available as audio here: "A Conversation with Dr. Hoby Wedler, Blind Chemist, About Wine Tasting, Sensory Literacy, and the Glorious Smell of Wet Pavement," *Aromatica Poetica.*
3. Rosenblum, "Scent Tracking, Dark Dining, & Other Sensations."
4. Rosenblum, *See What I'm Saying,* xv.
5. Rosenblum, "Scent Tracking, Dark Dining, & Other Sensations."

6. Rosenblum, "Scent Tracking, Dark Dining, & Other Sensations."
7. Herz, *The Scent of Desire*, 7.
8. Herz, *The Scent of Desire*, 4–5.
9. Charles, *Brother Ray*, 314.
10. Chabris and Simons, *The Invisible Gorilla*, 6.
11. Chabris and Simons, *The Invisible Gorilla*, 7.
12. Chabris and Simons, *The Invisible Gorilla*, 7.
13. Diderot, "Letter on the Blind," 117.
14. Pinker, *Enlightenment Now*, 214.
15. Tenenbaum, "A Vision for Genes."

17. Constructing Blind Pride out of Ancient and Evolutionary Blind Memes

1. Twersky, *Blindness in Literature*, 10.
2. National Federation of the Blind, "Blindness Statistics."
3. Girma, *Haben*, 164–65.
4. Bearden, *Monstrous Kinds*, 7.
5. Dawkins, *The Selfish Gene*, 249.
6. Dawkins, *The Selfish Gene*, 249.
7. Lawrence and Lee, *Inherit the Wind*, 67.
8. Dawkins, *The Blind Watchmaker*, 21.
9. Dawkins, *The Blind Watchmaker*, 37.
10. Harari, *Sapiens*, in "19 and They Lived Happily Ever After," Section "The Meaning of Life." Also in "6 Building Pyramids," Section "An Imagined Order": "There is only a blind evolutionary process, devoid of any purpose, leading to the birth of individuals."
11. Bérubé, *Life as We Know It*, 33.
12. Bérubé, *Life as We Know It*, 239.
13. Knighton, *Cockeyed*, 102–3.
14. Dawkins, *The Blind Watchmaker*, 41.
15. Kleege, *Sight Unseen*, 2.
16. Le Guin, *The Left Hand of Darkness*, 195.
17. Garland-Thomson, *Extraordinary Bodies*, 6.
18. Garland-Thomson, *Extraordinary Bodies*, 8.
19. American Foundation for the Blind, "Key Employment Statistics for People Who Are Blind or Visually Impaired."

Bibliography

American Foundation for the Blind. "Key Employment Statistics for People Who Are Blind or Visually Impaired." https://www.afb.org.

———. "Movie Magic: Helen Keller in Paris to Honor Louis Braille, 1952." Film clip (with audio description) and transcript.

Bacon, Francis. *The New Organon.* Edited by Lisa Jardine. Translated by Michael Silverthorne. Cambridge: Cambridge University Press, 2000.

Bearden, Elizabeth B. *Monstrous Kinds: Body, Space, and Narrative in Renaissance Representations of Disability.* Ann Arbor: University of Michigan Press, 2019.

Beckett, Samuel. *Beckett Remembering / Remembering Beckett.* Edited by James and Elizabeth Knowlson. New York: Arcade Publishing, 2011.

Bérubé, Michael. *Life as We Know It: A Father, a Family, and an Exceptional Child.* New York: Pantheon Books, 1996.

Beta, Andy. "Stevie Wonder's Journey Through the Secret Life of Plants." *Pitchfork,* August 4, 2019.

Beth Israel Deaconess Medical Center. "How the Brain Compensates for Vision Loss Shows Much More Versatility Than Previously Recognized." *ScienceDaily,* August 27, 2008. www.sciencedaily.com.

Birmingham, Kevin. *The Most Dangerous Book: The Battle for James Joyce's "Ulysses."* New York: Penguin Books, 2014.

Bloom, Harold. *Lear: The Great Image of Authority.* New York: Scribner, 2018.

Borges, Jorge Luis. "Blindness." *Seven Nights.* Translated by Eliot Weinberger. New York: New Directions, 2009.

———. "The Last Interview." Interview by Gloria López Lecube. Translated by Kit Maude. In *Jorge Luis Borges: The Last Interview.* Brooklyn: Melville House, 2013.

———. "Original Mythology." Interview by Richard Burgin. In *Jorge Luis Borges: The Last Interview.* Brooklyn: Melville House, 2013.

Bowles, Paul. *The Sheltering Sky.* New York: Ecco Press, 1977.

Bradley, Laura. "Stevie Wonder Reading the Envelope in Braille Was

Grammys 2016's Most Charming Moment." Video. *Slate,* February 15, 2016.

Brontë, Charlotte. *Jane Eyre.* New York: Signet Classics, 2008.

Brown, Eleanor Gertrude. *Corridors of Light.* Yellow Springs, OH: Antioch Press, 1958. Online at https://DaytonHistoryBooks.com.

———. *Milton's Blindness.* New York: Columbia University Press, 1934. Retrieved from archive.org.

Burton, Robert. *The Anatomy of Melancholy* (published under the name "Democritus Junior"). Project Gutenberg ebook #10800. Release date: January 13, 2004. Most recently updated: May 31, 2020.

Carver, Raymond. "Cathedral." *Cathedral: Stories.* New York: Knopf, 1983.

CBC Radio. "Punk Rock and Passion Plays." *Tapestry.* January 24, 2020.

Chabris, Christopher F., and Daniel J. Simons. *The Invisible Gorilla: And Other Ways Our Intuitions Deceive Us.* New York: Crown Publishers, 2010.

Charles, Ray, and David Ritz. *Brother Ray: Ray Charles' Own Story.* Cambridge, MA: Da Capo, 2004.

Cipriani, Belo Miguel. *Blind: A Memoir.* Tucson, AZ: Wheatmark, 2011.

Coetzee, J. M. *Waiting for the Barbarians.* New York: Penguin Books, 1982.

Cripple Punk. "Principles of Cripple Punk." 2016. https://crpl-pnk.tumblr .com.

Curran, Andrew S. *Diderot and the Art of Thinking Freely.* New York: Other Press, 2019.

Danielewski, Mark Z. *House of Leaves.* New York: Pantheon Books, 2000.

Darbishire, Helen, ed. "The Life of Mr. John Milton by John Phillips." *The Early Lives of Milton.* London: Constable, 1932.

Dawkins, Richard. *The Blind Watchmaker.* New York: Norton, 1996.

———. *The Selfish Gene.* 40th anniversary edition. New York: Oxford University Press, 2016.

Dickens, Charles. *American Notes for General Circulation.* Project Gutenberg ebook #675. Release date: February 18, 2013.

Diderot. "Letter on the Blind for the Use of Those Who See." *Diderot's Early Philosophical Works.* Translated and edited by Margaret Jourdain. Chicago: Open Court Publishing, 1916. 68–141.

Disability Justice. "Sexual Abuse: People with Disabilities Are Sexually Assaulted at Nearly Three Times the Rate of People without Disabilities." https://disabilityjustice.org.

Dobranski, Stephen B. *Milton's Visual Imagination: Imagery in "Paradise Lost."* New York: Cambridge University Press, 2015.

"Donald Glover on Singing with Stevie Wonder." *Jimmy Kimmel Live.* YouTube clip. May 11, 2018.

Eakes, Laurie Alice. "Yes, Blind People Read Books. We Write Them, Too." *HuffPost,* September 17, 2018.

Eliot, T. S. "Eliot on Milton: Milton I & II." Michigan Technological University. https://pages.mtu.edu.

———. "The Love Song of J. Alfred Prufrock." Representative Poetry Online (RPO). https://rpo.library.utoronto.ca.

Fitzgerald, Toni. "'See' Actress Marilee Talkington on What It's Like to Be Legally Blind in Hollywood." *Forbes,* November 25, 2019.

Flynn, Gillian. *Sharp Objects.* New York: Broadway Books, 2006.

Foucault, Michel. *Birth of the Clinic: An Archaeology of Medical Perception.* Translated by A. M. Sheridan. Abingdon, Oxon, UK: Routledge Classics, 2003.

FSCast. Episode 185. *Freedom Scientific,* June 2020. blog.freedomscientific.com/fscast.

Galilei, Galileo. *Sidereus Nuncius, or The Sidereal Messenger.* Translated by Albert Van Helden. 2nd ed. Chicago: University of Chicago Press, 2015.

Garland-Thomson, Rosemarie. *Extraordinary Bodies: Figuring Physical Disability in American Culture and Literature.* New York: Columbia University Press, 2017.

Girma, Haben. *Haben: The Deafblind Woman Who Conquered Harvard Law.* New York: Hachette Book Group, 2019.

Glenney, Brian, and José Filipe Silva, eds. *The Senses and the History of Philosophy.* New York: Routledge, 2019. Bookshare.org ebook.

Godin, M. Leona. "After Losing My Sight, Struggling to Be Seen." Modern Love. *New York Times,* January 17, 2020.

———. "Are Blind People Denied Their Sexuality?" A Blind Writer's Notebook. *Catapult,* July 17, 2018.

———. "The Brain-Smashing, Pity-Bashing Art of Blind Punks." A Blind Writer's Notebook. *Catapult,* November 21, 2019.

———. "How Helen Keller's Stint on Vaudeville Inspired Me as an Artist." A Blind Writer's Notebook. *Catapult,* January 29, 2019.

———. "Parting the Sea, and Why the White Cane Is a Symbol of Power, Not Helplessness." A Blind Writer's Notebook. *Catapult,* October 15, 2018.

———. "Reading Blind." A Blind Writer's Notebook. *Catapult,* March 6, 2018.

———. "The Real Story Behind Blind Dating." *Playboy* (online), April 13, 2018.

———. "The Spectator & the Blind Man: Seeing and Not-Seeing in the Wake of Empiricism." PhD diss., submitted under birth name, Michelle Leona Goodin. New York University, 2009.

———. "The Star of Happiness: Helen Keller on Vaudeville?!" Unpublished play. Performed in New York City, 2011, 2012.

———. "When People See Your Blindness as Superhuman, They Stop

Seeing You as Human." A Blind Writer's Notebook. *Catapult,* November 29, 2018.

Goffman, Erving. *Stigma: Notes on the Management of Spoiled Identity.* New York: Simon and Schuster, 1963.

Gregory, R. L. *Eye and Brain: The Psychology of Seeing.* Princeton, NJ: Princeton University Press, 1997.

Harari, Yuval Noah. *Sapiens: A Brief History of Humankind.* New York: HarperCollins, 2018. Bookshare.org ebook.

Harris, Thomas. *Red Dragon.* New York: Berkley, 2009.

Herbert, Frank. *Children of Dune.* New York: Berkley, 1976.

Herrmann, Dorothy. *Helen Keller: A Life.* New York: Knopf, 1998.

Herz, Rachel. *The Scent of Desire: Discovering Our Enigmatic Sense of Smell.* Sydney, Australia: HarperCollins, 2007.

Hiatt, Brian. "Jedi Confidential: Inside the Dark New 'Star Wars' Movie." *Rolling Stone,* November 29, 2017.

Holman, James. *A Voyage Round the World, Volume I: Including Travels in Africa, Asia, Australasia, America, etc., etc., from 1827 to 1832.* Project Gutenberg ebook #12528. Release date: April 13, 2019.

Homer. *The Odyssey.* Translated by Emily Wilson. New York: Norton, 2018.

Hooke, Robert. *Micrographia, or some Physiological Descriptions of Minute Bodies, made by Magnifying Glasses, with Observations and Inquiries thereupon.* Project Gutenberg ebook #15491. Release date: March 29, 2005.

Hull, John M. *Touching the Rock: An Experience of Blindness.* New York: Pantheon Books, 1991.

Hurt, Jeff. "Your Senses Are Your Raw Information Learning Portals." *Velvet Chainsaw,* May 23, 2012. https://velvetchainsaw.com.

Jay, Martin. *Downcast Eyes: The Denigration of Vision in Twentieth-Century French Thought.* Berkeley: University of California Press, 1993.

Johnson, Daisy. *Everything Under: A Novel.* Minneapolis, MN: Graywolf Press, 2018.

Johnson, Samuel. "Life of Milton." Edited by Jack Lynch, 2019. http://jacklynch.net.

———. "Life of Swift." *Lives of the English Poets: Addison, Savage, Swift.* Project Gutenberg ebook #4679. Release date: May 31, 2020.

Joyce, James. *Ulysses.* Project Gutenberg ebook #4300. Release date: December 27, 2019.

Kear, Nicole C. *Now I See You: A Memoir.* New York: St. Martin's Press, 2014.

Keller, Helen. *Midstream: My Later Life.* New York: Doubleday, Doran, 1930.

————. *The Story of My Life.* Edited by Roger Shattuck and Dorothy Herrmann. New York: Norton, 2003.

————. *The World I Live In.* New York: Century, 1908.

Kendrick, Baynard. "Country of the Blind; The Face of the Deep. By Jacob Twersky." *New York Times,* May 24, 1953.

King, Stephen. "The Langolieres." *Four Past Midnight.* New York: Pocket Books, 1990.

Kish, Daniel. "How I Use Flash Sonar to Navigate the World." TED Talk, 2015.

Kleege, Georgina. *Sight Unseen.* New Haven, CT: Yale University Press, 1999.

Knighton, Ryan. *Cockeyed: A Memoir.* New York: PublicAffairs, 2006.

Knipfel, Jim. "All the World's a Stage." *The Chiseler.* 2019. https://chiseler.org.

————. "The Cliff: 25 Years after the Americans with Disabilities Act, Why Can't the Disabled Find Work?" *Smashpipe,* February 15, 2016. (Website no longer exists. Manuscript furnished by author.)

————. "Hey, What's with the White Cane?" *Wall Street Journal,* October 11, 2016. (Manuscript furnished by author.)

————. *Slackjaw.* New York: Jeremy P. Tarcher/Putnam, 1999.

Kurson, Robert. *Crashing Through: A True Story of Risk, Adventure, and the Man Who Dared to See.* New York: Random House, 2007.

Kurzweil AI. "How Musician Stevie Wonder + Inventor Ray Kurzweil Made History." *On Air-Make It,* December 1, 2019. https://www.kurzweilai.net.

Kuusisto, Stephen. *Eavesdropping: A Life by Ear.* New York: Norton, 2006.

————. *Planet of the Blind.* New York: Dell, 1998.

Lawrence, Jerome, and Robert E. Lee. *Inherit the Wind.* New York: Ballantine, 2007.

Lee & Low. "Where Is the Diversity in Publishing? The 2019 Diversity Baseline Survey Results." The Lee & Low Blog. January 28, 2020. https://blog.leeandlow.com.

Le Guin, Ursula K. *The Left Hand of Darkness.* New York: Penguin Books, 2016.

Leland, Andrew. "The Secret Life of Plants." *The Organist.* KCRW, September 20, 2018.

Locke, John. *An Essay Concerning Human Understanding.* Edited by Peter H. Nidditch. New York: Oxford University Press, 1979.

Magee, Bryan, and Martin Milligan. *On Blindness: Letters between Bryan Magee and Martin Milligan.* New York: Oxford University Press, 1995.

Mahoney, Rosemary. "Why Do We Fear the Blind?" *New York Times,* January 4, 2014.

Mellor, C. Michael. *Louis Braille: A Touch of Genius.* Boston: National Braille Press, 2006.

Mervosh, Sarah. "Lego Is Making Braille Bricks. They May Give Blind Literacy a Needed Lift." *New York Times,* April 27, 2019.

Mills, Mara. "What Should We Call Reading?" New York University, December 3, 2012.

Milton, John. *Areopagitica.* In *The Complete Poetry and Essential Prose of John Milton,* edited by Stephen M. Fallon, William Kerrigan, and John Rumrich, 923–66. New York: Modern Library, 2007.

———. *Paradise Lost.* In *The Complete Poetry and Essential Prose of John Milton,* edited by Stephen M. Fallon, William Kerrigan, and John Rumrich, 283–630. New York: Modern Library, 2007.

———. "Selections from Second Defense of the English People." In *The Complete Poetry and Essential Prose of John Milton,* edited by Stephen M. Fallon, William Kerrigan, and John Rumrich, 1069–1110. New York: Modern Library, 2007.

———. "To Leonard Philaras." In *The Complete Poetry and Essential Prose of John Milton.* Edited by Stephen M. Fallon, William Kerrigan, and John Rumrich, 779–80. New York: Modern Library, 2007.

National Federation of the Blind. "Blindness Statistics." 2016. https://www.nfb.org.

———. "The Braille Literacy Crisis in America: Facing the Truth, Reversing the Trend, Empowering the Blind." March 26, 2009.

———. "National Federation of the Blind Comments on Foundation Fighting Blindness #HowEyeSeeIt Campaign." September 26, 2016.

Nelson, Maggie. *The Art of Cruelty: A Reckoning.* New York: Norton, 2011.

New York Times. "A Century of Louis Braille." June 23, 1952.

Nielsen, Kim E. *The Radical Lives of Helen Keller.* New York: NYU Press, 2004.

Orwell, George. "Lear, Tolstoy, and the Fool." *All Art Is Propaganda: Critical Essays.* New York: Mariner Books, 2009.

Ovid. *Metamorphoses.* Translated by Charles Martin. New York: Norton, 2004.

Pinker, Steven. *Enlightenment Now: The Case for Reason, Science, Humanism, and Progress.* New York: Penguin Books, 2018.

Plato. *Phaedo.* Translated by Eva Brann, Peter Kalkavage, and Eric Salem. Indianapolis: Focus, 1998.

Pollan, Michael. *How to Change Your Mind: What the New Science of Psychedelics Teaches Us about Consciousness, Dying, Addiction, Depression, and Transcendence.* New York: Penguin Books, 2019.

Pope, Alexander. "Essay on Man: Epistle I." Representative Poetry Online (RPO). University of Toronto. https://rpo.library.utoronto.ca.

Potok, Andrew. *Ordinary Daylight: Portrait of an Artist Going Blind.* New York: Bantam Books, 1980.

Powers, Hiram. AZQuotes.com, Wind and Fly, Ltd., 2020. https://www.azquotes.com.

Ribowsky, Mark. *Signed, Sealed, and Delivered: The Soulful Journey of Stevie Wonder.* Hoboken, NJ: John Wiley, 2010.

Roberts, Jason. "In the Realm of Blind Voices." http://jasonroberts.net.

———. *A Sense of the World: How a Blind Man Became History's Greatest Traveler.* New York: HarperCollins, 2007.

Rosenblum, Lawrence D. "Scent Tracking, Dark Dining, & Other Sensations: Interview with Lawrence Rosenblum, Perceptual Psychologist." By M. Leona Godin. *Aromatica Poetica,* November 20, 2019.

———. *See What I'm Saying: The Extraordinary Powers of Our Five Senses.* New York: Norton, 2010.

Ross, Ishbel. *Journey into Light: The Story of the Education of the Blind.* New York: Appleton-Century-Crofts, 1951.

Rubery, Matthew. *The Untold Story of the Talking Book.* Cambridge, MA: Harvard University Press, 2016.

Rubin, Laurie. *Do You Dream in Color?: Insights from a Girl without Sight.* New York: Seven Stories Press, 2012.

Russell, Robert. *To Catch an Angel: Adventures in the World I Cannot See.* Toronto: Copp Clark Publishing, 1962.

Sacks, Oliver. *The Island of the Colorblind.* New York: Vintage Books, 1998.

———. "A Man of Letters." In *The Mind's Eye.* New York: Knopf, 2010.

———. "To See and Not See." In *An Anthropologist on Mars: Seven Paradoxical Tales.* New York: Knopf, 1995.

Saramago, José. *Blindness: A Novel.* Translated by Juan Sager. New York: Harcourt Brace, 1997.

Shakespeare, William. *King Lear.* Folger Shakespeare Library. New York: Simon and Schuster, 2015.

Slater, Andy. "Is It Cool That We're Here?" SoVISA. Chicago Art Institute, 2019. Live performance recording. https://www.mixcloud.com.

———. "The Society of Visually Impaired Sound Artists Manifesto." YouTube. February 28, 2017.

———. *Unseen Reheard.* Album. March 21, 2020.

———. *Unseen Reheard.* Exhibit program. *The Chicago Sound Show.* University of Chicago, Smart Museum of Art, 2019. Draft furnished to author.

Sontag, Susan. *Illness as Metaphor* and *AIDS and Its Metaphors.* New York: Picador, 1989.

Sophocles. *The Three Theban Plays: Antigone, Oedipus the King, Oedipus at Colonus*. Translated by Robert Fagles. New York: Penguin Books, 1984.

Swift, Jonathan. *Gulliver's Travels: Into Several Remote Regions of the World*. Project Gutenberg ebook #829. Release date: June 15, 2009. Most recently updated: August 6, 2020.

Telson, Bob. "Now Let the Weeping Cease." *Gospel at Colonus*. Original cast recording. Rhino Entertainment, 2005.

Tenenbaum, David. "A Vision for Genes: One-of-a-Kind Geneticist Snags Ph.D." *News—University of Wisconsin, Madison,* November 3, 2016. https://news.wisc.edu.

Twersky, Jacob. *Blindness in Literature: Examples of Depictions and Attitudes*. New York: American Foundation for the Blind, 1955.

——. *The Face of the Deep*. New York: World Publishing, 1953. Bookshare.org ebook.

——. *The Sound of the Walls*. New York: Doubleday, 1959. Bookshare.org ebook.

Vendler, Helen. *The Art of Shakespeare's Sonnets*. Cambridge, MA: Harvard University Press, 1997.

Wedler, Hoby. "A Conversation with Dr. Hoby Wedler, Blind Chemist, about Wine Tasting, Sensory Literacy, and the Glorious Smell of Wet Pavement." Interview by M. Leona Godin. *Aromatica Poetica,* June 7, 2018. https://www.aromaticapoetica.com.

——. "Sensory Literacy." TEDx Talk, Sonoma County, December 1, 2017.

Weise, Jillian. "Cathedral by Raymond Carver." *Academia.* https://www.academia.edu.

West, Martin L., ed. and trans. "Proclus' *Life of Homer*." In *Homeric Hymns. Homeric Apocrypha. Lives of Homer,* 418–25. Cambridge, MA: Harvard University Press, 2003.

Weygand, Zina. *The Blind in French Society from the Middle Ages to the Century of Louis Braille*. Translated by Emily-Jane Cohen. Stanford, CA: Stanford University Press, 2009.

Winter, Bill. "10 Fascinating Facts about the White Cane." *Perkins School,* October 15, 2015. http://www.perkins.org.

Wonder, Stevie. *Talking Book*. Tamla Records, 1972.

Young, Élan. "disabled queer poet jillian weise upends ableist assumptions in *cyborg detective*." *3:AM Magazine,* September 26, 2019.

Index

M. Leona Godin is a writer, performer, and educator who is blind. Her writing has appeared in the *New York Times; Playboy; O, The Oprah Magazine;* and *Catapult,* where she writes the column A Blind Writer's Notebook. She was a 2019 Logan Nonfiction Fellow and has written and produced two theatrical works: "The Star of Happiness," based on Helen Keller's time performing on vaudeville, and *The Spectator & the Blind Man,* about the invention of braille. She founded *Aromatica Poetica,* an online magazine, as a venue for exploring the arts and sciences of smell and taste, not specifically for, but welcoming to, blind readers and writers.

A Note on the Type

This book was set in Granjon, a type named in compliment to Robert Granjon, a type cutter and printer active in Antwerp, Lyons, Rome, and Paris from 1523 to 1590. Granjon, the boldest and most original designer of his time, was one of the first to practice the trade of type-founder apart from that of printer.

Linotype Granjon was designed by George W. Jones, who based his drawings on a face used by Claude Garamond (ca. 1480–1561) in his beautiful French books. Granjon more closely resembles Garamond's own type than do any of the various modern faces that bear his name.

Typeset by Scribe, Philadelphia, Pennsylvania
Printed and bound by Berryville Graphics, Berryville, Virginia
Designed by Maria Carella